THE TIMES OF INDIA

THE BEST OF
SPEAKING TREE

Volume I

THE TIMES OF INDIA

THE BEST OF

SPEAKING TREE

Volume I

Times Group Books

Preface

T is in the very nature of a newspaper to focus on stories that unsettle the mind: stories about death and destruction, doom and decay, grief, suffering and anguish. Our endeavour in The Times of India has been to change the focus. We do not of course wish to ignore the dreadful events that brutalise our world. The aim rather is to place the events in a wider perspective to enable our readers to react to them with equanimity. At one level that perspective is analytical. The events are linked to trends and processes. This allows readers to make sense of the heaps of information put at their disposal.At another level, however, we propose a perspective that makes it possible for readers to look at events in a philosophical manner. It is to be found in two columns that appear on the editorial page of the paper. One is 'Sacred Space' and the other 'The Speaking Tree'. While the former consists of extracts from religious and spiritual texts of various faiths, the latter are spiritual reflections by contemporary thinkers. Both columns are meant to appeal to the higher consciousness of readers, a consciousness which rises above the din and grind of day-to-day happenings and, in the process, is able to sift the transient from the essential.The present volume brings together some of the more stimulating contributions to 'The Speaking Tree' column. They can be read at random since they are not linked to any specific news event. Each one gives an insight into how the inner self can accede to a realm where calm has replaced turbulence, peace has vanquished doubt and detachment has delivered the soul from the trappings of this worldly engagement.

Indu Jain
New Delhi
September 2002

THE BEST OF SPEAKING TREE - Volume 1

Copyright ©Bennett, Coleman & Co. Ltd., 2004

Published in 2004

Tenth reprint in 2013

by
Bennett, Coleman & Co. Ltd.
7, Bahadur Shah Zafar Marg
New Delhi-110002

Acknowledgements
We thank all those who have contributed to "The Speaking Tree" column in
The Times of India over the years.

Edit, Design, Marketed and Distributed by

Times Group Books
(A division of Bennett, Coleman and Co. Ltd.)
Times Annexe, 9-10, Bahadur Shah Zafar Marg, New Delhi-110002

ISBN 978-93-80942-06-3

Printed by
International Print-o-Pac Ltd.

Price: ₹250

CONTENTS

Questioning the Primacy of Violence

Ranjit Hoskote

 HE BUDDHA was no stranger to violence. He lived, as prince and sage, through one of the most turbulent periods in India's history. The expansionist tendencies of Magadha and Kosala had claimed the smaller oligarchies and republics. Every conquest was attended by massacre and often entire populations were enslaved and resettled. That political climate was not very different from our own. Among the Buddha's contemporaries were the bloodthirsty royal cousins Ajatashatru of Magadha and Viruddhaka of Kosala; bandit Angulimala; and Devadatta, the Buddha's cousin, who attempted to assassinate him. Then, as now, many states were controlled by courtiers and charlatans; stable regimes were toppled through agent provocateurs; violence was accepted as an instrument of policy.

Despite provocations, however, the Buddha never wavered in his insistence on ahimsa. In the *Dhammapada* (XIX, 256-57), he says: "They do not follow dharma who resort to violence to achieve their purpose". In the laboratory for ethical experiment that was his world the Buddha could see plainly the disastrous effects of violence. Its costs far outweighed its benefits; it was a whirlpool that sucked society, polity and economy towards its dark centre. By perpetuating the context of its origin, violence produces a state of permanent unrest, a cycle of assault and retaliation, a continuity of resentment and rage. The Buddha saw that these destructive energies corrode the soul and turn the world into an inferno.

The antidote, the Buddha held, was dharma: by perfecting ethical conduct, meditative abilities and wisdom; and by treating others with ahimsa, *karuna,* compassion, and *metta,* loving-kindness. This behaviour was based on karma, in which (as the commentator Eknath Easwaran notes) "no divine agency is needed to punish and reward us; we punish and reward ourselves". This ethic did away with the invocation of gods, the appeasement of ancestral spirits. Individuals took responsibility for their own actions, guided by the injunction (*Dhammapada,* XXI, 291): "Don't try to build your happiness on the unhappiness of others".

The Buddha asserts that no one can be transformed magically into a 'good' person; ethical practice is a deliberate effort. Those who accept this must reflect dispassionately upon their conduct; against the grain, they must develop those positive skills through which humankind's humane possibilities may be realised.

When concept and action flow as one, says the Buddha, ahimsa becomes an integral aspect of the practitioner's consciousness. In political terms, the Buddha's dharma would translate as an attentiveness to the unease of the other; a sharing in his anguish; a willingness to concede one's errors and establish a just peace. These are skills that India's political leaders conspicuously lack. If dharma were made the basis of politics, it might help resolve the crises on which the survival of India's parasitical ruling class depends.

An Agnostic's Faith in Universal Ahimsa

Khushwant Singh

 OW SHOULD we deal with evil? In Sikhism, the debate began when Guru Nanak was imprisoned by Babur. He questioned God why this suffering was being inflicted on his people. However, he never advocated revenge. The bhakti school has always advocated turning the other cheek. This pacific attitude continued up to the fifth guru Arjan Dev, who compiled the eclectic Granth Sahib. In 1665, Tegh Bahadur, the ninth guru, was tortured and executed. Yet, his hymns do not incite violence.

When the tenth guru, Gobind Singh, faced terror from the Mughals, he thought long and deep. He then wrote that when all other means have failed, it is righteous to draw the sword. On Baisakhi in 1699, he summoned all Sikhs and elected five 'beloved disciples', *panj piyare,* to form the nucleus of a new community: Khalsa, the pure. He created *sant-sipahis,* soldier-saints, who had no worldly interests. He spelt out specific conditions for *dharma yuddh* (righteous war). You could only fight the person perpetrating evil; not innocent people.

Guru Gobind Singh believed that once you launched a *dharma yuddh,* you didn't bother about winning or losing; you just fought to the finish. There would also be no vengeance. He wrote: "O Lord, these boons of Thee I ask, / Let me never shun a righteous task, / Let me be fearless when I go to battle, / Give me faith that victory will be mine, / Give me power to sing Thy praise, / And when comes the time to end my life, / Let me fall in a mighty strife".

Much has been said about waging an 'inner jehad' with the enemy within. Guru Nanak said that when you conquer the heart, you conquer the world: *man jeete, jag jeet.* Sikhism believes God to be *nirankar,* beyond life and death. But Guru Gobind Singh's concept of God underwent a martial metamorphosis after his father's violent death. Steel became a symbol of power. Sri Bhagwati was invoked: Sri, the goddess and Bhagwati, the sword.

Regarding American president Bush's statement: "You're either with us or with the terrorists", I want to say that I'm an agnostic Gandhian. I'm a pacifist like Gandhi. Whenever faced with a problem, I try to visualise Gandhi's approach to it. In today's context, with Osama bin Laden and the Taliban pitched against the US and its allies, Gandhi would have said: "Don't retaliate with violence". I don't know how realistic that would be. But my initial reaction would be 'no' to violence. It is sensible to be neutral.

As an agnostic, the only religious principle I subscribe to is ahimsa or non-violence. The rest is all marginal. Ahimsa bears the essence of all religions. This one word defines our relationship with all living beings, human or other. Don't hurt anyone. But, when your own existence is threatened, I'd rather live than die, then something has to be done. Adi Sankara asked: "Where have we come from? Who are our real parents? Where will we go when we die?" We don't know. There are no answers.

Ahimsa as the Way to Peace & Bliss

Binod Kumar Mishra

WO THOUSAND six hundred years ago, Mahavir Swami made the revolutionary statement: *ahimsa parmodharmaha,* non-violence is the supreme religion. This one sentence, thoughtfully uttered by the saint-saviour in the first millennium, changed the moral climate of the Indian subcontinent for all time to come. The key to the understanding of the psychology of violence could be found in the simple, ancient conclusion reached by Mahavir Swami that ahimsa and peace are born in the mind of man. Nothing can be achieved without the spiritual upliftment of the individual. A violent mind is not the place where peace could reside. His philosophy does not paint this world as a murky place, full of sorrow and pain. On the contrary, the door to peace and bliss is ever open. Just enter it. You don't even have to knock at it. The well-known Jain Dharmacharya and philosopher of modern times, Acharya Shri Mahaprajna has said that *bhava parivartan,* change at the spiritual plane, is of crucial importance. Nothing can be achieved without curing spiritual illness. He maintains that spiritual upliftment and purity of mind are essentially the same thing. But this spiritual change takes place on the condition that we have full faith in our *ista,* chosen divine ideal. Once a seeker completely identifies himself with his *ista,* he becomes part of that divinity; and attains to peace and unadulterated bliss.

The basic question, then, is how to bring about inner change. How to make ahimsa a way of life. Ahimsa cannot be practised by the weak. If war begins in the minds of men, peace too, according to the Indian spiritual tradition, emanates from the *chitta* — inner consciousness — of man. Ahimsa is not limited to 'not hitting', or 'not harming' others. It is not merely conceptual thinking. Ahimsa is the essence of a really civilised life. Ahimsa cannot pervade our inner self unless we get rid of dross, demeaning emotions, such as lust, anger, arrogance, fear and greed. An over-ambitious man panting with desires can never rest in peace. When corrupting and corroding desires are driven away from our mind, ahimsa reigns in all its glory. We are at peace with ourselves and with the society as a whole. The grand temple of world peace could be built only on the stable foundation of ahimsa. Only a changed man can change the world. This change could be brought about by creating a new man, a citizen of the world, by training the mind in moral and spiritual discipline.

Mahavir Swami's ahimsa goes beyond our concerns for mankind. Not only human life was precious; animals, birds, even plants and other kinds of vegetation needed man's protection. Man had no moral authority to destroy them as they too have life. If we destroyed nature, it will hit back in the shape of environmental degradation threatening the very existence of man. Thus, Mahavir Swami visualised man as a part of the organic whole of the life systems that inhabit this good, beautiful, ancient earth.

A Deep Dream of Peace

Rudolf C Heredia

EACE IS neither conquered nor imposed. It is received as a gift, discovered as a treasure. It must be founded on justice and built in harmony. It can never be a balance of terror, nor is it the re-establishment of a shattered order. Rather, peace is the creation of a new world. St Augustine's 'tranquillity of order' is too static an understanding of peace, for peace is essentially relational and dynamic.

True peace is not just a political affair premised on the dictum 'who desires peace must prepare for war'. Real peace is religious and spiritual, and demands a conversion of hearts. It looks ahead, so must include forgiveness, reconciliation and healing of hurtful memories. This might require a 'cultural disarmament': the abandonment of vested interests and non-negotiable positions, some of which might be so integral to our culture that we fail to notice them. We must accept, too, that many contents of our modern consciousness are deeply negative. Rationality is often mere aggression; 'progress' has degenerated into regressive consumerism; technology has instrumentalised us all.

Peace comprises harmony, freedom and justice. Sri Aurobindo once said that all problems of existence are problems of harmony. In our pluralist world, harmony must be more than a coincidence of opposites; it must create space for all. Such harmony can only prevail when it includes freedom and justice. Freedom cannot merely be individualistic liberty that regresses into licence. For, the ultimate subject of freedom is not the individual; it is the person in community, or rather persons in communion with others and with reality.

Freedom must be inclusive of both universal harmony and compelling justice. It is truth that can truly set us free. The justice we pursue must be the justice of God. One can fight for one's rights in a situation of injustice, of course; but the justice that brings peace must bring reconciliation and forgiveness.

The justice of God does not contradict love. To prepare ourselves to receive and treasure peace, we must realise that it is not simply a matter of rationality but one of our most basic myths. Modern man's tragedy is that he is no longer nourished by transcendental values.

We need value-bearing myths to sustain our world. The time has come to cherish the 'myth of peace', but we still lack common symbols and images by which to connote it. How inadequate and needlessly divisive our current devices are: the dove with the olive branch, the steel fist gloved in velvet! The peace of which we dream is an expansive and inclusive peace. It cannot be bound by the limitations and conditionalities we impose upon the Good. In our pluri-religious world, the myth of peace must be one that transcends boundaries of individual religions. This would make it more meaningful at a spiritual level, precisely for being the more secular at the outward one.

Let me conclude by suggesting an image that could become the symbol for our myth of peace — our blue planet seen from space. It is the only home we have, to care for and share in.

Balarama's Point of View

Devdutt Pattanaik

ALARAMA DID not participate in the Mahabharata war because he believed in peace at any cost. Balarama's point of view is often overlooked since he is dismissed as a 'partial incarnation' of Vishnu (Krishna was a 'complete' one). Yet, Balarama's alternative to the divine viewpoint reaffirms that there is no absolute in the empirical world.

Balarama, like Krishna, was born in response to the pleas of the earth-goddess, who had grown tired of man's greed. Balarama was Vasudeva's seventh son by Devaki. To protect him from the murderous Kamsa, the goddess Yogamaya transplanted him into the womb of Rohini, Vasudeva's other wife, who lived with her sister Yashoda in Gokul, across the river Yamuna.

In Jain mythology, Balarama is part of the 'Baladeva-Vasudeva-Prativasudeva' triad. Baladeva is the serene Jain hero who rejects violence while a Vasudeva is the hero who confronts the villain, the Prativasudeva, to establish order. Balarama's rejection of war makes him a 'Baladeva' and so, worthy of Jain adoration.

In Hindu mythology, Balarama is certainly not a non-violent hero, but his violence is impetuous, often fizzling out when he finds a reason to forgive. This is unlike Krishna, whose battles are determined efforts. While Krishna is charming and complex, Balarama appears candid and rustic. The two brothers represent union of opposites and thus the fullness of life.

As gods, Krishna and Balarama come across as patrons of man's primary occupations: Krishna with his cows is associated with animal husbandry while Balarama with his plough is linked to agriculture. Between them, loved and protected, stands Subhadra, a manifestation of the ancient and now forgotten earth-goddess, Ekanamsa.

In Puri, Orissa, stands the only temple where the three divine siblings are worshipped. Krishna represents the Vaishnava creed, Subhadra the Shakti cult and Balarama the Shaiva philosophy. Like Shiva, Balarama is associated with serpents and intoxicants (in iconography, he is always shown in a drunken state with his consort Revati). Like Shiva, Balarama has a quick temper but is easy to please, as many legends in the Mahabharata, *Bhagavatam* and *Harivamsa* demonstrate. And like Shiva, he prefers to renounce the complex politics of preservation and walk away from the battlefield.

To walk away from a battle is as tough as participating in one. If one chooses to fight, one must be prepared to accept responsibility for the bloodshed, rape and pillage that attend it. If one chooses not to fight, one must be willing to crush the ego that refuses to let one go. And one must be ready to be branded a coward and escapist.

After the Mahabharata, when Balarama condemned the unfair means by which his favourite disciple Duryodhana had been killed by Bhima, Krishna said: "You, who did not participate in the war, have no right to comment on it". Balarama sealed his lips, realising the price of non-participation — non-judgment.

The Axe-wielding Sage

Vidya Kamat

E HAS not slept for days, but his blood-shot eyes are as alert as those of a hungry tiger on the prowl. His nimble gait shows that he is well accustomed to the dense forest. His muscular body is almost bare, his matted hair loosely tied in a knot and his skin streaked with war paint. His left hand cradles a massive battle-axe while in his right hand is an arrow, a bow on his right shoulder. He is on a mission: To kill.

This may sound like a Hollywood action hero, but is actually a depiction of the sage Parashurama, believed to have roamed the earth in the fourth century BC and considered the sixth avatar of Vishnu. Parashurama's life is marked by controversy, mystery and violence, which suggest that he was a zealot, obsessed with personal vendetta. Born in the family of Bhrigu sages, he was the fifth son of Jamadagni and Renuka. Shiva was so pleased with Parashurama's devotion that he taught the young boy rare techniques in archery and warfare. Shiva also presented him a battle-axe, *parashu*, which became his hallmark.

There is an exceptional tale which reveals Parashurama's unflinching devotion to his parents. Once, when Jamadagni felt that his wife had lost her chastity, he commanded his sons to behead her. While his brothers stood horrified, Parashurama severed his mother's head with his axe. Jamadagni, pleased with his obedience, allowed him a boon. Parashurama promptly asked him to restore Renuka to life.

However, the deed that secured Parashurama the stature of an incarnation of Vishnu is his gruesome slaughter of kshatriyas, ancient India's warriors. Scriptures tell of how Parashurama 'cleared' the earth of kshatriyas 21 times. A kshatriya king, Kartavirya Arjuna of the Haihaya dynasty, once stole a magical cow from the hermitage of Parashurama's father. When Parashurama came to know this, he killed Kartavirya and recovered the cow. To avenge their father's death, Kartavirya's sons killed Jamadagni in Parashurama's absence.

Infuriated, Parashurama vowed to kill every living kshatriya and wipe the warrior caste from the face of the earth. The killing spree came to a halt only after he had destroyed 21 generations of kshatriyas, including 12,000 kings. He later offered a sacrifice to atone for this genocide, and invited the sage Kashyap to be the officiating priest. As *dakshina* or fee, Parashurama offered Kashyap all the land he had seized from the kshatriyas. Taking this opportunity to restore order, Kashyap ordered Parashurama to vacate the land at once. Homeless, Parashurama scaled Mount Mahendra and flung his axe in the west towards the ocean. Where it fell, the land of Shurparika (present-day Sopara, a coastal town in Maharashtra) was created.

Parashurama represents a period in the history of ancient India when the existing social order was threatened by a power struggle between two dominant segments of society. Then, as now, the genocide, that Parashurama, an 'avatar' of Vishnu, wreaked, raises an unsettling question: Can violence really be justified as a solution to social problems?

Cosmic Awareness is True Human Identity

Daisaku Ikeda

CONOMIC GLOBALISATION is proceeding at a furious pace today. The heart of the problem is not capitalism per se but indifference to global justice and ethical standards. Can we afford to reject everything alien to market principles and enforce ideas across the board in the name of global standards?

We must strive to create value. In economic terms, this means a transition from a consumer economy to a constructive one. What interests me as a Buddhist is the problem of identity. The correct identity base must be global, even cosmic, awareness. A borderless economy results in homogenisation and a standardised consumer culture. The inability of the human spirit to be satisfied with a consumer's impersonal identity generates friction, which in turn engenders a kind of isolationism.

There is no greater good than empowering humanity. Religion also should help people discover themselves anew, find liberation, reform their consciousness and elevate their souls. Only then can it contribute to overcoming the identity crisis and bridging the gap between 'local concerns' and the 'overarching goals of global civilisation'.

Gautama Buddha's *Lotus Sutra* describes a Bodhisattva as a person committed to the work of restoring a sense of cosmology to contemporary society. This means being a master of the art of dialogue and a standard-bearer of soft power. The following three traits summarise the character and mindset of a Bodhisattva of the earth: To be strict towards oneself, like a sharp, autumn frost. To be warm and embracing towards others, like a soft, spring breeze. To be uncompromising when confronting evil, like a lion monarch.

Only a person embodying all three can be a master of dialogue, which is the most reliable tool to firm foundations for peace. We must first identify the nature of the problem and then employ dialogue — the essence of soft power — to remove, one by one, the obstacles to its solution. In our information-saturated society, we are inundated with readymade stereotypes obscuring the truth of people and situations. This is why person-to-person dialogue is more than ever in demand.

No one wants war. Unfortunately, isolation breeds mistrust, which breeds conflict. To make the new millennium an age of peace, we must explore means of deinstitutionalising war. The best way to start is by encouraging dialogue. The second is the reduction of the international traffic in arms. To profit from warfare in other countries, to callously sacrifice human life for one's private gain. To view the future as an extension of the present is passive and defeatist. The future is something we ourselves must create. We must not passively wait for things to change, we must make the 21st century an era free of nuclear weapons, the start of a new millennium of harmony and peaceful coexistence founded on respect for the sanctity of life. We can and must create a global civil society that is truly of the people, by the people, and for the people.

Taoist Approach to Resolving Conflict

Marguerite Theophil

AO ROUGHLY translates as 'path' or 'way'. It refers to a power, which envelops all things. Tao embodies the harmony of opposites, maintaining that there would be no love without hate, no light without dark. A 'Taoist', then, is someone whose life is marked by a search for harmony and balance in all aspects of living.

Since Tao suggests understanding alternatives, it is also a potent approach to handling conflict. Conflict arises from imbalance and can be resolved by rebalancing whatever is disproportionate. Thus conflict handling is seen not as a 'go-in-and-sort-it-out-now' approach, but as an ongoing process.

The western linear process of handling conflict is: "Establish a conflict-free society and keep it that way. Always. Fight anything that disturbs this 'ideal' state". The Taoist would say that nothing stays the same always. Conflict arises in response to the disharmony that any one-sided approach is bound to bring. Conflict acts to balance 'too much' of any kind — too much good as much as too much bad. Conflict is seen then not as an evil force, but a teaching call.

Taoist ideas suggest that a conflict between two opponents persists often because the person who tries to attain harmony with the other does not know more alternatives than the other, who, in turn, attempts to intensify the confrontation. 'Alternatives' here would include ways to analyse, categorise, evaluate, explain, and act in the situation.

Some other approaches of Taoism seem baffling. For instance, it holds that 'non-action' is more effective than action. *Wu-wei,* the non-action talked of in Taoist texts, does not imply passiveness. *Wu-wei* is 'to do without doing' or 'to act without action'. Non-action does not evoke no action, but a different kind of action. *Wu-wei* implies that the individual's part may at times be to take action while at others, simply to be still, so that the Way may act through one without hindrance. Our "do something, do anything" culture completely overlooks this.

A difficult-to-grasp Taoist idea maintains that "weakness is the usage of Tao", and the metaphor used is of water. Water, though soft and flexible, can vanquish hard and strong obstacles by selecting alternatives to reach its goals. Mahatma Gandhi understood this and used it to great effect. In dealing with conflict, according to Tao, technique is important but secondary. First comes a deep understanding of ourselves, our intentions and motives. Anyone who intends to change others' actions or perceptions, or even simply influence them, must understand how Tao operates in himself, between one individual and others, how it operates in the universe. Then comes the need to consider all other alternative factors — social, natural, external, psychological — that interact with one another. The effective (but oh-so-tough) options in human interaction listed by Lao-Tsu in the *Tao Te Ching* include: working yet not taking credit, leading yet not dominating, creating without claiming ownership, and guiding without interfering.

Violent Images
Make Us Insensitive

Sudhamahi Regunathan

 NE MORNING the faculty of Jain Vishva Bharati University and I were discussing the need for education in non-violence. It seemed to attract few students and yet, it had relevance to all sections of society.

On the same day, the heinous attacks on the World Trade Center in the US were carried out. Our senses recoiled. That people could move to such levels of cruelty was beyond imagination. We could imagine the anguish of those trapped in the hijacked aircraft. We lamented the snuffing out of the lives of so many innocent people. Tears seemed to dry up in horror. As Harshavardhana writes in his play *Nagananda:* "Patience has become helpless, where has benevolence gone? Charity has vanished and compassion seems to be dead".

TV networks played the horrific scenes over and over again. As the images reappeared, shock was replaced with sadness and helplessness. Soon, we will accept this act as a distinct possibility and look towards the sky as unrestricted space for destructive imagination. Here begins the process of desensitisation and of widening frontiers of violence; by accepting and tolerating acts, which are so violent that they negate the very meaning of life.

This is an opportunity to understand non-violence, and to explore and expand its potential. Since both violence and non-violence are states of mind, social intervention is possible. Let us endorse our faith in non-violence. Let us try and change our mindset. It should not be difficult. We have all recoiled on witnessing this incident, which means we have a natural tendency towards non-violence.

Acharya Mahaprajna says that non-violence is founded on amity, tolerance and fearlessness. If we go further, we arrive at a step-by-step methodology to reach a non-violent or peaceful state of mind. That is the first step towards global peace. Policy decisions and global actions may be bound by administrative considerations to keep discipline and order. This may seemingly keep them away from opting for non-violence immediately. But as individuals who form society, we can make a beginning.

Each individual's step is significant and contributory. A story is told about Chanakya. Touring the countryside in disguise, he halted in a small village. An old woman offered him a meal. Chanakya was ravenous and so accepted the invitation. He was served steaming hot rice. Chanakya delved into the centre of the rice on his plate, which resulted in his burning his fingers. "Oh dear!" exclaimed the old woman. "You are indeed like our stupid minister Chanakya". Chanakya was taken aback. The old lady explained: "Never begin at the centre of the problem. Chanakya plans his attacks on the capital city and loses. He should begin at the periphery and slowly make towards the centre". Chanakya had learnt a new technique for success. The beginning is always small and at the periphery. But it will unfailingly lead to the centre, one day.

Individual Will No Match for Mad Mobs

Manoj Das

N THE 1960s, communal riots shook a certain town. I was surprised, for it was a new settlement around a huge industry. There was no tradition of animosity between communities; and they were united by common necessity.

On a visit to the town, I asked my friends: "Where did so many violent people come from?" "They were absolutely indigenous", revealed one. He directed my attention to a young man at a roadside kiosk. "What do you think of him?" he asked me. "A nice lad", I said. "While buying batteries from him I found that I'd forgotten my purse. I decided to come back later, but he pressed the batteries into my hand and assured me I could pay later".

"On that fateful night I saw him preparing to hurl a child into a burning house when he was prevented by some other guys of his own community", informed my friend. I realised how right Euripedes was when he said: "The mob gets out of hand, runs wild, worse / Than raging fire, while the man who stands apart / Is called a coward".

I recounted an old tale to my friends. A young farmer, Raju, worked hard on his land. One evening, the royal herald rode by announcing that whoever could interpret the king's dream will receive 100 gold coins. The king had seen a sneering jackal trying to jump onto his lap. "If only I knew the answer", murmured Raju. "I'll tell you, provided you give me half the reward", said a little bird to him. Raju agreed. "The jackal symbolises treachery. Ask the king to be cautious", said the bird.

Raju conveyed this interpretation to the king and received his reward. "What a pity I have to part with half the reward", thought Raju. He took a detour, avoiding the bird.

He invested the money prudently and grew rich. Five years passed. One evening, the king's general galloped to Raju's house and called out: "His Majesty has had another dream. He saw a bloody dagger circling his head". Scared, Raju went in search of the bird. As he approached the banyan tree, the familiar voice said: "Will you give me half the reward if I interpret the dream?" Raju promised. The bird said that the dagger represented violence and that the king should be on his guard. This time, Raju won 1,000 gold coins.

He was in no mood to oblige the bird. But what if the bird reported the matter to the king? He kept a stone handy and hurled it at the bird. Luckily, the bird escaped unhurt. As the years rolled by, Raju forgot all about it, until the king had another dream. This time he saw a dove on his lap. Once again Raju went to the bird and was told the dove symbolised peace. Raju was awarded 10,000 gold coins.

This time, he surrendered the entire amount to the bird. But the bird had no use for it. "Please tell me that you have pardoned me", pleaded Raju. Said the bird: "On the first occasion there was treachery in the atmosphere and you proved treacherous. The second time there was violence in the air and you were violent. Now there is trust and you have acted accordingly. Few can act according to their own inner will".

Islam Says Peace is one of God' s Names

Maulana Wahiduddin Khan

HERE ARE, in this world, two types of movements. One is based on love whose aim is to reform human beings. Such a movement awakens in its adherents feelings of generosity and good wishes towards others. Its exponents strive peacefully to pass on the truth they have discovered for the benefit of their fellowmen. Such a movement becomes a driving force towards the moral and social uplift of people in all walks of life.

The other kind of movement is based on hatred. Its adherents consider those who are not like-minded to be enemies. They have an overriding desire to wipe them off the face of the earth. So-called Islamic fundamentalism is a movement of this nature.

This negative thinking divides humanity into two camps; one comprises enemies, the other friends. If the incentives for the members of the movement based on love are generosity and goodwill, those for members of the movement based on hatred are ill-will and animosity.

The hatred felt by religious fundamentalists becomes inseparable from their ideology. Experience shows that of all kinds of hatred, that based on an ideology is the most rabid. Personal hatred, on the other hand, arises from temporary factors, and seldom takes long to dissipate in the ordinary course of events. But there is little chance of ideological hatred abating. And its target is the obliteration of enemies. Not until this end is achieved will it ever die down. This is the reason that ideological hatred takes no time in assuming the shape of violence. When it is found that peaceful means of persuasion are showing no results, arms are resorted to, so that all enemies may be removed forever.

Islamic fundamentalists justify their actions with a couplet by the poet Iqbal which can be translated as: "To every vein of falsehood every Muslim is like a surgical knife". We, however, find that it is implied in a different manner in the Qur'an: "When it is said to them: 'Do not commit evil in the land', they reply: 'We do nothing but good'. But it then is they who are the evil-doers, though they may not perceive it".

Islam is a name for peaceful struggle, while the so-called Islamic fundamentalism is quite the reverse. Islam is a religion which preaches non-violence. According to the Qur'an, God does not love *fasad* or violence. Basically, *fasad* is that action which results in disruption of the social system, causing huge losses in terms of lives and property.

Conversely, we can say with certainty that God loves non-violence. He abhors violent activity being indulged in human society, as a result of which people have to pay the price with their possessions and lives. This is supported by other statements in the Qur'an. For instance, we are told that peace is one of God's names. Those who seek to please God are assured in the sixteenth surah that they will be guided by Him to "paths of peace". Paradise, which is the final destination of the society of God's choice, is referred to in the Qur'an as "the home of peace".

Duty & Conscience:
Gandhi on War

Glyn Richards

AHATMA GANDHI'S attitude to war is unequivocal; he sees it as degrading, demoralising, and brutalising for men trained for it. It is totally opposed to qualities of gentleness, patience and self-restraint. Gandhi's opposition to war as a means of solving problems is total, and yet ahimsa does not mean a failure to recognise that there might be situations of moral dilemma in which different moral considerations apply for different people.

Gandhi's repugnance, for example, does not take him to the point of seeking to prevent those who wished to take part in war. He prefers simply to place the issue before them, and allow them to make their own decisions. It means that one is not forcing one's moral decisions on someone else. But Gandhi goes a step further. When those who believe in war refuse to do their duty, that is, when they refuse to fight, Gandhi feels it to be his moral duty to enlighten them as to their responsibilities as soldiers, while at the same time presenting them with the alternative path of ahimsa. By relating belief to duty, Gandhi is able to claim that he would have no compunction under Swaraj, a self-governing India, in recommending those who had no objection to taking up arms to fight for their country. Yet, he is able to maintain that the person who participates in war should strive to free himself and the world from war. He justifies this by claiming that "one's life is not a single straight line; it is a bundle of duties very often conflicting. And one is called upon continually to make one's choice between one duty and another".

If we were to argue that, as a firm believer in ahimsa, Gandhi's moral responsibility could hardly be regarded as recommending people to fight, it might seem difficult at first to know what his response would be other than that if a man is unable to choose the higher path of ahimsa, he should be encouraged to fulfil the obligations of the choice of the lower path of duty to his country.

Gandhi does not equate ahimsa with non-killing and notes the distinction between ahimsa and *himsa* (violence) by indicating that *himsa* means killing from anger or selfishness and ahimsa means refraining from so doing, in which case, it might be possible to be a believer in ahimsa and yet kill, provided the killing is performed with detachment, as one's duty. This is in consonance with the Bhagavad Gita.

Different moral considerations apply for different people in similar situations. Yet even when a person maintains the principle of non-violence, it is absolute only in the sense that it informs the spirit and circumstances in which violence is done, and not in the sense of a rule that permits no exceptions. This does not mean that Gandhi is not aware of the wrong that is being done when violence is committed or tolerated, or that he does not share in the feelings of guilt that result from so acting. What it means is that as life "is not a single straight line", he does what he thinks must be done and what it is morally possible for him to do in situations of moral dilemma.

Man not Measure of All Things

Kailash Vajpeyi

AN IS no longer to be the measure of all things. When Leonard B Meyer yanked man down from his exalted status in his 1963 book, *The End of Renaissance?* he triggered a radical shift between man and nature. Today, that understanding goes variously by the name of Gaia or Deep Ecology. Traditional Indian hypotheses postulate that the earth is a living organism that regulates like any other organism and that for 3.5 billion years, life on earth has co-evolved with the environment.

The Gaia hypothesis, propounded by James Lovelock, suggests that some parts of the earth are vital organs which if disrupted would cause the earth (Gaia) to malfunction. Interestingly, in Indian scriptures we come across such examples. The *Bhumi Sukta* says: "O Purifying Earth, I you invoke / O Patient Earth, by sacred word / Enhanced bearer of nourishment and / strength of food and butter / O Earth we would approach you with / due praise".

For Vedic seers, the idea of subjugating the earth was incomprehensible. The prime concern of deep ecology is to know that however ugly the parts appear, the whole remains beautiful. Integrity is wholeness. The Buddha, in his religion of mind management, also said that the world couldn't be any other way. It simply is. Everything is that which Is. There is nothing which is not that which Is.

The idea of non-violence in Jain philosophy can easily be compared with the basic tenets of Ecotopia or Deep Ecology. It is so subtle and deep that it includes every form of life (visible and invisible) which needs the attention of homo sapiens. Cause no unnecessary harm to others is the teaching of Jinas. Jinas are entirely free from attachment or aversion to any person or thing; they have neither love nor hate; nor do they have any delusion.

Influenced by this vision, the Indian way of life was integral, its purpose the well-being of all creation. In the western hemisphere Martin Heidegger, famous philosopher and author of *Being and Time,* got interested in Ecotopia near the end of his life. He concluded that all anthropocentric development paved the way for the technocratic mentality which espouses domination over nature. He requested his readers to dwell with alertness to the nature processes on this earth. David Ehrenfield, author of *The Arrogance of Humanism* was perhaps one of the first major ecologists to systematically look at the world view from a perspective that is close to Ecotopia.

The basic laws of Deep Ecology are: Everything is connected to Everything; Everything must go to somewhere; Nature is our mother, she knows best and We are earthlings. As early as in 1250 AD, the mystic Baba Farid in one of his sardonic notes had said: "Do not despise the Earth, though you tread it underfoot. When you pass away, the earth on you they will put".

The Godzilla Parishad Takes Over

Amrit Gangar

SOMETIMES, THE monsters we glorify on screen tell us about the things we dare not face. Remember Godzilla, the Japanese monster first seen in the film of the same name in 1954? His family has grown since—Son of Godzilla, Baby Godzilla, Godzilla Junior, and Super Mecha Godzilla. With these, his enemies have also grown to include fantastic figures as King Ghidorah, Rodan, Mothra, Battra and so forth. The film *Godzilla vs Mothra,* which jelled well with popular imagination, shows how years of nuclear testing have reduced the large mystical moth Mothra's egg to a hideous wasteland. Greedy businessmen turn the ruined egg into a billion-dollar tourist attraction, which the great moth wants back. And then Godzilla rises from his slumber to trample Japan. Mothra is asked for help. But Godzilla, mother of all monsters, is too deadly for any power to prevail over him. Now, Godzilla has stomped across New York as well. *Godzilla in America* is said to have shattered the previous screening record set by the film *Jurassic Park.* This brings to mind Godzilla's predecessor, King Kong.

King Kong hit public imagination in the US just around the Depression (1932-33). Recovering from the Depression, the western world began to develop an industrial model built on an inexhaustible demand for weapons. Burgeoning armament and consumer goods factories in the cities destroyed towns and villages. Progress was dictated by minds that clamoured for profits and power at any cost, and this is still the vision that drives most of the world today. One answer to this mad rush was Mahatma Gandhi. Unfortunately, there is no place for him in the jingoistic and hysterical climate that inevitably emerges in a society shored up by weaponisation. Popular culture then craves for a macho self-image, the scarier the better. And so Godzilla, who could breathe thermonuclear air and spit death rays, swelled in popularity during the Cold War. Now that the post-industrial technological complex has created new and ever more fantastic special effects, we have an increasing number of monsters in whose exploits we may rejoice.

The Godzilla sequel-fest may have taken on the look of a formulaic ritual, but it does echo the deadly sounds of the nuclear attacks on Hiroshima and Nagasaki, the carpet bombing of Vietnam. Dangerously enough, political immediacy decides the fate of mankind. However, the pantheon of monsters can easily make us believe that our collective nightmares are actually our dreams. And even the most innocent pleasures turn out to have poisoned roots. Not surprisingly, for instance, the first major commercial application of virtual reality betrays its military origins: Battle Tech is a game based on networked military tank simulators.

A promo-line for the latest Godzilla movie announces: "Twice the monster, twice the fun". Godzilla has returned, equipped with brand-new technology. He will find more cities to devastate, more minds to overwhelm. No wonder the recent nuclear tests in South Asia have been welcomed with public jubilation. Twice the bomb, twice the fun?

Long Night of the Unsheathed Sword

Esther David

The season changes.
In the midday sun, the squirrels multiply.
One more troubled night passes in the shadow of unknown ghosts.
The Koel and the Bulbul
continue to call.
You tell yourself, it's nothing. It will be a normal sort of day.
It will pass.

***

You watch in wonder at the new white shoots dyed in pink and
orange, sprouting out of the dry branch of the Bougainvillea.
The Kesuda, erect, tall, thorny, stands shedding leaves in
emptiness.
It's red flowers, smooth as velvet, blossom in a bed of thorns.
Blood flows in our city of sorrow.
Clogging our lives with shrouds without forms.
Bags of ashes stand alone and unattended like funerary stones.
Columns of smoke lick the sky with demonic tongues of fire.

***

Take what you can.
Objects.
Remnants of an inferno.
Fill your bags with all that is not yours.
Connect objects with memory.
And how? dear friend, are we going to live with this loot.
These votive offerings to death.

***

Why do you shudder?
When did you last hear the stampede of human feet, clanging with
the sounds of swords, spears, guns.
Did you hear the sound of feet trampling the book of life.
Do swords and spears have a sound of their own?
Do you hear them,
moving closer?
In tens, hundreds, thousands.
With shouts of victory or defeat?
War-cries of death, destruction?
Or was it just a cry?
Tread softly on stones with sharp edges and shards
of broken glass.

***

We break the barricades of
herded animals.
Birds flutter without wings.

How many did you get?
Carry them home, in twos and twenties, upside down, legs tied,
necks hanging.
Chop them with hands dipped in blood, and fill the sky with
clouds of feathers, tufts of hair, hooves, ears, entrails and
stifled bleats.
Cook slowly on a low fire, the night is long,
the swords unsheathed.

***

The favourite *sari* with the paisley design, crumples in the dust,
turns to ashes.
The mind wanders into nooks and corners, in places known-
unknown.
And a Tear-bomb falls at your feet.
Filling your being with the fear of death.
A face cracks and breaks like a mirror.
Something dark like a bullet whizzes past.
Or was it a bottle of acid?
A can of petrol.
A lighted matchstick?
Do you feel the tears sting your eyes?

***

Your blood turns into petrol, ready to blow up in
a fountain of fire.
You have forgotten the meaning of fragrances.
Fragrances of life, love.
Homes transform into ovens and gas cylinders burst like crackers.
You wonder, in which bakery did you last smell the fragrance of
freshly baked bread and breathe into a bouquet of flowers.
When did you last walk without fear?
When did you last think about death, disaster and funerals.

***

The mind strolls in the familiar alleys of the city, taking this,
leaving that, moving away from heaps of ashes and wondering at
the meaning of freedom?
Beauty? Home?
In the empty lane under the shadow of a bullet-ridden curfew,
silence flutters overhead like a frightened bird.

(The author is a poet and lives in Ahmedabad.)

A Battle that is Eternally Waged in the Soul

Vinod Dhawan

RI KRISHNA reveals to Arjuna in the Bhagavad Gita (chapter IV, shloka 8) that he incarnates on earth as an avatar in every age to restore dharma. The evidence available to us, however, suggests that this promise has not been kept in the present age. For have we not violated dharma with impunity as to provoke the birth of an avatar? Beset as we are by the apparent triumph of negative forces, what consolation can we derive from the belief that Krishna protected the good and destroyed the evil? How, indeed, does the idea of divine intervention affect our ongoing struggles within our innermost selves and also in the external world? The concept of the avatar will not help us at all if we interpret it as a narrative sequence of deeds of one wondrous divine hero after another, who descended in times gone by to perform miracles and vanish.

Yogi Krishna Prem points out that the real meaning of an avatar is symbolic: it stands for the dawn of truth within us. He says: "It is by the mind that the whole mass of suffering that we call the world has evolved, and it is in the mind that the dread spectre must be exorcised so that in its stead the vision of harmonious Reality may dawn".

Krishna Prem (1898-1965) was a Briton who underwent Vaishnavite disciplines and possessed the remarkable ability to express, in clear English, the depth and inner resonance of ancient Sanskrit texts. Who are those wicked ones who are destroyed by the Lord, he asks. "We like to flatter ourselves that we are the good, and that those who oppose us are the wicked... It pleases us to think that all our misfortunes are the result of the wickedness of our oppressors and that, if they are destroyed or converted, we should be perfectly all right. But this is a delusion. It is not external enemies who oppress us, but we ourselves", he writes.

"He who oppresses me from without is but the instrument of my own karma; his destruction would in no way lessen my sufferings", he continues. "It is my own evil desires and tendencies that are my oppressors; it is they who cause me to suffer; and it is they who must be destroyed in the Kurukshetra which is within". Krishna Prem notes that the narratives of Vishnu avatars are metaphorical and intended to convey those inner truths that we are unable to recognise unaided: "It is not that Sri Krishna is forever beheading an eternally terrified Kamsa in an eternal Mathura, but that the spiritual laws which are symbolised for our benefit by these acts are always operating in our hearts and in the world, now as much as 5,000 years ago".

Krishna Prem concludes: "Now, as then, people are oppressed by evil rulers, but those rulers are not any material kings. It is *kama* (desire), *krodha* (anger), *lobha* (greed), *moha* (delusion) and *ahankar* (pride), who are our so-called kings. It is they who shut us up in the prison of the body. There, in the darkness of our hearts, the birth of Sri Krishna, of truth, has to take place".

The Cosmic Web of Life

Swami Satya Vedant

TODAY, MOST religions seem to have lost connection with their source. Encrusted with superstition, they lead people astray from truth. So religion as currently practised is social hypnosis; and has helped undermine human values and social responsibility. How can we restore dharma to its rightful place in the lives of people without their becoming captives of its peripheral manifestations? For this, we must be ready to accept and grapple with religion's transcendental core, which the contemporary mystic Osho called 'religiousness'.

Recent ecological studies have revealed that the earth's living and non-living entities function together as one organism. Vedic literature embodies this ecological understanding through deification of the elements. A Vedic prayer to the earth reflects this: "To you, who wear the ocean as a robe, and whose sacred breasts are the mountains/ O wife of Vishnu, forgive me, for now I must touch you with my feet". In the Rig Veda, the befriending of the universe is expressed thus: "I shall look at all beings with eyes of friendliness. And all beings will, therefore, look at me with friendly eyes".

A truly religious person is one who is aware of himself, of life around him, of his place in the universe: such a person is unlikely to cause harm either to himself or to the world. In this context, Osho remarks: "As you become more and more silent, serene, calm, and quiet, as you start understanding your own consciousness, as your inner being becomes more centred, your actions will reflect morality. It will not be something that you decide to do, it will be something as natural as roses on a rosebush".

As we begin to understand our relationship with the world, it becomes clear that religion and science are not mutually exclusive quests. Science now acknowledges that the universe is essentially an energy presence: this world picture corresponds to the religious understanding of the Divine as energy. Again, science has recognised that we live in an expanding universe; the Vedantic term 'Brahmn', the cosmic Overself, literally means 'that which is ever expanding'. In other words, God is not the creator, but rather the catalyst for an uninterrupted process of creativity. As Krishna says in the Bhagavad Gita (9:10): "My presence alone creates the universe, and in my presence the universe dissolves and recreates itself again and again".

To be religious, then, is to realise that we are manifestations of God's creativity; as humans, our ultimate fulfilment lies in manifesting our energy creatively. And religiousness consists in recognising that we need to create God every moment—we are the rock, the sculptor, and the carved image as well. As Osho declares: "The urge to create is the first stirring of the divine within you. The urge to create is the presence of God. You have the first message, the first ripple has reached you. It is the beginning and the birth of prayer... To be creative is to be religious".

The Relevance of the Saint

Ranjit Hoskote

CRITIC of this column once told me that the world has no real need for saints and that we ought not to confer a spurious acceptability on religious figures by dressing them up as scientists, feminists or environmentalists. Observing that a saint is concerned with the private quest for communion with the Divine, he contended that this could not possibly concern humanity at large. This argument needs to be treated seriously. While believers enshrine the saint as a mystic given to bursts of revolution, activists extol him/her as a revolutionary slowed down by embarrassing mystical baggage. In this separation lies the danger of distortion. A religious genius bears the values of transformation at many, sometimes irreconcilable levels, and the mystic cannot be isolated from the revolutionary.

When we speak of St Francis of Assisi, for instance, do we mean the holy man who mortified his vanity by kissing lepers' sores, or do we mean the spirited protector of animals and birds? Do we praise Mira's *Krishna bhakti* as a rebellion against feudal patriarchy, or deplore it as an act of abject self-surrender? Do we cherish Kabir as the serene celebrant of the Holy Name, or as the weaver who attacked the dogmas of the established order?

It is a mistake to straitjacket saints as perfect machines of righteousness. Often, one component of a saint's work achieves universal significance, while another remains imprisoned within its time horizon. In the same personality, radical creative insight may exist beside conformity with tradition. The saint inhabits a spiritual minefield and may become trapped by the routine performance of good acts and expectations of the devout. Sometimes, also, history overtakes the saint: the emancipatory language of divine love fades before the cadences of subjection. Or we may emulate the saint's love for created beings without particularly desiring communion with the Creator. And yet we cannot seem to exist without saints: if none are available, we invent them.

Before our eyes, a woman who led a life of tragic, confused impulses has been transmuted into an icon of compassion. If Princess Diana's was a case of canonisation by television, millions of people do turn, in their distress, to such genuine bearers of hope and resilience as Baba Amte, Pandurang Shastri Athavale, Anna Hazare, Sunderlal Bahuguna and Medha Patkar... but do I hear my critic splutter in rage?

It is not perfection, but the tenacious striving after it that makes a saint. Hamstrung though s/he be by temptations or adversities, the saint remains committed to extending human potentiality to its limits. Hobbled by negative emotions, s/he nevertheless aspires to achieve the natural, unforced practice of compassion, charity, faith. Perhaps we return to the saints because we see in them an image of what we could be. Or possibly what we could never be, but the example offered by such a life of self-experiment and self-discovery is reassuring. In this lies the continuing relevance of the saint.

In Praise of the Waters of Life

Vidya Kamat

HE BELIEF that water is the origin of life was shared by most ancient civilisations, including the Egyptian, Mesopotamian and the Indic. Since these flourished on banks of rivers, their worship of water is not surprising. In each case, the river acted as a catalyst in the evolution of socio-economic and cultural patterns. This development is celebrated in the myths that form the core of most ancient religions.

Many modern-day Hindu beliefs about rivers are inherited from the Indo-European or Aryan tribes thought to have settled beside the river Sindhu. Millions of people are convinced, for instance, that a bath in the Ganga can wash away their sins. Renowned scholar Ananda Coomaraswamy observed that the magical quality of water was akin to feminine fecundity. Indeed, Vedic seers held that rivers were females possessed of extraordinary powers. Saraswati, the most celebrated river in the Vedas, is personified as a goddess and principal mother. Rig Veda (VII.95) addresses Saraswati as the 'celestial cow' who nourishes with her milk.

The divinity attached to the river waters can be explained by the fact that Vedic seers made a clear distinction between celestial waters from rain and rivers, and terrestrial water, comprising primarily the oceans. It was the celestial waters that had the magical procreative powers. This is reiterated in mythical accounts of superhuman endeavours employed to bring these waters from the abode of the gods to the earth.

It was also proposed through myths that water, like fire, was the divine witness to all human deeds. As a result, no Hindu rite is complete without its presence. In Hindu rituals, rivers are symbolically represented by a pitcher or *kalasha*. But the most significant value attached to a river is that as the source of knowledge. Thus, Saraswati represents the goddess of knowledge without which it is impossible to attain *moksha*, liberation.

The Bhagavad Gita asserts that knowledge can help even the most sinful of beings to cross the ocean of *samsara*. Since only knowledge, and action based on knowledge, can destroy accumulated karma, nothing is purer than knowledge. And since the metaphors of revelation and passage and the values of sustenance and mystery meet in the image of the river, Saraswati is therefore worshipped both as a bestower of knowledge and as a guide who leads the devotee to *moksha*.

But with the passage of time, the traditional content of a mythic symbol is lost; and the symbol is then often confused with reality. The function of a mythic symbol is to lead from conviction based on faith to a genuine spiritual experience. Mythic symbols, which rely on tradition legitimise the experience of the seers and assure the continuity of a culture. As Carl Jung warned us, however, such faith can easily degenerate into spiritual inertia, thoughtless compliance with dogma, and cultural stagnation. After all, cultural consciousness must be characterised by the fluid energy of the river, not by the sluggishness of the swamp.

Overcoming the Dark Cloud of Despair

Sanjay Ranade

HISHMA, THE *pitamaha*, and Drona, the acharya, looked on while Dushasana dragged Draupadi by her hair into the middle of the Kuru court. Her husbands, the Pandavas, sat helpless. Arjuna's legendary bow, the Gandiva, lay useless by his side, and Bhima could only roar an oath to avenge the insult. Later, when the battle was about to begin, Arjuna lost his nerve. Throughout the battle, Bhishma's conflicts plagued him. Where did his responsibility lie? In protecting Hastinapur or its king? Drona, the teacher, asked for Eklavya's thumb without any compunction whatsoever. But in battle, his arrows found it difficult to find Arjuna. All these men knew what virtue meant and yet got so confused that they just watched helplessly as events unfolded. Their minds were clouded with thoughts and questions that had never occurred to them before.

Often, when there is economic and political uncertainty, moral and ethical values come under pressure. When the time is ripe for a change, long-held opinions suddenly come under scrutiny. Solutions, tried and tested, fail; conventional explanations and rationalisations appear obsolete. This is vividly described in the Mahabharata when Arjuna, at the threshold of war, tells Krishna that his limbs have gone limp, his mouth is dry and the Gandiva slips through his fingers. Nothing seems worthwhile. Many people feel like this during unrest and chaos.

The citizens of Magadha faced a similar conflict during the rule of the Nandas. The acharyas, who were the source of values, had been sidelined; the ministers were yes-men, and those who opposed the king simply disappeared. The entire northern region was ruled by kings who were not willing to bury their differences even when faced with Alexander's invasion. At this time Chanakya took on the responsibility of uniting people; and also educated the young rebel Chandragupta in his responsibilities as a ruler.

Chanakya, in his *Arthashastra,* offers a solution to this problem of hopelessness. He notes that *rajniti,* statecraft, is necessary for maintaining *niti,* moral order. Ethical values, however sound they might be, must have the backing of *samarthya,* power. Otherwise they are like a bow and arrows without an archer to use them. The weapon has neither strength nor accuracy nor purpose by itself. Power can be political or economic in its nature; it may emerge from the sword or the pen, or from the common voice of a collective. Power can also come out of faith, the conviction that one's way is the right (and righteous) one. It is this belief in oneself that we see at work in the mission of Mahatma Gandhi, in his practice of *satyagraha,* insistence on truth. Such faith presumes that one has meditated upon the situation, evaluated the options, understood the implications and is prepared for the consequences of one's action. It is, therefore, the most difficult of the routes to power, because it turns the wielding of power from a gratification into a responsibility.

Stop Fighting Over the Artha of Dharma

Sanjay Ranade

NE CANNOT preach religion on an empty stomach. In that one observation, Swami Vivekananda underscored the delicate relationship between religion and economics. In all struggles, control or distribution of wealth has played a key role. While perception of opposed interests promotes conflict, the perception of shared interests pacifies it.

In a market-driven world, one cannot emphasise the importance of wealth enough. Where all activity is directed towards the maximisation of advantage, it is no surprise that wealth becomes an end in itself.

In such a world, Hinduism and the Hindu face two challenges: First, Hinduism cannot be easily defined: there is no single definition quantifying or describing the 33 crore gods and goddesses of the Hindu tradition; no single version of its history; no fixed dictionary of the castes and sub-castes that make up the social realm of Hinduism; no encyclopaedia of the diverse dreams, rituals, philosophies and mythologies of the millions of people who call themselves Hindus. Secondly, there is the problem of defining a Hindu. One does not become a Hindu, one is born one.

Some, not helpfully, call Hinduism a way of life. And here, liberalisation has created a third difficulty. India's cities are melting pots where cultures, castes, histories and religions are being stirred together. Where productivity, efficiency and strategies matter. One's personal history is of little consequence. It does not always lead people to wealth or prestige as it may have done in the past; nor does it exclude people from high status, as, too, it might have done in the past. India's caste system can no longer fully contain socio-economic change. It has finally reached a point where it can no longer fit the dharma of a chief executive officer into a caste. One is not born a CEO, one becomes one.

Slowly, the karma of living action is finding its right place over karma interpreted as a birthright secured by deeds performed in previous lives. And this is the final dilemma before the Hindu. How does one fit the present-day Hindu's 'way of life' into the way described, say, in the Vedas, Upanishads or the Bhagavad Gita? With individual identities dissolving in the cosmopolitan reality of modern India, the security that one's caste and history provided is gone. Characteristically, one finds people grasping at rituals handed down by word of mouth. But, just as a temple and its idols are empty without the faith that animates them, rituals without purpose are meaningless.

Hinduism as a religion, a philosophy, a guide to better living, a dharma is facing its toughest challenge yet. This challenge does not come from other religions. It comes from within and the sooner the Hindu realises this, the better it will be for Hinduism, and for other religions too. Because, like Hinduism, other religions too will soon reach a point when their inner contradictions will strain the delicate arguments, the complicated stories, myths and hierarchies they have established over the centuries.

Dosage of Atma in Place of Adrenalin

S H Venkatramani

PIRITUAL PREACHERS straddling the spectrum of world's religions have exhorted man to remain unattached. Krishna in the Bhagavad Gita wishes man to go through life as a *sthitaprajna,* one situated in equanimity. It is the same philosophy of supreme non-attachment that St Catherine of Genoa preaches when she says: "We must not wish anything other than what happens from moment to moment, all the while, however exercising ourselves in goodness".

The Bhagavad Gita, however, does not hold before us a lazy lotus-eater's life. It preaches karma yoga, the philosophy of right action without attachment. Enthusiasm for action calls for motivation. Some adrenalin must flow in your system. The critical question is: How can you get that motivation if you live in supreme non-attachment?

In his *The Perennial Philosophy,* Aldous Huxley explains non-attachment: "In the practice of mortification as in most other fields, advancement is along a knife-edge. On one side lurks the Scylla of egocentric austerity, on the other the Charybdis of an uncaring quietism. The holy indifference inculcated by the exponents of the Perennial Philosophy is neither stoicism nor mere passivity. Self-will is renounced, not that there may be a total holiday from willing, but that the divine will may use the mortified mind and body as its instrument for good".

Non-attachment and equanimity do not mean the abnegation of will, but the transcendence of all private desires, so that the individual self can totally become an instrument of divine will. As St John of the Cross explains: "The soul that is attached to anything, however much good there may be in it, will not arrive at the liberty of divine union. For whether it be a strong wire rope or a slender and delicate thread that holds the bird, it matters not, if it really holds fast; for until the cord be broken, the bird cannot fly. So the soul, held by the bonds of human affections, however slight they may be, cannot, while they last, make its way to God".

In action without attachment, the motivation comes not from the heart's passions, but from the soul's clear perception of the indivisible oneness of reality, the *advaita* of Adi Shankara. In this perception, there is no dualism between the perceiver and the perceived: You cannot tell the dancer from the dance, as W B Yeats described it. "The goods of God", said St John of the Cross, "can only be contained in an empty and solitary heart". You have to empty yourself of all private purpose so that you may be imbued with the divine purpose. That is the poverty of the spirit which Jesus Christ repeatedly spoke about.

The Sufi woman saint, Rabi'a, says: "God, if I worship Thee in fear of hell, burn me in hell. And if I worship Thee in hope of Paradise, exclude me from paradise, but if I worship Thee for Thine own sake, withhold not Thine everlasting Beauty". When you see that "everlasting Beauty" in your soul, and yourself as one with it, your action will spring from an awareness born of atma, not of adrenalin.

War and the Dharma of a Journalist

Siddharth Varadarajan

URING A war, what does a journalist do when his dharma as a journalist comes into conflict with what the State holds to be his dharma as a patriot? Even though the Kargil war did not jeopardise the existence of the country, the fact that young soldiers were fighting and dying placed a heavy moral burden on society. For journalists, the dilemma was: Was it justified to compromise truth to further the State's 'war effort'?

Two weeks into the conflict, the country was appalled to learn that the bodies of six Indian soldiers had been returned by Pakistan in a mutilated condition. Every newspaper carried the gory details, as supplied by the Army to UNI, without waiting for independent or even official confirmation. Strangely, such confirmation never arrived. At least two newspapers received information that only one of the six bodies had shown signs of mutilation. Yet, the journalists who received this information chose to remain silent. As the battle progressed, at least one newspaper and one magazine also received reports from correspondents at the front of incidents where Indian soldiers had mutilated the bodies of some dead Pakistani soldiers. After a heated editorial debate, the decision was taken to 'kill' these stories.

In the Mahabharata, truth-telling often clashes with other obligations. Arjuna decides that he must obey his vow to kill anyone who insults Gandiva, his bow, even though this means he must slay his brother Yudhisthira. Krishna counsels Arjuna that his duty to avoid fratricide must take precedence over his duty to be true to his word. Promise-keeping and truth-telling can be compromised, said Krishna, if lives are saved as a result. He narrated the story of Kaushika, a hermit who always spoke the truth. One day, some merchants passed by. Soon after, a gang of robbers asked Kaushika where the merchants had gone. Kaushika truthfully told them. The merchants were robbed and killed.

As B K Matilal argued in an essay on moral dilemmas in the Mahabharata, Krishna believed that "under situational constraints, there might be stronger grounds for rejecting truth-telling as a duty and accepting the stronger duty of saving an innocent life". Acknowledging that dharma cannot be known by us as universally fixed, Matilal nevertheless adds: "But the acknowledgement of possible flexibility does not mean that the fixity and universality of ethical laws will be entirely negotiable... Krishna allows for flexibility of dharma but this flexibility never means the 'anything goes' kind of morality".

Does Krishna offer the Indian journalist a way out of his moral dilemma during war? He certainly does. The journalist must abide by his dharma so long as nothing he does leads to the loss of an innocent life. To reveal crucial details of strategy when the war is being fought would be an act of moral stupidity equal to that of Kaushika. But the suppression of truth about unpleasant incidents and the dissemination of half-truths and innuendoes alluded to above did not save lives. All it did was undermine the reputation of the Indian media.

Five Lessons in the Dharma of War

Muthusamy Varadarajan

HE SOUND and fury of Kargil has led to the dharma of the politician and the journalist being debated. It is time, however, to look at the dharma of war itself. Opening words of the Bhagavad Gita hail Kurukshetra as *Dharmakshetra,* field of dharma, because it is an unavoidable, just war. The injured party, the Pandavas, made reasoned pleas, sent objective negotiators but were told they would not get even five villages. Thus the Pandavas' hands were forced.

Lesson one: Fight if you have right on your side and you are left with no alternative. But the very first hiatus occurs when the most redoubtable Pandava warrior throws down the Gandiva in despair, unable to face the thought of killing uncles and cousins, playmates and friends. He prefers death and disgrace to fratricide. Not all of Krishna's mellifluous eloquence and 18 chapters of sustained logic and elucidation can convert him until he sees the Divine Charioteer's *Vishwaroopa* and finally awakens to the awesome realisation of his inescapable karma, duty.

Lesson two: Once you have decided, and rightly, to fight, then fight unto the finish. The battle rages. Dronacharya's arrows fly with fierce fury and deadly effect. At this point, Yudhishtra, verily the Dharmaputra is inveigled into uttering a white lie in Drona's hearing: "Ashwattama (Drona's son) is dead", and whispers, "not the human but an elephant". The valiant Drona loses heart and is promptly killed. Why does Dharmaputra lie? The thought that a small lie would end Drona and save thousands of lives was what does the trick. Lesson Three: All is fair in love and war, half-truths are permitted, even for journalists provided your cause is just and you can ensure thereby a swift conclusion. What really stands out is what the Tamil *Kamba Ramayanam* reveals about Rama's conduct in battle. As he sees Ravana bloodied and fatigued, Rama tells him: "Take thyself off the battlefield today, you are exhausted, go refresh yourself and come back and fight tomorrow". Lesson four: Display compassion even at the height of battle and even if you are the victor.

Finally and most importantly, heroism on the battlefield: There is the famous verse in *Purananooru,* an old Tamil classic, that begins thus: *Mandu amarku Udainthanan ayin.* It recounts the trauma of a heroic mother. Someone has told her that they saw her soldier son's body in the battlefield, with an arrow that had pierced him in the back, implying thereby that he was fleeing for his life. Instead of grieving, the mother rages at this ultimate ignominy. Lesson five: In a just war, victory or death, that should be the motto.

Having said all this, as we ask ourselves if legend and history, literature and epic, have any lessons at all in this hour of euphoria. Albeit punctuated by dark and perilous premonitions, we should also look for sage counsel. The best advice, of course, is what the Shankaracharya of Kanchi, Chandrasekarendra Saraswati gave: "Foreswear war, abandon competition".

Beyond Parochialism
and History's Limits

Shalan Savur

 UR REAL problem in India is not political, it is social", said Rabindranath Tagore. His words reach out to us to be *sadhaks,* not *sainiks.* In post-independent India, a *sadhak* is a multiplexed personality: sage, scientist, executive, self-educationist, environmentalist, believer in self and others, statesperson, gender blender, artist, thinker.

Just as a word reveals a meaning from its alphabetical composition, so the world reveals a divine genesis from its human composition. To understand this is to comprehend the shallowness of diversity, the weakness of divisibility, the strength and beauty of unity. Such comprehension can be cultivated through the attitude outlined by Sri Aurobindo: "Either a quiet equality to all regardless of their friendliness or hostility, or a general goodwill". The key word here is 'quiet', entreating us to still our consciousness and regard one another with equanimity. Similar messages filter through our scriptures: *tat twam asi,* 'you are', a recognition of the other as self.

Nature has woven this pattern of achieving tranquil vastness in our living design. In sleep, we banish consciousness of our identity, we become *sadhaks* beyond boundaries, awash in bliss. When we awaken, we shrink ourselves to a stream, a *sainik* guarding his territorial identity.

To be in harmony in waking hours is everybody's dream. We can be, if we see ourselves as *sadhaks* contributing to the strength of the whole; not as *sainiks* defending our stretches of water. We can be, if we lower our egoistic dams of diversity, flow in a mental mainstream of oneness, ever-opening our minds so that the thinkprisons of silhouetted identities fade as the sun of unity brightens to prism a larger panorama. Implicit in such living is a greater understanding, that there is no culture that is exclusive but inclusive in the culture of humanity; no language that barricades but unites in its dignity of diction and depth of truth. To reach that divineness, we need to understand that the *sadhak's* world is a self-empowering ocean; a *sainik's* is merely an organised power. The former's calls for civilisation through conscience; the latter's for survival through might where, oftentimes, conscience is sacrificed to maintain might. Which is why the *sadhak* accepts harmonious oneness as the baseline for his growth to divinity; the *sainik* fears it as a threat to his power-base.

Today, we need to paddle midstream to contemplate, re-examine our attitudes, realise that only a balance in our inner ecology would harmonise the environment without. And float in the *sadhak's* ocean to expand through the fluid freeways of fearlessness and trust. That is what Tagore meant. In a democracy, politics is nothing but a mirror reflecting a magnified, high-profile image of our social mindset. If we become *sadhaks,* those in power will have no recourse but to become *sadhaks* themselves. If we recognise divinity, not diversity, as our destiny, so will they. A power-seeker who tries to fan our identity-passions will find his words stilled in our healing hush of harmony.

Give Sattva a Chance

Ranjit Hoskote

Dear Arjuna,

It's been quite a shock coming back to India. It's not the events; that I can cope with; remember the Bhagavad Gita (II, 64): "The soul that moves in the world of the senses and yet keeps the senses in harmony, free from attraction and aversion, finds rest in quietness". It's the newspapers that worry me. Their windows always open over the roughest view. I know it's the sensational that make the headlines. But surely life doesn't revolve around death, disease, disaster and decay alone? Where do I read about fulfilment, reflection, joy?

In the Bhagavad Gita (XIV, 5), I said that all things exist in an ever-varying combination of three *gunas* or qualities: *sattva* (serene knowledge), *rajas* (passionate action) and *tamas* (dark inertia). In the newspaper, it turns out there's a great spread of *tamas;* a fair splash of *rajas;* and here and there, a small dosage of *sattva.* The ratio of *tamas* to *sattva* is at all times overwhelmingly in favour of the former. That wise thinker, the Buddha, opened his *Dhammapada* with the crisp observation: "Our life is shaped by our mind; we become what we think". If *tamas* is what you think, I need hardly underline the consequences. Picture a spiritual Chernobyl, and you will have got the idea.

The newspaper's been described as a supermarket satisfying a spectrum of needs and tastes, where every reader can pick up what s/he wants. But we might think of the newspaper as a large temple complex where readers can stop to worship in any corridor they wish. If their temperament leads to sensual satisfaction at the periphery, they can stop there. But some may want to visit the sanctuaries of powerful deities, the cupola of leisure and lifestyle, the temple of national debate. And some might want to press still further, to reach the still point where the *sattva* is, where they read about the themes of the inner life, about bearing witness to one's actions rather than treating life as self-forgetting.

I'm not saying that *tamas* should be eliminated entirely, but get the balance right. The good newspaper designs itself on the grand temple, because the grand temple is a model of how we approach the world, a model of *jnana,* an orientation that permits you to maintain your balance while you negotiate the involvements which bind you to the world. Some have called this orientation 'spiritual literacy', a competence in attention, a mindfulness that helps you hang on to your raft in the floodwaters of experience, getting across with your compassion and creativity intact.

It's a thought, anyway. Things are quite confusing down here, and I haven't been able to figure out who's in charge. But I expect the readers have something to do with it. After all, they're the community the newspaper serves, aren't they? Ask them, Arjuna. Maybe they want to give sattva a chance.

Yours ever,
Krishna

Follow the Right Religious Path

Swami Sunirmalananda

HAT WHICH brings supreme good to the soul is called dharma. The simplest definition of dharma is *dharati lokam iti,* that which protects the world is dharma. Coming to the individual, I may be born with a thousand bad thoughts and evil tendencies. But by following dharma, my mind will become pure, and there will come a time when no evil thought will rise. The religious strive consciously to become pure and perfect. In them, no evil tendency exists; their life is a blessing and a source of inspiration to one and all. This is the effect of dharma.

Dharma is like an ocean: it has a thousand faces. In the Bhagavad Gita there are a thousand ideas, as also in the Bible and the Qur'an. Can one practise all of them? It's simply impossible. All of us are born with some inherent tendencies and select ideas and ideals which suit our temperament and follow them. If I love to meditate, I take up ideas on meditation. If I love work, I take up the path of karma yoga. All religions have views on killing but these are contextualised.

The Durga Saptashati talks only about war and killing. The Mahabharata and the Ramayana speak of violence and war. In fact, in the Mahabharata, Krishna tells Arjuna specifically that he must kill enemies. Why do we not give importance only to such teachings and go on killing our kith and kin as Arjuna did? Because these teachings were only meant to be followed under certain circumstances as guided by dharma. In the *Bhagavata* there are details of how Hiranyakashipu performed austerities. Brahma himself became pleased with his austerities since, mentions the *Bhagavata,* nobody had ever done such *tapas.* Ravana, Narakasura, Bhasmasura and a host of other religious mythical 'villains' all thought they were religious, only, they did *tapas* selfishly, to gain power. Our scriptures praise their *tapas,* their prowess, but say that they did get punished. Our bhakti scriptures go so far as to say that of the nine types of devotion, hatred is one type. Kamsa got liberation through his hatred for Lord Krishna, because he always thought of Him. However, they are careful to point out that God loves those who follow Him with love.

Some people are demonic. Their ideals are different. Although they say they practise religion, they are using religion for selfish ends. Please be reminded of that famous saying that a knife can be used both for killing others as well as serving the patient by cutting nutritious fruits for him. Religion contains so many ideals. Some are meant to warn us, while some others to guide us. There are ideas about how to destroy enemies as there are ideas about how to elevate one's own self by serving all. The simple test is to check our own conscience to see if we have chosen the right path.

Igniting the Fire in the Mind, Cleaning the Windows of Perception

Nagesh D Sondhe

T ANY given time, millions are reciting stotras, psalms, surahs and hymns in adoration of the Divine. This *japa* to the exclusion of all other thoughts leads to complete absorption in the Divine. For this practice to be effective, one must possess *shraddha*, which is often translated as faith. *Shraddha* does not mean belief in a religious creed. Since no human being's perception of reality is final, any faith or belief that we may arrive at on the basis of such a perception would also be incomplete. For seers, *shraddha* signifies the state of being in constant receptivity to intimations from beyond the boundaries of ordinary experience. Significantly, the Vedic poets sang: "My ears are open to listen; my eyes are open to perceive; what shall I speak, what shall I speak?"

This vision also informs Patanjali's aphorism, *yogah chittavritti nirodhaha,* which indicates that one must practise restraining of thought. By doing so, we may establish the true nature of humankind, which is *ananda* or bliss. To be receptive to the intimations of transcendence, we must first empty our minds of the opinions, preconceptions and beliefs that have been stored there ever since we were born. We must turn the mind from a storehouse into a sensitive and finely tuned instrument; we must leave ourselves free to perceive with our eyes, listen with our ears and savour with our intellect the expressions of the seers, without any impediment from our own thoughts, their acceptance or rejection of fresh knowledge. Only in this way can we open ourselves to receive and be attentive.

It is only in a spirit of receptivity that we can grasp reality in all its grandeur; with the exultant seer of the Yajur Veda (31.28), we may sing: "I have perceived the Supreme Person, of golden hue, abiding beyond darkness". The Vedas, Upanishads, sermons of saints and pronounce-ments of prophets are all the outcome of their *shraddha*. It is *shraddha* again that is enjoined upon the brilliant Shvetaketu in the Chandogya Upanishad: sensing the young scholar's arrogance, his father Uddalaka counsels him to be receptive to "what he has not heard, not thought, not known". In the Brihadaranyaka Upanishad, Yajnavalkya urges us to "perceive rather than merely see, listen rather than merely hear, meditate rather than merely think". And Yama, in similar vein, cautions Nachiketa in the Katha Upanishad that the path to enlightenment is "sharp as a razor's edge, hard to cross and difficult to tread".

In the Rig Veda, the poet-seer is called 'Shraddha-kamayani', one who desires *shraddha,* and invokes receptivity in the form of the divinity Shraddha (X.151). Having surrendered all his energies, the seer seeks Shraddha's grace. He knows that only the mind which has unlearned earlier habits of thought, which receives as freely as it responds, can be truly creative. Only by burning old thoughts can the mind forge a new plane of thought for itself, rejuvenate itself. And only through such renewal by spiritual fire does the mind approach illumination.

Letting the Mind's Bow-string Draw Itself

Nergis Dalal

ZEN, DERIVED from the Sanskrit *dhyana* (meditation), arrived in Japan shortly after the military dictator Minamato Yoritomo and his samurai warriors seized power. This conjunction of events provided the samurai with a religion that appealed to them strongly because of its directness and simplicity. Zen holds that the mind should be let alone, so that it may function spontaneously. So used, the mind remains unaffected by outward circumstance.

Samurai warriors incorporated Zen into such activities as swordsmanship, archery, wrestling and judo. But Zen was not confined to the warrior class: it entered Japanese architecture, poetry, painting, even the tea ceremony. Zen practitioners believe that after the formal techniques have been mastered, they must be discarded: this act releases the ingenuity and creativity of the mind.

Japanese painting and poetry are the supreme examples of Zen. Sumi-i painting, first perfected in China, was quickly adopted by Japanese artists for its 'painting by not painting'. The artist shows a world of mountains, trees, birds and large empty spaces. Every tree, every mountain is the echo of a mood. The relative emptiness of the painting is not only the background but an integral part of the picture. The secret lies in knowing how to balance form with emptiness. These paintings are often used to illustrate haiku poems which express the inner state "of going nowhere in a timeless moment". The emphasis is always on the inner life and the communication of ideas is reduced to the barest minimum. For instance: 'In a dark forest/ A berry drops./ The sound of water'. A haiku does not strive for effect. It is an expression of a state of mind and should spring complete from one's inner depths.

In his *Zen in the Art of Archery,* Eugen Herrigel writes of his own training under a Japanese master. For five years, Herrigel practised, trying to find the right way to release the bow-string so that it would "intentionally go without intention". Then came the day when the arrow flew to its target without mind and without choice.

In Zen, the brush must draw by itself, the sword-thrust be made without reflection, the meditation engaged in without desire for *satori,* enlightenment. Peter Matthiessen, author and dedicated follower of Zen, writes: "To practise Zen means to realise one's existence moment to moment rather than letting life unravel in regret of the past or day-dreaming of the future. To 'rest in the present' is a state of magical simplicity, although attainment of this state is not as simple as it sounds. At the very least, the sitting Zen, practice called *zazen,* will bring about a strong sense of well-being. To travel this path one does not need to be a Zen Buddhist, which is only another idea to discard, like enlightenment, like the Buddha, and like God".

This sentiment is perfectly expressed in these lines by a Zen Master:
"The wild geese do not intend to cast their reflection
The water has no mind to receive the image".

Solitude is a Blessed State

Sonu Rangnekar

S O MANY of us complain of loneliness, when we should cherish being alone. Are we not born alone; live our unique experiences alone, and die alone? Loneliness does not necessarily arise out of isolation from others. We can be lonely even in a crowd. On the contrary, it is when we are isolated from ourselves, when we lose contact with the quiet voice of our inner self that loneliness makes its presence felt.

How, then, can we attain the blessed state of solitude? Only when we cease to identify ourselves with the 'I' consciousness. In solitude, the mind is silent and uncluttered; we live from within. As Sri Aurobindo remarks: "You must gather yourself within more firmly. If you disperse yourself constantly and go out of the inner circle, you will constantly move about in the pettiness of the ordinary outer nature".

As slaves of the mind, we look at all our unfulfilled longings and desires through a magnifying glass and make ourselves miserable. We are totally consumed by the external reality and lose all touch with our deeper self. The more we look for external supports to pull us out of this misery, the deeper we get into it. In solitude, on the other hand, all external support is abandoned and we are alone, open and facing ourselves. Many religions draw our attention to the importance of 'non-reactional attentiveness'. Lao Tzu emphasises non-action, which is not idleness or inertia, but a total receptiveness to that which wells up from the deepest wellsprings of being. This non-action is not different from the quiet watchfulness that the Buddha commends in the *Dhammapada*.

The nearer we are to our centre, the better we can watch all events and say 'they happen', as the Bhagavad Gita tells us. Or, as Jesus summed it: "Watch and pray". In a similar vein, Guru Nanak teaches us the value of unconditional surrender to God and His will. By whatever name we may identify it, whether as non-reactional attentiveness, total receptiveness, quiet watchfulness or unconditional submission, this quality of being brings about calm.

The feeling of loneliness prevents us from living in the present moment: it crowds the mind with memories of the past and anxieties about the future. And this crowded, clouded mind is unable to attain non-reactional alertness: it cannot stop craving and learn to observe without clinging to attachment. The non-action which Lao Tzu describes is actually a key to free ourselves from our mind, into a condition where we feel at one with the universe and experience a solitude that is also communion. It is in this solitude that we are able to relax into the present moment and live in the trust that, at the appropriate moment, all the pieces of the jigsaw puzzle will fall in place. And it is in this solitude that we learn to laugh in the way that the Tibetan master, Long Chenpa, urges us to: "Since everything is but an apparition/ Perfect in being what it is,/ Having nothing to do with good or bad,/ Acceptance or rejection,/ You might as well burst out laughing".

Evolving Through the Mediation of Fire

Marzban Hathiram

IRE HAS been revered by all religions. The dominant role it has played, both in the material and spiritual life of the human race, has been reiterated in many scriptures including the Vedas and the Bible. But nowhere has fire been so revered and eulogised as in the Zend Avesta, the principal scripture of Zoroastrianism. Indeed, Zoroastrians have often been described as *atash parast,* or 'fire worshippers'.

Atash is roughly translated as fire, but the word has other resonances. Avesta says: "Fire is the son of Ahura Mazda". Further, *atash* is eulogised as: "Homage unto thee, O fire, thou created by Mazda, possessing great wisdom; of all the worshipful beings, the greatest and most worthy of worship". The Avesta reveals that fire is the physical manifestation of divine energy, or *athra,* present in all things. This divine energy is the cause of all motion: it animates everything from the smallest particles to the largest forces that drive the universe. And fire as the 'son' of Ahura Mazda is the entity that best furthers the work of Ahura Mazda, which is universal salvation.

The Avestan account holds that every fire, whether it is the warmth-giving fire of the pavement dweller or the searing one of a steel furnace, contains the divine energy, *athra,* that connects every object in the universe with Ahura Mazda. This energy is dormant. It is when an *athravan,* a priest, prays over a fire and performs various rituals over it that the dormant *athra* reveals its true nature. Such a fire is transformed into a living entity working selflessly for Ahura Mazda. It becomes *atash,* son of Ahura Mazda. A collection of four such *atash,* from the houses of a priest, a warrior, a cultivator and an artisan, forms the *atash* of an agiary or fire temple, whereas the Atash Behram, or principal fire temple, is a collection of 16 *atashes.* Of these, 15 are connected with a particular trade, while the last is created from lightning.

Agiaries and Atash Behrams are sanctuaries where the live *atash* is constantly fed and kept ablaze through prayers of the *athravans* who zealously guard its sanctity. The devout express their obeisance through the prayer: "O Ahura, cleanse me. Give me that spirit of perfect devotion that Armaiti possesses. Give me, O Mazda, the state of the Best Spirit, and the strength that comes through the observance of righteousness. Bestow unto me, a flock of goodness". Thus, rather than being worshippers of fire, Zoroastrians are worshippers of Ahura Mazda, who use the mediation of His son, Atash, to earn their redemption. Nearly 1,300 years ago, a group of 2,000 men, women and children had to leave the shores of Iran to escape the religious persecution of invading Islam. Ironically, the concept of fire worship was clearly understood and articulated by a Muslim, the celebrated Persian poet Firdausi, only 200 years after this forced migration. In his *Shah Nameh,* a legendary history of the kings of Iran, Firdausi wrote: "Do not call them fire-worshippers,/for they are worshippers of the Holy Lord through fire".

In Transit Between Darkness and Light

Homayun Taba

THE METAPHOR of light is often used to describe spiritual realities. Buddhists tell us we are "all Buddhas, but densely clouded", living in the cloud of unknowing. Another eastern metaphor refers to the opacity of the mind: by clearing and polishing it, we can turn it into a 'mirror-mind'. Upanishadic sages pray: "Lead us from darkness to light". The Buddha on his death-bed advises: "Become a light unto yourselves". Zaddiks, Jewish mystics believed that the heavenly heart was a shrine where the divine spark was hidden.

Islam is also replete with the symbology of light. Architecturally, luminosity is reflected in golden domes. In the Quran, besides innumerable references to *nur* or light, there is a chapter called *Al-nur,* which says that Allah leads "from the depths of darkness into the light". A traditional Celtic fire-lighting prayer allows a householder to turn an everyday act into a meaningful ritual: "As I light this fire, Lord, I bend my knee and lay myself before you; kindle in my heart a flame of love... Be a bright flame before me, a guiding light above me, a warm welcome ahead of me, today, tomorrow, forever".

In John (I, 10-12), we read: "That which the world had not known is the light which came into the world but which the world knew not, those however who received it became the sons of God". These sons of God, or enlightened ones, are almost always depicted with a nimbus or halo. Metaphors of light continue into the conception of the body as a spiritual vessel. Three nodal points in the body are associated with light: the heart, the forehead and the crown. The heart is often said to have been kindled by the divine spark, a vision that lives on in the image of Christ with the Sacred Heart; and St Augustine prays, "Let the flame of Thy love set on fire my whole heart".

The forehead in yoga is the location of the *ajna chakra:* the abode of that Divinity whose 'nature is light'. The opening of this chakra is the sign of illumination. Understood spiritually, enlightened men and women really see the world, as it were, 'in a new light'. The third nodal point is at the crown of the head. In Tantric symbology, the movement of the *kundalini* is directed towards the thousand-petalled lotus in the *sahasrara chakra* in the cranial region, the place of transcendental light. This union is an indication that all the lower chakras have been opened, cleared and lit up for this passage of energy. First contact with transcendent light can be quite shattering. St Paul on his way to Damascus is thrown to the ground by a light of fierce radiance. Arjuna had a no less momentous encounter with Krishna's divine form: "If the light of a thousand suns were to blaze forth all at once in the sky, that might resemble the splendour of that exalted Being". In *The Inward Odyssey,* Edith Schnapper writes that this yearning to which so many of the world's traditions bear witness "is not a promise of a future gift of light but the realisation that to receive the light is the inalienable birthright of man".

The Rest is Silence

Mrinalini Sarabhai

N THE midst of the constant noise of city life, there is need for silence. Not in an escape to the Himalayas, but in the quietude of the inner self. It is only in silence that we can seek the melody of our lives. Yet our days are filled with meaningless talk. Walk through the streets and loud voices, blaring music and the constant honking of vehicles mar the stillness of the air. Are these signs of the unhappy restlessness of our minds, which has to be covered by the din of ugly noise?

Meditation teaches us to be one with the infinite. This meditative spirit can be with us all the time. Pause a moment beside a tree and feel the love of the green forest. Look at the humble serenity of a flower, and imagine a world without flowers. Flowers ask for nothing but to give colour and fragrance to our world. Spare them some moments of silent thought as you pass by. From which garden did they come? Who gave them such lovely hues? Lift your thoughts to the garden glades that you may have walked through silently sometime in your life, perhaps as a child holding the hand of your mother. Or later with a loved one. Then, the nature of each sensation was perhaps enjoyed in silence.

Can we not continue in that gentleness even through the din of dusty, crowded roads? At twilight, the stars shine beyond the haze of polluted air, radiant, luminous. When the moon rises in a blaze of glory, the sense of serenity is overwhelming. If one only looks, seeing beyond ordinary mundane thought: in that moment of lifting one's eyes to the sky, there is a quiet lifting of the consciousness.

Use these silent, inward moments throughout the day and the clamour will become gentler and softer. For silence teaches us to recognise the useless cacophony of sound. When a centre of silence is created within ourselves, it radiates all around and in its turn spreads into larger and larger circles that reach out into infinity.

To observe silence for long periods of time is considered in all religions as a way of attuning oneself to the Supreme. But even in our busy everyday life, moments of silence can be snatched throughout the day. Is it necessary to talk continually? To air one's opinion? To listen quietly is a great virtue, but few are blessed with it. Listen not only to words but to the movement of clouds in the sky, the rustle of the earth you tread upon, the sound of water, the lilting music of nature's gifts.

The power of silence leads to a heightening of thought, of creativity and of understanding. It makes for a dynamic balance in our daily lives. For a few moments during the day, let the world go by. In the words of the revered Buddhist seeker, Lama Anagarika Govinda: "You listen and hear the Silence/ You listen and see the Silence/ You listen and smell the Silence/ You listen and taste the Silence/ You listen and feel the embrace of the Silence".

A Teacher who was not Afraid to Learn

Luis S R Vas

EVEN IN an age when the written word has yielded to the TV, certain books can revolutionise one's outlook on life. Father Anthony de Mello, the Indian Jesuit and writer who died 11 years ago, recounts one such incident in his book, *Contact with God*: "I was giving a conference to a group of sisters one evening and telling them how few are the books that really teach us to pray...One sister said, 'I've discovered a book that teaches you how to pray. Would you care to read it?'"

Having begun reading the book after supper, Fr de Mello found it so fascinating that he stayed up late into the night. Titled *The Way of a Pilgrim,* the book was discovered at the beginning of this century in the cell of a monk at Mount Athos. It soon became a spiritual classic.

The book is the story of a Russian pilgrim who wants to know how to pray without ceasing, and is in search of someone who will show him how to do this. One day, he finds a monk and entreats him to teach him how to pray. He tells him to repeat the prayer 'Lord Jesus Christ have mercy on me' in rhythm with his breathing.

Fr de Mello took up the practice: "Within less than a month I noticed that there was a marked change in my prayer. All I did was repeat this... as often during the day as I remembered to". The change he experienced was difficult to describe. "It was nothing sensational. I began to feel somewhat more peaceful, more integrated: to feel a certain depth within me. I also noticed that the prayer had the habit of springing to my lips almost automatically anytime I was not occupied with some mental activity; then I would begin to repeat it, sometimes just mechanically, sometimes meaningfully".

Fr de Mello goes on to discuss the Jesus prayer, tying it up with the psychology of the unconscious and drawing parallels with the effects of reciting the rosary. His earliest book, *Sadhana,* drew heavily on insights of vipassana meditation, he also studied Zen and was attracted to the teachings of Jiddu Krishnamurti. From these experiences emerged, not scholarly tomes, but books like *The Song of the Bird, One-Minute Wisdom* and *The Prayer of the Frog.* These are collections of spiritual stories gathered from diverse traditions, countries and cultures and are written "not to instruct but to awaken".

Fr Parmananda Divarkar observed in his introduction to one of Fr de Mello's books, that he (de Mello) evolved through three distinct stages: outwardly from spiritual director through therapist to guru; and inwardly, "from holiness through love to freedom".

In his last letter to a friend, written a day before his death on June 2, 1987, Tony de Mello observed: "I find the whole of my interest is now focused on something else, on the 'world of the spirit', and I see everything else as trifling and so irrelevant... never before in my life have I felt so happy, so free..."

Calm and Insight

Michael McGhee

BUDDHISM DISTINGUISHES between two kinds of meditation, *samatha* and *vipassana,* the former being 'calming' while the latter is an 'insight' practice. The distinction is to some extent artificial, since insight is available through samatha and calming through vipassana too. What precisely is this calming and what kind of practice is involved?

There are at least two forms of samatha meditation. One is mindfulness of breathing, *anapanasati;* the other is *metta bhavana* or development of loving-kindness. Both are exercises in learning to give your full attention to what you are doing, whether observing your breath or relating to others. Their effect may be likened to that of aesthetic experience. When the Greek god Orpheus starts to sing, forest animals fall silent, their appetites and desires recede to the periphery. That interlude allows new thoughts and feelings to be released into a consciousness which expands to receive them. And so emerges the possibility of a struggle between contending forces, where before there was only engulfment. This is perhaps what the ancient Buddhist writers had in mind when they talked about the *parikalpita* or 'imagined' nature of experience.

By contrast, samatha gives us moments of freedom from habitual grasping, not just during the practice itself, but also in liberated moments during the day. And that experience gives us intimations of the possibility of a *parinispanna* or 'perfected' consciousness, one in which grasping has completely disappeared, though it remains to be seen whether that could ever be realised. On the other hand, we start to see that consciousness itself depends upon conditions, is capable of change, and that is a form of vipassana.

Essentially, the insight is into possibilities of living and of relationships, whose possibility recedes or advances as the obscuring passions advance or recede. The implication of all this is that meditation is by no means an end in itself, but an instrument of transformation, the means of a change of being. And that raises the question of why anyone should want to meditate in the first place. In traditional Buddhism, right meditation is only one aspect of the noble eightfold path, which represents the testing of the truth, if it is one, that *dukkha*, suffering, can be overcome. So *dukkha* is the source of interest, the disease that seeks a remedy.

But this disease or uneasiness or feeling of unsatisfactoriness already opens up the possibility of an ethical dimension. The feeling is news from the future, an announcement from the periphery that things are not as they should be, new thoughts and feelings making themselves felt even in the midst of craving, for we are rarely after all wholly engulfed by the dark passions of the *alayavijnana* or storehouse consciousness. The *alayavijnana* contains other seeds that are pushing upwards, seeds which need to be seen in order to grow, just as other growths need to be seen in order that they may start to wither.

Krishnamurti's Theory of Creative Void

Kailash Vajpeyi

HIS WORLD is afflicted by neurosis. Can peace prevail in the world, or is it only a dream entertained by poets, philosophers and other such cranks? This was discussed during the last five decades by philosopher Jiddu Krishnamurti. What he struggled against were the rigid, fixed reflexes of humankind. People conditioned to accept half-truths fight for their religion, which is nothing but an amalgam of convictions borrowed from the scriptures. Even when there is much else to do, nations wage wars; only to sign peace treaties in bad faith and resume hostilities. More wars, it seems, have been fought in the name of religion than in that of love or universal brotherhood.

For Krishnamurti, there is no fixed path to truth. Sorrow is a reality and will remain so as long as desire keeps man competing with others. He explains the havoc caused by desire: "Pleasure is the guiding principle in our life. Pleasure is the thing that we want most. Here in this world and in the spiritual world in heaven, we want pleasure in any form". And when the moment of excitement is over, the event is recorded in the memory; thought wants it to be repeated. But the trouble with pleasure is that it also nourishes fear, leads to conflict and produces an unsound mind.

"The element of conflict ceases when a person realises that 'I', the observer, am the observed", notes Krishnamurti. His experience of the silent mind has its roots in the Bhagavad Gita, where Krishna tells Arjuna: "One who is not disturbed in spite of threefold miseries, who is not elated when there is happiness and who is free from attachment, fear and anger, is called a sage of steady mind". Similarly, for Krishnamurti: "A disciplined mind is never a free mind, nor can a mind that has suppressed desire ever be free. It is only through understanding the process of desire that the mind can be free. The mind that is limited by envy, by the 'me', by the acquisitive desire for things or for virtue, can never be a truly religious mind. The religious mind is not a comparative mind. The religious mind sees and understands the full significance of what is".

In one of his talks, Krishnamurti said: "The state of direct experiencing is attention without motive. When there is the desire to achieve a result, there is experiencing with a motive which only leads to further conditioning of the mind". Krishnamurti reaches the conclusion that the problems created by the mind can never be solved by the mind, divided as it is against itself. His theory of the creative void is not new to the student of Indian philosophy either. Nagarjuna, while discussing the root of conflict and suffering in his *Mahaprajnaparmita Shastra*, emphasises the fact that man's ultimate nature is his undivided being. As long as man is divided, he is bound to feel isolated and fragmentary. Nagarjuna lays bare the absurdities of life, as conceived by the imagination; he then describes the conditionedness of the conditioned as void, *shunyata*.

The Home and the Ephemeral World

Vinod Dhawan

HOW IS one to conduct oneself as a householder? King Janaka is held out as an example of the ideal householder, who through the dint of self-enquiry, realised the unsubstantial nature of the world. Though ruling a mighty kingdom, having to look after the interests of multitudes, his mind ceased to desire for anything at all, on any ground, for the sake of any cause whatsoever.

Sukhdev, a young ascetic proud of his spiritual standing, was denied entry into Vishnu's abode because he had no guru. He was vain and thought that since he was the son of a great sage, there was no need for him to have a guru. His father advised him to go to King Janaka, "the only perfect Master" at that time. Sukhdev was not satisfied. He said: "Janaka is a king while I am a sage. He is a householder and I am an ascetic. He holds court in a palace while I am a hermit. How can he be my guru?" At the intervention of Narada, Sukhdev finally went into the palace. Janaka, knowing that Sukhdev was proud of his renunciation, staged a drama. He had one leg massaged by a beautiful woman, while the other rested on hot coals. Seeing this, Sukhdev realised his mistake.

Janaka created yet another spectacle. A servant came running to report that the town was on fire. The king was unperturbed. Soon another report came that the entire countryside was now in flames. "God's will", repeated the king. A further report came that all the king's courts had gone up in flames. "It is God's will", said the king serenely. Finally the news came that his own palace was on fire. Still the king was content to resign himself to God's will. Sukhdev now thought that the king was a great fool, because he did nothing to prevent the fire from spreading. He picked up his bundle and stick and was ready to run for it. The king caught him by the arm, saying: "Look, all my wealth and possessions have been reduced to ashes, and I haven't bothered about them. Yet you are worried about your cheap bundle and stick. You are so proud to be a sage; so tell me now, which one of us is truly the hermit?"

There was another, final test in store for Sukhdev. The king ordered his officials to arrange celebrations in Sukhdev's honour. To Sukhdev he said: "Carry a cup of milk filled to the brim wherever you go today". He instructed the escort: "Let him see everything. But if he should spill a single drop, behead him on the spot". When Sukhdev returned late that night, Janaka welcomed him and asked: "How did you enjoy the entertainment?" "O King, I saw nothing of the show", Sukhdev replied, "for at every moment all my thoughts were concentrated on this cup". Janaka smiled. "Sukhdev", he said, "that is how I live in the midst of all this luxury and grandeur. I see nothing, for at every moment my thoughts are concentrated on the Lord".

Sukhdev understood that this is the supreme path, where one engages in daily activities, but does not get bogged down by them. Like the lotus, one should live in muddy water but not get muddied.

Atma is Hoo-Hoo, a Whiff of Breath

Sadhu T L Vaswani

CCORDING TO Krishna: "You are not the body, you are the atman". Just as you are in this body, there is another thing inside this body we call atman. Our physical body is like a building, where the atman comes to dwell for a while. Body is the abode of soul, house of that great *shakti*. You are not the house but its resident, the atman. 'What is atman?' A young girl asked me. Atman is a breath, a whiff of breath. From where does it come? It comes from our real home, the home we yearn to know, the home we aspire to reach, the home which is every human being's ultimate destination, the home we do not know, yet long for. Sadly, we have lost the vision of that home. This whiff of breath comes from that home. That breath is atman.

If we examine closely, we find that soul is *shakti*. What is soul-shakti? There is reference to it in the Bhagavad Gita. Atma is wonder! Atma is enigma! It has a strange composition. No one can perceive it. No one can describe it. Very few can understand it. Those few seldom speak of it and when they do, hardly anyone understands. So how should atma be described? Atma is wonder, surprise, enigma. Sri Ramkrishna Paramahansa describes it so. It cannot be put into words. Rishis contemplated on it. It is above mind, head, heart and senses. Its path is unseen, its *shakti* unfolded. The child has that wonder in the purest form. But as we grow old, we lose that wonder. Anyone who has lost this wonder, this innocence, this purity will not experience soul/ soul- shakti.

Before I left Sind for India, I went to that sacred place, Shah-ji-Bhit. Every year hundreds of fakirs, dervishes and pirs throng the place and sing in their loud desert voices. The first words which fell on my ears were Hooo Hoo/ Hooo/ Hoo. Clad in their long black robes, these pirs and fakirs sat huddled, puffing out the mysterious word, Hoo/ Hoo/ Hoo/ Hoo. The soul is Hoo/ Hoo. It is difficult to describe atma in words. All one can say is Hoo/ Hoo — a whiff of breath! I gazed at those faces lit with the wonder of that mystical chant. They were gifted with that unique faculty of wonder, through which they could perceive Hoo/ Hoo. The great Persian poet of the 13th century, Jalaluddin Rumi, too refers to the soul, as Ya-hoo.

How to grasp the soul? Often we forget that soul is *Param Khazano*. Often we violate the soul by entertaining vicious thoughts. When we sit in the company of holy men whose atma is awakened, when we interact with men of enlightened consciousness, we recover atma. The one most important lesson we should learn is to renounce. To renounce does not mean we wear ochre robes, forget our duties, or eschew our responsibilities. To renounce is *tyag*. It comes from within. It is the renunciation of our senses, our desires. A question was put to Ramakrishna. What is the essence of the Gita? He said it is *tyag*. When you renounce, you will understand *tyag*. You will enter the wonder of the soul.

You are the Father and Son of God

Trishla Jain

 NOWLEDGE IS divided between phenomenology, science of the changeable and ontology, science of the unchangeable. Ontology is the realm of being and phenomenology that of becoming. To explain it to the laity, Christianity uses the word 'Father' for ontology and 'Son' for phenomenology. The Holy Spirit is individualised consciousness that mediates the two.

Phenomenology is the mixing and constant flux of the five elements: solid, liquid, gas, space and heat. The five elements are interdependent and are created from one another. For anything to be solid, it must have been liquid previously. For anything to be liquid, heat is required. For eons, the sun has caused the earth to revolve in a manner that H_2O remains in liquid form in a narrow temperature range of zero to a hundred degrees. This is a feat of wondrous exactitude as temperatures in the cosmos range from negative to positive infinity. In order to have heat, some combustive gas is required. All this interplay occurs in space, which is the womb or mother element. Matter occupies infinitely less than one-zillionth of cosmic space, where the *leela* of phenomenology takes place.

Science limits itself in scope to this zillionth of cosmic space occupied by matter. Hence, it has been said that science is an incomplete philosophy, but philosophy is a complete science. Ontologists posit that we are pure spirit, trying to learn how to be human. At birth, we are pure; pure consciousness. The difficulty lies not in being pure consciousness, but in being human. Completely alien to our Being, we are constantly trying to master manmade functions ranging from table manners to law, family governance to human love. It's a comedown, a 'thud' that keeps us in febrile fever.

Ontology is the science of the unchangeable, undivided, pure consciousness. Knowledge of pure consciousness makes us realise that the entire universe is nothing but consciousness. I Am That. I am the entire universe, and the functioning of the universe is my responsibility. The brain is incapable of grasping the essence of ontology. This is because it can only categorise, divide and choose, assuming separateness, that there are two to choose from. The higher the IQ, the more divisive the brain. Since pure consciousness is One, the brain cannot grasp it in a thousand lifetimes.

To know your Being or virginal ontological state is to resolve, 'I am a pure virgin'. A virgin is one who is untouched by man. Hence, no thought emanating from any man can touch you. No political, economic or scientific theism penetrates your pure state. The very concept of a universe is a creation of man; even the Creator is a creation of man. If the universe and God do exist, they are a part of your pure consciousness. Once stabilised in your virgin state, everything that emanates from you is pure. Thus, Christ emanates from the Virgin Mary. This is no mere historical phenomenon; it is happening moment to moment, even as you grasp this, as only your virgin purity can. If only Christ had said, "You are the Son of God", instead of seeing purity only in himself...

What the world calls knowledge, ontologists define as ignorance. Armed with this ignorance, they can be billionaires, presidents or physicists. Even as they watch, their wealth will be surpassed, nations subjugated, scientific ideas bombed. They are at the feet of the masters of ontology, the masters of truth. Newton defined truth as 'that which is invariant in all frames of reference'. All frames of reference lean on the inventive constructs of time and space. Ontologists would simply say that they are changeable and hence are untruths—even by Newton's definition. Know the truth, and truth will set you free. The phenomenological world will be at your beck and call. Pity, you'll have no use for it, having sublimated it...

Life is Death's Gift to Humankind

Vithal C Nadkarni

TORIES OF the afterlife have fascinated the human imagination for thousands of years. Among the earliest are the adventures of King Gilgamesh, written 1,500 years before Homer. It narrates the saga of Gilgamesh of Uruk in Mesopotamia, who obtains the herb of eternal youth from the ferryman who lives forever in Dilmun, the land "where the bird of death does not utter the cry of death".

Gilgamesh intends to use the plant to revive his dead friend Enkidu. But first he must bring it out of the netherworld without succumbing to sleep. Therein lies a catch. For it is only the living who are yoked to sleep. By eschewing it, Gilgamesh joins the non-human horde and will thus be unable to cross the country from the clasp of which no one returns. And if he should sleep, he forsakes the secret of immortality, equated with ever-wakefulness. In the end, Gilgamesh nods off for a second and becomes the first human to discover the burden of mortality. He accepts the futility of struggling for what goddess Siduri calls "searching for the wind".

Divisions between life and death are not so inflexible in the Indian tradition. The well-known story of Satyavan and Savitri illustrates how Death's noose could be untied. Satyavan, Savitri's husband, dies prematurely. Yama, god of death, comes to collect his soul. When Savitri fearlessly follows the god, he offers her any boon except that of her husband's life. An only child, she asks that her father be granted grandchildren. Death assents, only to discover that he must restore Satyavan to life. Unlike Gilgamesh, Savitri returns victorious. Equally marvellous is the dialogue between Yama and Nachiketa in the *Kathopanishad*. Nachiketa, a truth-loving boy, faults his father for giving away barren cows during a sacrifice. The incensed father gives the boy away to Death. Death offers to let Nachiketa go, but he refuses to leave and will not stop asking the most awkward of questions: about the secret of life and death. He declines all temptations, choosing instead to listen to the science of liberating the soul.

The personification of Death in the Indian tradition has changed over the ages. In the earliest Vedic verses, Yama was the first man to die. Later, he became the terrifying club-wielding, noose-swishing herder of souls astride his fearsome water buffalo. He presided over a secretariat of soul-inspectors headed by Chitragupta, chronicler of deeds, who sits in judgment over the dead. By the time of the Mahabharata, Yama was identified with Dharma or Law. Whether death liberates one from life or not is debatable; but it is the absolute finality and inevitability of death that has resulted in its being associated with the defining conditions of law, morality and ethics in traditional cultures. While doctors and healers may delay its sting, eventually death bites everyone who is born. To be aware of the gaping jaws of Mahakala, time as Death, in the midst of life is wisdom, not fatalism. For only then does one realise how fleeting and precious are life's gifts, which, once spent, can never be regained from Death's unyielding grasp.

Gazing Upon the Goddess

Ranjit Hoskote

NE OF the most celebrated images of Saraswati is the 11th century marble sculpture from Dhar, Madhya Pradesh, now in London's British Museum. Installed by the Paramar king Bhoja, a legendary patron of the arts, it is a vivid tribute to the deity of musicians, artists and scholars. In this image, the goddess is clothed only in ornaments. Her breasts are emphasised; the highly stylised conception draws upon the female body's fecund sensuousness to signify nature's wider fertility. Saraswati, the 'swift-flowing one', is most often depicted as a beautiful young woman clothed in white, seated on a white lotus. Conceived of as the consort of Brahma, Saraswati is also presented in some Tantric and Puranic accounts as the wife of Vishnu; she plays an autonomous role in Hindu worship. Saraswati's cult arose during the Rig Vedic period. In later Vedic times, she had become Vak, goddess of the spoken word. The importance of the spoken word, *mantra,* in Brahminical ritual ensures a pre-eminent position for Saraswati in the Hindu pantheon.

In the light of the controversy over M F Husain's depiction of a nude Saraswati, we might usefully examine the significance of the naked female icon in India. It is unfortunate that our sensibilities have come to be conditioned by conventions of post-Renaissance western art, which almost always treats the unclothed female body as an object, a commodity on display before the male gaze. But the nakedness of the Indian icon asserts the very opposite. It is a visionary magnificence that challenges and overwhelms the viewer. The bare-breasted goddesses are no simpering nymphs baring their pink bosoms; nor are they plump, pretty dolls in the Ravi Varma manner. Rather, they are tremendous presences, manifestations of the primeval feminine principle of Shakti. Even as we gaze upon these icons, we realise that the act of viewing tells us as much about ourselves as it does about the object of our attention. Do we not usually find in something that which is in our nature to see? Indeed, there are three modes of vision by which humans approach reality: Depending upon their personality, they may use the *mamsa chakshu* (the fleshly eye of ordinary experience), *divya chakshu* (the angelic eye of the intellect) or the *prajna chakshu* (the penetrating eye of wisdom).

Viewing the naked female image, then, is in fact a test of the viewer. It reveals him as one possessed of a gross, prurient appetite, or an analytical understanding, or as one who has attained communion with the Divine, and can (in the Vedantist's phrase) look past the image at the universal ground reality of which it is an emanation. As Kshiti Mohan Sen, that distinguished commentator on Hinduism, puts it: "It would be quite naive to assume that a Hindu taking part in the Saraswati Puja believes that in heaven there is a fair young lady sitting on a white swan. It would require more imagination than this to appreciate the personification of abstract concepts so popular in Hindu culture". It is to be hoped that contemporary worshippers of Saraswati will conduct themselves in such a way as to honour Sen's faith in their sophistication.

Religion as the Marriage of Ritual and Reason

Meenakshi Bana

ANY PEOPLE regard ritual and reason as antithetical. For others, however, these are complementary in spiritual growth. Rituals are born of man's adoration for the unseen power underlying life. Worship and sacrifice encourage humility and surrender, resulting in *chitta shuddhi* or spiritual purification. Patterned as they are into traditional cultures, some rituals grow to such proportions that their real significance is lost. History affirms that rituals never die out, so long as they can offer the devout a sense of security. They must evolve with changing times to serve the purpose of self-discipline.

The attitude and intent of the performer are important. One must perform rituals with a yogic attitude, untainted by ego, lust or greed. This is the ideal of the karmayogi, expressed in T S Eliot's *The Rock:* "I say to you, make perfect your will/ I say: take no thought of that harvest/ But only of proper sowing". Yoga is the culmination of the process of refinement that leads to inner grace, soul expansion. When one learns to detach oneself from the fruits of worldly activities, one surrenders to the Divine.

Each one approaches religious practices according to his predominant *guna* or tendency: the *sattvic* devotee will appeal to God with incense and flowers, the *rajasic* will pay homage with pomp, and the *tamasic* devotee will resort to animal sacrifices. Swami Atmananda writes in *Sankara's Teachings:* "Rituals and *svadharma* are the essential atmosphere for detachment. But performance of rituals as such does not lead to this detachment, there is a method of doing it in a proper attitude of mind. This in turn paves the way of an easy ethical life".

What is this proper attitude of mind? Understanding karma as a cause and effect principle, we realise the reasonableness of leading an ethical life. Belief supported by reason and experience culminates in realisation. The reasoning power, cleansed of ego, strengthens the discerning intelligence and so helps dispel ignorance. When one is firmly established in leading an ethical life, ritual fades away. Negativities melt into courage and cheerfulness. Let us not, therefore, squander our power of reason on questioning the suitability of rituals. Let us, instead, concentrate on ethical excellence and on the transformation of knowledge into wisdom, or *jnana*.

Yoga shows how to channelise this knowledge to achieve ultimate harmony: it helps us evolve from the accumulation of knowledge to the actualisation of belief and theory. Reason, enriched by intuition and revelation, grows into consciousness of the Divine. As Parmahansa Yogananda writes: "If you work all the time, you become mechanical and lose Him in preoccupation with your duties and if you seek Him only through discriminative thought you may lose Him in the labyrinths of endless reasoning; and if you cultivate only devotion for God your development may become merely emotional. But meditation combines and balances all these approaches".

The Serpent as Lord of Nectar and Poison

Ranjit Hoskote

UR RESPONSES to the snake range from awe to revulsion; and yet, if it symbolises the fear of death, it also signifies a celebration of fertility. The serpent god who can assume human form and deceive wives in the guise of their husbands, the snake maiden who poisons her human lovers, who returns to avenge her dead mate, the dragon who guards the elixir of life — these are the stuff of childhood terror, folk belief and popular cinema. One has only to consider the tenacious persistence of the *nagin* theme in Hindi cinema and the mesmerism of the street-side *sapera* to recognise that the serpent haunts India's collective unconscious.

Snake worship in India forms part of that prehistoric cultural substratum which far predates Vedic religion. The snake is Shiva's garland and Ganesha's waistband; it forms a canopy for the Shivalingam with its hood. The thousand-headed Ananta Shesha serves as Vishnu's bed upon the cosmic waters. Snakes have long been worshipped as lords of nectar and poison and guardians of immortality. Figures who both bestow and withhold favours, they are at once benign and hostile. Naga cults originated among forest tribes of the subcontinent long before the coming of the Aryans. As the Aryans began to penetrate the forests, alliances sprang up that led to a fusion of cultures, which explains the importance accorded to *nagas* in texts like the Mahabharata. Serpent kings Vasuki, Takshaka and Nilmata play an important role in various traditional accounts; dynasties, including the Shishunaga and the Satvahana, took nagas for their tutelary deities and founder figures.

The naga is also the Indian peasant's favourite 'guardian of the field', *kshetrapala,* and is often carved in relief on stone. In an agrarian economy, snakes perform the crucial function of keeping fields free of pests. When rains flush them out, they can be a deadly threat. This is why Naga Panchami, the serpent festival, is celebrated during the monsoon: women throughout India make milk offerings to snakes (the fact that they choke on milk does not deter the devout). Many regions commemorate a specific mythic event from serpent lore on Naga Panchami. In Mathura, the focus of the celebration is Krishna's defeat of the serpent king Kaliya in combat. In Bihar, Naga Panchami is dedicated to Manasa, the goddess who offers protection from snakebite. In Mithila, newly-wed couples offer the Madhu Shravani Puja, worshipping the divine snake couple. Some of the *aripans* or ritual drawings associated with the puja trace the motif of the *naga-bhaga,* two snakes coiled around one another in passionate embrace.

Significantly, the vital energy described in Tantra as the *kundalini* is visualised as a potent snake coiled at the base of the spine, which can be aroused by yogic practices to rise through the body's psychic centres to the lotus-crown of liberation. If Judeo-Christian thought trains us to stigmatise the snake as an emblem of sin and sexual temptation, Indian thought revels in the opposite: the snake as the archetypal symbol of life's irrepressible powers of renewal.

Getting Down to the Basics

Narayani Ganesh

 INDUISM IS often regarded as a 'way of life' rather than as a strictly institutionalised entity. Religion and culture are so indistinguishably entwined that it would be sacrilegious to even try to separate the two. To those not familiar with the basics, this must seem rather odd. On the other hand, it could be this very adaptability that has enabled it to survive all kinds of onslaughts from within and without; it has retained its essential character while being embellished from varied sources.

Hindu philosophy, thought, religion, culture are rooted in the application of the laws of the universe to human life. Hence, any study of this subject begins not with scriptures but with observing the universe, from our home to the stars. The Rig Veda says: "Enlightened sages first observe, then make a deep study of God's creation. Then they repeatedly form their own versions filled with new vigour and suited to the times". The sages observed that the universe is changing ceaselessly. In their quest for immortality, they identified that what remained unchanged was infinity. This could be found within our own selves. Our body is not real, only apparent. What remains unchanged is your real Self. This was named by the ancient sages as Brahmn or atman. This is the final goal or destination of all creation. However, humans are closest to achieving it because we have developed our consciousness enough to be aware of Brahmn.

Having thus zoomed in on Brahmn, the sages honed the skills that would be required to achieve it. Six methods were developed, which are extant even today, the most popular among them being Patanjali's yoga. Yoga refers to union with the atman by elevating the individual consciousness from the body to the atman within or Brahmn without, which are, in fact, the same infinity. Yoga teaches that, in order to reach atman, you must first work off the outer layers of body and mind. Swami Prabhavananda compares yoga to seeing the bottom of a lake. "If the surface of a lake is lashed into waves, or if the water is muddy, the bottom cannot be seen. The lake represents the mind, and the bottom of the lake the atman". So the mind must be clear, calm, steady. Only then does the atman reveal itself.

When your consciousness is detached from the body and focused instead towards the atman, then the sensory perceptions of the body do not matter. The detached mind remains calm, steady, undisturbed. Then the atman comes within reach. All this and more is presented in a simple, lucid manner by Mrinal Bali in his recent publication, *The Hindu Culture,* where he leads the reader by the hand into the magical world of discovery. "I was taught about Rama and Krishna but not the basics of Hindu culture", he writes. "Rama and Krishna came much later. The basics, the foundations, of Hindu culture were laid long before them. Leave aside Rama and Krishna for a moment. Focus instead on the basics. The basics of Hindu culture are really simple for the young mind to grasp; and when the basics are clear, Rama and Krishna come closer".

Taming the Drunken Monkey

Abhijit Majumder

NCE S/HE has waded to a reasonable depth in Hindu scriptures, the reader is initiated into the art of representation by which the mundane illuminates the Divine. The self's journey through Raja Yoga, the path of spiritual integration leading to *samadhi,* is an instance. While its first phase deals with the ethical preparation of the aspirant for enlightenment, its second phase is the transformation of *chitta,* the human psyche. In this, we come across an extensive coding of transcendental experiences in physical images. The image of the restless monkey is used to represent the anarchy of the unconscious. In its normal state, the *chitta* is compared to the monkey who drinks wine and runs amok.

A less dramatic visual image is that of a lake whose muddy, agitated waters send up waves, or *vrittis,* that hide its serene floor, which is the 'I' that is visible only when the ripples have subsided. As Swami Vivekananda writes: "A word is like a stone thrown into the lake of *chitta;* it causes a ripple which sparks a series of ripples. This is memory". The treatment of *chitta* is crucial to *samadhi* because it provides the base for all mental processes. The first step of transformation, *pratyahara,* is the "gathering process". Speaking of *pratyahara,* Vivekananda invokes the monkey metaphor: "The first lesson is to sit for some time and let the mind run on...let the monkey jump as much as it can, just wait and watch... Many hideous thoughts may come into the mind; but you will find, each day, that *chitta's* vagaries are becoming less violent. Only after a patient struggle can you succeed".

The final transformation of the *chitta* to a one-pointed form of consciousness takes place in the third and last phase of Raja Yoga, through *samyama* or concentrated meditation. During the three stages *dharana, dhyana* and *samadhi* the monkey is tamed and the yogi moves closer to becoming one with the Infinite or Brahmn. With *samyama,* the yogi enters the stage where he focuses on the stone, the lake, the sun, the tree and the river as itself, participating in its 'is-ness' without binding himself into a possessive attachment. Even the otherwise pioneering Freud was ill at ease describing states like *samadhi* or *moksha;* he incorporated them under the collective term 'oceanic feeling'. In *The Inner World,* social psychologist Sudhir Kakar cites a parallel analogy drawn by Ramana Maharshi, who compared *samadhi* to a bucket of water immersed in a well: the self is immersed in the greater Self, but the rope "symbolic of the ego" is there to draw it out again.

In the *moksha* state, the ego is rendered harmless, "like the skeleton of a burnt rope", though it has a form, it is of no use to tie anything with. And so the drunken monkey is tamed to perform the rope trick: an example of how the simplest puppetry of the street flashes us a glimpse of the sacred mysteries of evolution that lie at the heart of the yogic tradition.

Ten Degrees of Evolution

Namita Devidayal

N KEEPING with the times, words take on new meanings. The Sanskrit word 'avatar' originally meant a divine incarnation. The most compelling example of it is the *dashavatar,* the ten forms believed to have been assumed by Vishnu through the ages. It has interesting contemporary resonances. For the rationalist, it sounds like an uncanny illustration of Darwin's theory of evolution, which traces the graph of species from fish-like forms to Homo sapiens. For the modern mystic, it is the story of every man's life — an allegory of physical and spiritual evolution.

Early incarnations of Vishnu are described through exotic myths — Matsya, the fish which rescued humanity from the cosmic deluge, and Kurma, the turtle that drew nectar from the ocean. Matsya might symbolise the zygote that floats in the womb; Kurma is the developed foetus, while Varaha, the boar with its head pointing down, could be the baby ready to come into the world. Narasimha, the man-lion, is perhaps a metaphor for the animal instincts men are born with, and which they must gradually overcome through the intellect. Some continue to behave like wild beasts, but others graduate to Vamana, the child state. One of the most interesting incarnations is Parashurama, the volatile Brahmin sent into the world to destroy the kshatriyas. Who has not seen vestiges of him in the self-destructive adolescent? A society which glorifies the angry young man, through cardboard cut-out Bollywood heroes, clearly has a hard time evolving out of 'Parashuramitis'.

Rama represents the *grihastha.* He personifies discipline and duty, but not necessarily the wisdom it takes to manoeuvre around law. For, in his enthusiasm to be a good king, he banishes his wife. It is rather Krishna who is wise. His charm, savvy and understanding of human nature make him a profoundly attractive personality. He serenely unravels the greatest mysteries of life even during battle, "when all around you are losing their heads". Contemporary Krishnas are hard to come by. Some might see traces of the saint-politician in Gandhi who, recognising India's military limitations and Britain's sense of propriety, used non-violence to good effect. Or in Sardar Patel, whose diplomatic acumen helped shape independent India. Yet even Krishna was, to an extent, passionately entrenched in the world. The ninth avatar, the Buddha, symbolises compassionate detachment. His teachings have a curiously modern, existentialist ring. For the Buddha, there is no external God. You are the master of your destiny through your thoughts, words and actions.

The idea of constantly reinventing yourself applies not only to individuals, but also to organisations and, indeed, nations. The allegory of the *dasha-avatar* is deeply embedded in our collective consciousness, but funnily enough, the ostrich-avatar, which exemplifies this country's current state, doesn't figure anywhere in that genealogy. It's time, therefore, to introspect, evolve and aspire towards some semblance of that elusive and most intriguing tenth incarnation, Kalki, the flawless one. It's time, in other words, to get our heads out of the sand.

Reading the Scriptures Through Women's Eyes

Geetanjali Gangoli and Gopika Solanki

LL RELIGIONS have evolved within social frameworks controlled by men: they have, accordingly, tended to propagate patriarchal ideologies. While acknowledging that religion has been the most effective tool to oppress women, some contemporary feminist scholars have argued that religion ought to be reinterpreted from a women-centred perspective. There is space for women to intervene. Religion also plays an important role in the lives of women: they are the 'carriers' of rites and traditions.

Riffat Hassan, a scholar of Pakistani origin who now lives in the US, has contributed significantly to a feminist interpretation of the Qur'an. She suggests that egalitarianism, humanism and social justice are at the heart of all religions. It has been the misrepresentation, mostly deliberate, by male scholars and theologians that has led to the degeneration of religions into oppressive and punitive practices, especially for women. Ms Hassan uses three tools of analysis: politics of language, philosophical consistency and ethical principles. Language is central in identifying the vested interests of patriarchy. She adduces the common practice of collating Allah with *miyan* (literally husband) in speech, which equates husbands in general with God. This is impermissible and blasphemous in Islam. Besides, the Qur'an has a logical consistency of equality discernible when it is studied in its entirety. Finally, she points out that the central ethical principle of the Qur'an is justice, as Allah is just. Any interpretation of the text which perpetuates injustice violates the intentions of God.

While interpreting texts in monotheistic religions like Islam and Christianity might be easy, religions like Hinduism (with their multiplicity of traditions) present a problem. Usually, those readings that have been backed by the most powerful interests have succeeded in imposing themselves and popularising their versions of religion. Women most often are powerless. How can women be empowered to push into practice a feminist understanding of their religions? In India, feminist scholars have explored folk versions of the Ramayana and the Mahabharata in an effort to recast Sita and Draupadi as feminist icons. Uma Chakravarti, a historian, has demonstrated that earlier versions of the Ramayana invest a far greater degree of autonomy in Sita than does Tulsidas's Ramacharitmanas. The research of Nabaneeta Deb Sen has led to the discovery of a women's version of the Ramayana where Rama is castigated for deserting his wife.

The importance of such efforts as a strategy to work in a pluralistic society like India is obvious. It may bring about, in some women, a newer understanding of themselves vis-a-vis their religion, family and society. But this must be combined with other strategies like legal reform, the creation of alternative social spaces, the raising of consciousness and the establishment of a programme for economic independence. This will enable women to become, through action and reflection, subjects rather than objects of their destiny.

Ganesha's Grace and Past, Present & Future

Bejan Daruwalla

ANESHA POINTS out that Indians do not say astrology. They say *jyotish,* which means light of God. In India there exists a holy umbilical cord between religion and astrology. To possess total and terrifying objectivity, knowledge, dexterity in handling planets ('energies' as I call them), on the chessboard of life and death; an abiding compassion for all life; a fervent desire to heal sorrows and augment joy; and an ability to evolve without losing a sense of fun, wonder, creativity and tranquillity. This, to me, is what an astrologer ideally is.

The *jyotishi* vibes with a family or an individual from womb to tomb. Marriage, divorce, birth of a child, starting a venture, finding out stolen valuables, auspicious occasions, buying/selling, investing/ shopping, laying the foundation stone of a building, and so on, are the areas which fall under the astrologer's orbit. The greatest lesson astrology has taught me is tolerance. People are so different in their attitudes, opinions, behaviour patterns, reactions, hates and loves. In this difference lies the magic of life. Life is a mosaic. Astrology reflects, refracts it. Therefore, it is wildly alive, tremendously challenging. This is not to suggest that astrology is the only key to life. There are other equally important disciplines, such as art, science, medicine, psychology, anthropology. I respect their contributions to understanding life.

Fate may be fully inexorable. But the glory of humans is that we have the courage to go to the end of the line and even beyond. The West has marriage counsellors, psychologists and psychiatrists. India has her astrologers and it is in our right royal tradition to go to them and be helped. This is particularly so, because we have our Vedic *mantras* and pujas for the propitiation of planets. Astrology is in our collective unconscious. Call it auto-suggestion, but it still helps, and that's what finally matters, namely public weal and good.

Sitting solid as a slab of night with a dot of radiance in the centre is the astrologer, juggling, interpreting, operating, discovering trends and directions of planets; above all, by intuition, which I call Ganesha's grace, coming to a final and sure conclusion about the track of destiny for an individual or a nation. It is this, his puja and his faith in his maker that sets him apart from other mortals.

According to Einstein's four-dimensional space and time concept, "the future is already out there and laid out. Time itself is frozen". Astrology is all about the right person, at the right place and the right time. Astrology, simply put, is timing, like the sweet smack of bat to ball. Who am I? From whence do I come and whither do I go? These are the imponderables the Indian astrologer tackles, because Vedic astrology has sections or houses in the horoscope which deal with the past life, the present one, and rebirth, or the next life. That's why it is soul food.

The Loneliness of the Short-distance Intellectual

Jyotirmaya Sharma

HE TWO armies face each other, brought together by deception, treachery and half-truths. The war, however, will have to wait for two intellects to finish an all-important conversation. The dialogue revolves around issues of this world and beyond. Early in the dialogue, they will define the *sthitaprajna*. In doing so, they will define the intellect blessed with clarity. Having done this there will be no yearning on their part for certainties normally beyond the reach of human capacities.

What lies between Pokhran and Chagai is no Kurukshetra. There is no anguished Arjuna, nor is there a wise Krishna. Any talk of an ethical and spiritual universe translates into smugness and pride since intellects do not converse, intellectuals do. The intellectual defines himself from the mirror gaze of others, not from self-possession. Yet, he is incapable of becoming part of a community.

Liberty, equality and fraternity make the intellectual free but introduce a ruthless dissolution of meaning. Scepticism and debate make nonsense of fidelity to a predetermined truth, but that also results in restlessness. The intellectual can conceive everything and dares to do everything, but exhausts himself in activities that are lonely and trivial. Capable of nothing more than restatement of prejudices, he confuses unity with unanimity. To achieve organic solidarity, he commits himself to the re-establishment of inhuman and antiquated structures. The intellectual becomes an accomplice of power and legitimises it. He knows he will encounter death and suffering, yet abdicates intellectual responsibility in the face of brute force and cruelty. Otherwise, the thought of innovative ways of death and suffering is transformed into grand systems of timeless civilisational discourse. Finally, he surrenders to the magic of technology. In times of crises, technology assumes quasi-religious dimensions. He convinces himself of technology's neutrality. But technology serves all, and because of that, it is not neutral. In the end it serves most efficiently the one who has the maximum power. The modern state inevitably utilises it most effectively.

It is not that we have ceased to ask where the centre of a human being was, what is that core of commitment which neither the senses nor the powers of nature can impregnate, what is that point of steadfastness that was immovable. Only, the answers have changed and the language has changed. The armies face each other on the tract of land between Pokhran and Chagai. War may begin any moment. The conches have been blown; no, they are not called Panchajanya and Devadatta. No intellects will converse, however. The intellects are silent, while the intellectuals create a din. One sees a lonely, solitary figure in the distance. No, it is no character from the Mahabharata. It is the philosopher Montaigne. He is saying: "In the last scene, between death and ourselves, there is no more pretending; we must talk plain French". Or plain Hindi, Urdu, Tamil, even English if you must. But is anyone listening?

True Faith is not the Tool of Ideology

Rudolf C Heredia

LL RELIGIOUS language limps in articulating mystical experience, on which faith is founded. Faith cannot ground itself in religious institutions alone; for it is in the experience, not the institutions, that we encounter the religious mystery. Precisely because a religious experience is by nature 'extra-ordinary', it both needs institutionalisation and is affected by it. To limit religious experience to individual expression subverts its necessary social dimension; to absolutise it by alienating it from human experience perverts its liberating potential.

Without grounding in religious experience, religion easily becomes an ideology, a set of ideas through which one controls one's world. This kind of religious ideology is the opposite of, and indeed, a betrayal of faith. For, while faith expresses itself in self-surrender and trust, ideology does so in terms of control and security. If self-surrender and trust are truly mutual, they cannot lead to confrontation and conflict. However, the quest for security and control only too easily becomes competitive and mutually exclusive when two or more persons are involved. The exact opposite is true for faith encounters. Here we can have a win-win situation in which each benefits oneself while enlightening the other in the exchange. This is what dialogue is all about: It is not about 'converting' the other, but about enriching both oneself and other through the foundational experience of one's religious tradition.

Of course, there are people who refuse to accept any 'mystery' to human existence. They reduce themselves and their world to a positivist perspective. Theirs is a deterministic world of cause and effect: there is no room here for hope and freedom, for moral responsibility and love. It is a closed world without transcendence. But surely human life in such an impoverished world can only be a reduction ad absurdum of the human and its potentialities? What we must address today is the brazen mobilisation of religion as an ideology, not just as a social and cultural affirmation of a group's identity, but as an orchestrated political campaign to capture and manipulate collective power. This only alienates religion from the well-springs of its religious experience and empties it of all genuine faith.

Unfortunately, the fundamentalism that is so pervasive in the religious traditions today readily lends itself to such political exploitation. For it mistakenly emphasises religious institutions, rites, rituals, scriptures, taboos, rather than personalising religious experience. This straitjackets religion into stereotypes: rather than renewing religion by reintegrating the foundational religious experience into a contemporary response of faith, fundamentalism fossilises structures and values which are then corrupted by politicisation. Here, religion is no longer just 'the opium of the masses', it becomes a tool of dehumanisation and oppression. Whereas if it is true to its foundational faith, and the experience that grounds it, it could very well be a mystic grace, an instrument of peace and liberation. The choice is a collective one, but it is still ours to make.

Balancing Between Thought and Action

Marguerite Theophil

HAVE been reflecting on the polarity that many of us believe to exist between the 'contemplative' and the 'activist'. The prevalent notion is that one excludes the other; that they are two distinct ways of being; that every individual must make a choice between them while defining his or her identity. Recently, I read in an article by Vicki Robin and Joe Dominguez, in which they said: "Activists are learning that they must also nurture themselves and their relationships; meditators are learning that they must also act".

Many who have meditated over a long period report a growing discomfort as their practice deepens; it takes the positive form of "moving to the verb", towards action. And what are the words that the activist, so busy righting all wrongs, tries to ignore? Perhaps these words of Kafka: "Stay at your table and listen. Don't even listen, just wait; be completely quiet and alone. The world will offer itself to you to be unmasked". Today, people who would ordinarily be silent are being thrust into campaigns for the environment, for human rights. It seems harder, though, for those in the thick of action to step back and reflect.

Some can doubtless respond to the wisdom of Buddhaghosha: "He who is strong in concentration, weak in energy, is overcome by idleness, since concentration partakes of the nature of idleness. He who is the opposite is overcome by distractions. Therefore, they should be made in balance to one another; from balance comes contemplation and ecstasy". Teachers in all traditions have understood the need for 'whole persons'. One wise swami would assign an intellectual seeker the task of peeling potatoes or rolling out stacks of *chapatis*. To the hands-on, sweat-it-out who came to the ashram, he gave the job of research. The balance between these two aspects of our identity can come through the intervention of a wise guide or teacher, or through our own Inner Teacher awareness or some sudden, awakening event.

An ancient story from the Chinese master Chuang Tzu tells of Shan Po, who did not act for gain like other people. Unfortunately, he met a hungry tiger who killed and ate him. Another man, Chang Yi, was quite the opposite, and lived an active life. He developed an internal fever and died. Chuang Tzu observes: "Shan Po looked after what was on the inside and the tiger ate up his outside. Chang Yi looked after what was on the outside and the sickness attacked him from inside. In my own life, I am aware of long phases when my thinking, analytical identity slides into reflection and then into contemplation. As this intensifies, I find a growing need to move, to act on my insights, to begin something, to involve myself, to invite the involvement of others. This is cyclical, as all process is. Then, the intense build-up of my action leads to a point where, if I don't consciously slow down and rein in the activist identity, my body in its wisdom will fling up a cautioning illness; it will insist that I listen".

Nature or Consciousness will not tolerate any imbalance for long!

Evil is a Necessary Evil

Sheryar Ookerjee

THE 'PROBLEM of evil' arises for two kinds of philosophies: the theistic and the absolutist, that is, for those who believe that God exists and governs the world; and for those who believe that the universe is perfect. The theistic problem is if God exists and is good, why does evil exist? He must be powerless to stop it; but if He has the power to stop it, and doesn't, He could not be all that good. Naturally neither horn of this dilemma is acceptable to the theist. One escape route is usually suggested: evil is God's instrument of soul-making and soul- testing.

But there are calamities where the question of testing or character-building just does not arise: sudden and unexpected death, for instance, of a good person who leaves no relatives or friends behind. For the theist, then, God is either omniscient omnipotent or all-benevolent, but not all three together. I know of no convincing solution offered from the theist position.

For the absolutist, Reality or the Universe or the Absolute is perfect. But, then, how can evil exist in such an Absolute? Morality and good and evil pertain to the sphere of human activity. They have no supra-human reality. The binary concept of good/evil arises only for human minds, which judge according to certain values. Further, although such judgments are not purely subjective, they are often framed within particular contexts of norm-formation and behaviour, and their 'objectivity' might therefore be somewhat relative. What is important is to realise that Reality is, for the absolutist, not a conscious quasi-human or divine being with purposes and a sense of values. For such a Reality, therefore, there is no thwarting of purpose and consequently no evil. The theist's three-horned dilemma does not bother the absolutist.

Then in what sense is Reality said, by the absolutist, to be perfect? Firstly, it is so in the sense that it is completely self-contained; there is no 'other' outside it, to which it is related. Secondly, it is a system of inter-related parts where everything is ultimately related to everything else and nothing is left isolated. Thirdly, it is not a chaotic, disorderly conglomeration, but a coherent whole subject to laws, for example, the law of causation. Because of this, human purposes are often fulfilled and are also often frustrated in such a system, giving rise to evil.

An orderly, law-dominated reality could not possibly satisfy both of two conflicting purposes. And because of the law of causation, there are millions upon millions of conflicting purposes. This is unfortunate but, on the whole, it is better this way than otherwise. In a universe not subject to laws, nobody could plan his or her life, or hope to have any purpose fulfilled. It would be a totally bewildering, Kafkaesque universe in which life is a perpetual nightmare. Thus the existence of evil is really the fallout of a perfect orderly universe; and the solution of the problem of evil is that though there is evil, there is no problem of evil. In an orderly universe, evil not only exists but must exist. This is cold comfort to those who have to face evil, but an alternative universe would have been more uncomfortable still.

The Serene Flame of Action

Vidyadhar Date

HAT BUDDHISM is not passive was demonstrated by the self-immolation of the Buddhist monk Thich Quang Duc on a Saigon street in 1963 in protest against the war launched by the US in Vietnam. Shown on TV and front-paged in newspapers in the US, it aroused the conscience of the American people against the war. Subsequently, the expression 'engaged Buddhism' was introduced by the Vietnamese Zen Master Thich Nhat Hanh, who contributed to the fall of the repressive Ngo Dinh Diem regime. In India, B R Ambedkar had adopted Buddhism as a liberating force for millions of oppressed Dalits in October 1956. The recently published book *Engaged Buddhism* edited by Christopher S Queen and Sallie B King focuses on the emancipatory role of Buddhism. The editors point out that the contribution of Buddhism to non-violent action in the cause of social justice has been so great that two recent Nobel Peace prizes have gone to Buddhists: the Dalai Lama and Aung San Suu Kyi.

There are differing views on Buddhism as an instrument of social change. Buddhism is based on service to others, wrote Walpola Rahula, the eminent Sinhalese scholar-monk and activist, in 1946. The occasion was a heated debate over the social role of the Buddhist monk in Sinhalese society in the final months before Sri Lanka's independence. Rahula founded the United Bhikkhu Council to promote an awakening of monks and laymen to current social, economic and political problems. In Max Weber's account, however, Buddhism appears as an anti-political religion, a radical mode of salvation-striving. Many scholars disagree with Weber, pointing out that the radical aspect of Buddhism was toned down by royal patronage and the institutionalisation of the *sangha*. Rarely would Buddhist rulers, even pious ones, tolerate a Buddhist judgment which criticised the existing socio-political order.

Buddhism, as practised in most Asian countries today, is seen mainly to legitimise dictatorial regimes and multinational corporations. A radical Thai Buddhist leader, Sulak Sivaraksa, contrasts the 'capital B' Buddhists, who cultivate relations with the military and financial brokers of state power, against the 'small b' buddhists, who change society by manifesting the qualities of wisdom, compassion and peace. In India, the Trailokya Bauddha Mahasangh established by the English-born Buddhist scholar-monk, Sangharakshita, has been conducting social work among Dalits. Its activities include the running of day-care centres, kindergartens, healthcare programmes, adult literacy classes and so forth.

A very different response to Buddhism was provoked recently when the foundation stone was laid for a mammoth 350-ft pagoda in Mumbai. The project is the culmination of the remarkable work done by S N Goenka, who has popularised vipassana meditation throughout the world. A nagging question persists: Why is the pagoda to be built on such a large scale? In this consumerist age, does the *saddhama*, the True Law, require flamboyance to attract seekers?

The Active Power of the Pledge

Sanjay Ranade

THE MAN has been at it for almost 30 years now. As children, we heard adults call him names and repeated them. But he continued, serenely. Every Sunday morning, he would clean gutters in the area. He would carefully pick up the stones, bottles, pieces of plastic that choked the gutters, clearing the way for the water to run smoothly. As we grew older, the realisation dawned on us that this was our filth the man was cleaning. He was not a municipal employee. He lived amongst us in a flat. He had a good job. Why were we making fun of him? Why didn't we join him? But we never took the crucial step from thought to action. The man is still alone at his task.

This is an interesting pattern. Millions of people work with sick men and women. They watch illness, deprivation, pain and suffering. Hundreds work at morgues, and death is their everyday neighbour. But only the prince Siddhartha was led to ask questions about the meaning of life when he saw sickness and death. During the mediaeval period, hundreds of women in the Deccan were married to Maratha sardars. But only one woman questioned their mode of existence and raised a son like Shivaji. Early in life, Stephen Hawking was struck with a disease that crippled him. But that did not stop him from becoming one of the greatest physicists of our time.

Where did these men and women get the *samarthya,* the power, to do what they did? All these people had their own limitations; some imposed by background and upbringing, others by disease, yet others by economic factors. But none of them allowed limitations to become mental blocks. These are traps we set ourselves and get caught in: 'I am too young', 'I am too old', 'I am poor', 'I am rich', 'I am a woman', 'I am just one person against the world', and so on. We can turn any of our limitations into a mental block; the special achievers among us demonstrate that limitations are meant to be understood and overcome. Of these mental blocks, the one that bothers us the most today is the idea that our values and opinions do not really matter.

But don't we have any influence on what is happening around us? We would be lying if we said this. Consciously or unconsciously, we influence everything around us; and, in turn, everything around us has an effect on us. In India, we have had the tradition of *vrata:* a promise made to oneself. Under a *vrata,* there are some who don't eat meat, others who abstain from liquor, or wear only khadi.

In a world that is becoming ever more consumerist, such pledges of self-restraint may seem a joke. Other pledges can replace these. One can vow, for instance, to reduce the use of plastic in one's life, or to have one's vehicle checked for pollution. Such pledges record our awareness of the optimal balance between our personal needs and those of society. This, in turn, creates a feeling of participation and purpose, of *samarthya* and it is then that we realise that no effort can go waste, however small or limited in scope it may seem to be.

The Tragic Offering of the Archer's Thumb

Damodar Prabhu

N 1928, Bihar was struck by an earthquake; and Mahatma Gandhi commented that it was caused by the 'bad karma' of people. This was met by protest, and he retracted. But can he really be blamed for holding this opinion? For the law of karma, extending along actions and consequences connecting successive rebirths has long been accepted as reality in our ethos. For instance, the Mahar saint Sant Chokhamela suffered humiliation quietly for being born 'untouchable', blaming it on sins committed in a previous life. The point is: Can a society that nurses such beliefs ever become truly egalitarian? For despite brave reformers who have battled this belief, it has hardly declined.

We routinely hear of atrocities on Dalits, tribals and other marginalised sections of society. However, today they no longer suffer oppression passively, as in the past, when they meekly allowed the caste system to dominate India's social life. One such person who acquiesced in the humiliation of the subaltern has become a permanent symbol of injustice: Eklavya, prince of the Nishads, the original hunter-gatherers of upper India. Hearing of Dronacharya, the archery teacher of the Kurus, Nishad king Hiranyadhanu sent his son Eklavya to him; naively not taking into account the racial arrogance of the Aryas.

Drona refused to instruct Eklavya. Undaunted, Eklavya made a wooden statuette of Drona and, under the eye of this symbolic guru, taught himself the skills of archery. Once, while they were out hunting in the jungle, the Pandava brothers found that their dog's mouth had been sealed by arrows, a feat impossible even for the gifted Arjuna. Searching for the wondrous archer who could perform such a feat, they came upon Eklavya. They learnt that the dog had barked at him, Vyas says because of his dark complexion and unkempt looks, so he shut its mouth with arrows. Who was his guru? Eklavya pointed to Drona's statuette.

Peeved, Arjuna went to Drona, complaining that none should be able to surpass him in archery. Drona in turn, rushed off into the jungle to meet Eklavya, who fell at his feet in reverence. Drona asked for his *guru-dakshina,* the offering made to the master for his instruction and demanded Eklavya's right thumb. By offering his thumb, Eklavya was marginalised forever.

During my schooldays, this story was told as an ideal the *guru-shishya* relationship. With its customary impartiality, the Mahabharata, on the other hand, tells it as a sordid story of one-upmanship (Arjuna), lack of moral scruples (Drona) and an excessive respect for systems and authority (Eklavya). This drama has been played out in every society, whether with Native Americans and Africans in the US, or in the caste system in India. The moral of the story is simple: The privileged fear the possibility of an Eklavya arising among the exploited. And so the thumbs of innumerable Eklavyas fall to the ground, cut off before they can guide another arrow unerringly to its mark.

A Tale of Two Yogis

Rajni Bakshi

T IS widely known that Sri Aurobindo refused to meet Mahatma Gandhi. For some people, this signifies a tussle between 'other-worldly' spirituality and social activism. There is a substantial difference between the two, but is there necessarily a conflict? Sri Aurobindo's thoughts on Gandhi's death do not indicate any conflict. He wrote: "The Light that led us to Freedom, though not yet to unity, still burns and will burn on till it conquers. The Power that brought us through so much struggle and suffering to freedom will achieve the aim which so poignantly occupied the thoughts of the fallen leader at the time of his tragic ending". Yet, at least three generations of political activists, who have admired Gandhi as an inspiration for radical action, have dismissed Aurobindo. For them, struggling against social injustices is a far more worthwhile goal than undertaking the uncharted quest for the self.

As the lives of Gandhi and Aurobindo demonstrate, this is only an apparent divide. Gandhi remained a politician while striving for the purity of a *sanyasin*. Even in old age he did not flinch from hands-on action. Thus the journey to riot-torn Noakhali where he, at age 78, walked from village to village to restore communal harmony. Aurobindo gave up the life of a bureaucrat and a revolutionary to delve into the spirit. For the last three decades of his life, he remained within his ashram, apparently aloof from worldly affairs. He answered queries in writing and composed large volumes of poetry and prose on the inward journey.

Jayantilal Parekh, member of the Aurobindo Ashram since 1938 and head of its archives, suggested that Gandhi and Sri Aurobindo represented different kinds of light, each destined to play a vital, distinctive role. There is fertile ground for those who seek the complementary elements in these great lives. For the raison d'etre of Gandhi's worldly involvement was the possibility that the self can be perfected and ultimate truth sought within. At the core of Sri Aurobindo's life-journey, correspondingly, was the exploration of ways by which the consciousness of humanity could be raised. This is why, even half a century after they both left this world, it is relevant to address Sri Aurobindo's refusal to meet Gandhi.

Jayantilal Parekh believed that Sri Aurobindo's decision was born "out of a deep spiritual consideration for him (Gandhi) and the work he had come to accomplish". Parekh appealed that, in order to grasp the truth, they ought to understand the nature of spiritual consciousness. "Sri Aurobindo's seeing Gandhi would have disturbed the work Gandhi was doing and in which he was being led by a moral force. Sri Aurobindo represented a different Light, if not quite a different and contrary nature..."

The precise nature of these differences may not be easy for most of us to grasp. However, the very attempt holds a promise of enrichment and deeper perception. But, as Jayantilal Parekh cautions, the ways of spiritual consciousness can only be understood by those who approach the spiritual path in humility.

Spiritual Pornography of the Terrorist

Jug Suraiya

HE 'SPIRITUALITY' of the so-called 'propaganda by deed', a euphemism for terrorism, has spawned monstrous paradoxes. Russian anarchists like Bakunin saw themselves as soldier-priests, preaching revolutionary ideology through the rhetoric of action: 'Destruction is also a form of creation'. In an unjust scheme of things it was not only the right, but the sacred duty of the revolutionary to unleash violence against the established order. But this gave rise to a moral dilemma.

How could a crusader for higher justice keep his cause unbesmirched by the innocent blood he shed? The anarchist's 'solution' was simple: he would sacrifice his own life along with his victim's. Writing about the freedom struggle in Ireland, W B Yeats paid a tribute to the soldier-martyrs: "All is changed, changed utterly;/A terrible beauty is born". Blood-stained history has shown up the murderous fallacy of such narcissism. There is no scruple of the heroic in modern-day terrorism. No principle, no transcendent utopia can condone or mitigate premeditated savagery against defenceless humans. This is no revolutionary fight for freedom; it is barbarism that must redefine our understanding of man's capacity for evil at the turn of the millennium.

Stripped of his romantic camouflage of rebellion, the terrorist emerges as both the product and the propagator of what could be called 'spiritual pornography'. The terrorist acts under the aegis of justice, a dispensation divinely ordained. So he seeks not just exculpation but even glory for his atrocities. He destroys not just the order which he sees to be repressive but also hope of future redemption for humanity.

The terrorist's so-called idealism or spiritual calling, is to genuine faith what pornography is to love; a perversion of a gift which offers the only hope of a link between our common dust and its uncommon, singular origin. Like the pornographer, the terrorist by sleight of mind substitutes rage for passion, isolation for oneness beyond the one; in the name of humanity he corrupts the only thing that allows us to call ourselves human. As in other products of pornography, terrorism has its exploiters and users. The most obvious is political cynicism, which time and again covers it in a cloak of legitimacy. It is aided and abetted by a media increasingly voracious for sensation. Using denunciation, such reportage highlights the most gruesome detail, transgresses the most intimate privacy. In the name of a sacred right to know, competitive elements of the media act as an unwitting tout for terrorism.

The subversive allure of the rebel casts a long shadow, from Milton's Lucifer and Michael Madhusudan Dutt's Meghnath to Melville's Ahab, ready to "strike the sun in its face if it should insult me". Our "proud and angry dust" has found in a rage of angels an apt metaphor for our unique enigma: That condemned to be free, in the name of liberation we shackle ourselves to that which must deprive us of what was already inescapably ours had we been able to see it. Blinded not by love, or even only too human lust, but by robotic pornography.

Belief in Science Can be Superstitious

Bryan Appleyard

EOFF HOON, the British defence secretary, commenting on the depleted uranium shells used by the army, said: "It does worry me that we as a society are being so sceptical about scientific investigation when we all benefit in such a staggering way from it". But what, he was asked, if his advisers are wrong? "What other advice can I rely on? We have scientists, we have doctors and, with the best will in the world, I don't really think we can go to the lowest common denominator of people's fears". This quandary is the defining puzzle of the public life of our time.

The cluster of issues based on this conflict grows by the day: the MMR vaccine, therapeutic cloning, genetically modified foods, damaging effects of mobile phones and, of course, mad cow disease (BSE). In each case we are asked to take scientists at their word and yet many of us are reluctant to do so. Most scientists told us that BSE was not a threat to human beings. They were wrong. In the case of MMR, it is now clear that the recent Finnish study did not, as doctors claimed, prove complete safety of the vaccination. This survey did not catch on the cases of autism that another dissident scientist, Andrew Wakefield, a consultant at the Royal Free Hospital, north London, believes may result from MMR.

Knowing the limitations of the Finnish study, scientists would nevertheless decide to make large claims for it on the basis that the suffering caused by any epidemic resulting from a fall in vaccination numbers would be greater than suffering caused by some cases of autism. This is a humane position to take, but the calculation cannot be made explicit because many people will inevitably conclude that their own children are at risk in the name of greater good.

Both sides are trapped in misconception. The sceptical public is unwilling to accept the probability involved in any scientific calculation and even the most well-meaning scientists are lured into claiming a degree of certainty which they know to be impossible. Both sides are haunted by the elusive spectre of a simple-minded conception of truth as a final statement about the material world. But neither side is, in fact, capable of speaking the truth in a much larger sense.

In his book, *The Tyranny of Numbers*, journalist David Boyle pins the blame on our obsession with numbers. Modern man is fatally drawn to simple numerical indices, such as intelligence quotient, as ways of measuring human affairs. Convinced that these represent 'hard truth', we find to our bewilderment that messy reality does not agree. Our response is simply to generate more numbers, rather than seek out more subtle forms of understanding. He is right, but I'm not sure he correctly identifies the problem which is, in essence, superstition. These days it most commonly means an excessive belief in science. The reality of science is that, for all its startling achievements, it remains a tentative series of guesses about nature of reality. As Isaiah Berlin said: "To claim the possibility of some infallible scientific key in this realm is one of the most grotesque claims ever made".

Nature Keeps its Secrets, Defies our Limited Perceptions

Ananda Wood

THE ANSWER to the question, 'Was Einstein a relativist?' is not quite yes. He did show that space, time, matter and energy are not real in themselves but are only observations made in relation to varying points of view. But Einstein went on to ask: If all observations of the world are relative, then what isn't? To us the world seems made of various objects, which have somehow been placed in space. But this is only a momentary picture of matter placed in three-dimensional space, to which we add the fourth dimension of time as a succession of moments.

The theory of relativity does not see the world like this. Matter and energy are treated as a single totality. They are only manifestations of a single continuity that extends through all events, past, present and future. This is the 'space-time continuum'. As we seem to travel through space and time, we get a partial and changing view of small localities. But mathematically, the continuum is described as a seamless whole through four-dimensional geometry. Each object travels along a path of events. This path is always a straight line.

Near the places where matter appears, the continuum is curved and its geometry gets complicated, thus giving the appearance of movement accelerated by force. This is just a misleading appearance seen from the narrow perspective of visualising only the three dimensions of space at each particular moment. In a single continuity, extending through space and time, all movement can be understood as naturally straight at its location within the continuity. Thus, the idea of 'force' is superficial. Einstein's approach is that reality is essentially invariant and definite; and the way to truth is a search for unity and certainty.

When quantum physics was in its infancy, he made contributions for one of which he got the Nobel prize. But he always regarded quantum theories as showing up the uncertainties of current perception in order to look for a deeper principle of truth that would resolve them. When quantum theory made discontinuity and uncertainty its fundamental principles, he was appalled. As he put it: "Nature hides her secret because of her essential loftiness, not by means of ruse". He thought it quite wrong that a theory should legislate on final barriers of uncertainty, which nature will not allow us to get past. After all, wherever we find uncertainty, it just shows up our ignorance, and ignorance shows unreality. No such ignorance or unreality can ever be final. To take it as such is to shut the door blindly on deeper knowledge.

Einstein recognised that quantum physics had shown up a difficult barrier to his further work on a 'unified field theory' that would go on from gravitation to include other forces. He cheerfully accepted that no great breakthrough was in sight. His real interest was not in spectacular or imposing theories, but in a dedication to underlying truth, which is its own reward. In his later years, he said, "One thing I have learned in a long life: that all our science, measured against reality, is primitive and childlike and yet it is the most precious thing we have".

Selfhood in the Time of the Cyborg

Baiju Parthan

N 1984, when William Gibson, who coined the term 'cyberspace' in his novel *Neuromancer*, floated the notion of a man-machine link-up suggestive of a futuristic mode of transcendence and symbiosis, it found few takers. Today, we have the World Wide Web and the Internet, which hint at the ominous potential of the all-knowing cyberspace matrix onto which everyone is physically hooked on in Gibson's vision of the future. Recent attempts at a man-machine link-up show that the Gibsonian world of cyborg life might be around the corner.

These attempts began in 1997 when Eduardo Kac, a Brazilian media artist, implanted a microchip beaming a signal indicating his identity to a database in the US through the Internet. He was making a statement about how our freedom is sacrificed to technology. At the opposite end of the ideological spectrum is the chip implant on Kevin Warwick, a professor of cybernetics in Britain. The chip switched on his computer, made his office welcome him, opened doors, even helped his secretary track him. The issue is, whether we are losing our human qualities through over-dependence on techno-intelligence. But, as Professor Warwick points out, almost all our activities will take place within a machine-augmented world in the next decade, and the only way we can fully participate in such a reality will be by developing a symbiotic relationship with machines through implants and wearable prostheses.

Science in the 20th century has been based largely on what is invisible to the human vision and offers us a world of forces and fields. Pitted against this, our everyday reality becomes a phantom reality maintained through consensual devices like semiotic stability, cultural continuity and uniformity of dogma. The machines that confront us today belong to the world of fields and forces, with operational limits defined through phenomena like quantum tunnelling, which are beyond the scope of normal human experience.

Writers like Gibson foresee a hope for a better life, even a sort of transcendence of the immediate situation that is accomplished through cybernetic prosthetics or an escape to off-planet life by living in virtual worlds. In these visions of our future, technology intrudes into the hitherto sacred space of the human body and morphs into a tool for achieving transformation. The future is not out there for the cyberpunk, where life is full of pain and all-too-human suffering. His hope lies inward, in nerves guided by the supreme all-knowing machines. This venture, it may be argued, is intrinsically similar to the one that has always been the domain of religion, except that religion has been legislated through ethical directives while the cyberpunk may give in to unregulated fantasy.

Images of the future provided by writers of science fiction have always had an insidious tendency to crystallise into reality. The outlandish vision of man machine melding is fast becoming a reality and provoking us to re-examine our traditional ideas of emancipation as achieved through religious and ethical means.

Maths and Theology in Search of God

T Kashinath

T IS interesting to examine the way the idea of God has figured in the lives of those one would think as the most rational: mathematicians and physicists. They have often had mystical beliefs, seeing the beauty of natural laws or mathematical theorems as the objective correlative of a divine order. Some have even proven the existence of God through rigorous mathematical arguments. Notable amongst such mathematicians was Pascal. He was the inventor of probability, the idea of which to a certain extent sits ill with the idea of a God ruling over our destinies. Only in a universe that is not pre-ordained can one have the play of chance. Pascal's argument supporting God was somewhat disingenuous. He said that even if one did not know that God existed, the benefits of believing in him far outweighed the drawbacks of such a belief.

Another amusing apocryphal story of a mathematician trying to prove the existence of God was of Euler, an 18th century Swiss mathematician. He was summoned to the court of Catherine the Great to dispute with the atheist Denis Diderot. At that time, rulers took their sanction to rule directly from God, the Higher Majesty, and thus this was a grave matter. Euler was a pious man. He came to the court and said: "Sir, e....=-1, therefore God exists!" The flummoxed atheist was apparently booted out amidst jeers.

Newton had a passionate interest in alchemy and the esoteric and was a Unitarian. He did not believe in the Trinity, though he swallowed his disbelief to teach at Trinity College, Cambridge. But in private he is thought to have believed himself to be one of the chosen ones, a secret apostle, and in his old age, he gave his mind increasingly over to speculations about the unfathomable mysteries of God.

Mathematicians routinely dabble in the infinite, and one can say that the idea of God is an infinity that is more numerous than any other. Given infinity, there is always a greater infinity, and thus God is the blind spot of mathematical thought. Mathematicians are also comfortable with the idea of nothingness or *shunyata*, another concept important in Indian philosophical thought. It is then perhaps no wonder that it was the Indians who invented zero, a number that denotes the presence of an absence.

Amongst mathematicians some believe that they discover mathematical truths pre-existing in God's mind. While some others believe mathematics to be a human activity, its truths being the ones we create, and thus mathematical creation is more invention than discovery. The God of the physicists is often the God of Spinoza, immanent in nature, and physical laws are seen as His divine writ that runs through the natural world. The idea of God is so subtle that it has fallen through the finest sieves mathematicians and physicists have come up with. In any case, spirituality is a matter of experience rather than learned disquisition. God is an enigma before which the hubris of the intellect is tamed, and its finitude exposed.

Pecking Order in Evolution of Life

S H Venkatramani

MOST OF us have conditioned ourselves to think of man as the pinnacle of evolution, but no one has really bothered to check whether the crows and chrysanthemums concur with this flattering self-assessment. The large size to which the brain has evolved in the human being, and the formation and shape of the cerebral cortex, are superficially observable; but even then, the quintessential humanness of this mystery called man is yet to be revealed. An ancient philosopher-poet rhapsodised: "I died as a plant to be born as an animal. I died as an animal to be born as a man. I will die as a man to be born as an angel". Even this imaginatively profound prose poem subliminally assumes that animals belong to a higher order of creation as compared to plants, and that human beings occupy an even more superior position.

Perhaps the closest we have come to putting our finger on what marks man out amid the entire kaleidoscope of creation is to have identified the human capacity for self-awareness. Man is not only aware of what happens around him by virtue of his faculties of perception; he is also conscious of the fact that he is capable of sense perception. In fact, he is even capable of being cognisant of his own awareness of beholding himself in a mirror. It is because of this unique human capacity for self-awareness that ancient seers emphasised the supreme importance of knowledge of the self. As the Brihadaranyaka Upanishad expounds: "Let men worship Him, Brahmn, as self, for in the self all these, our breath, eyes, ears and mind, are one. This Self is the footstep of everything, for through it one knows everything. And as one can find again by footsteps what was lost, thus he who knows this finds glory and praise".

Western philosophers and poets too have exhorted man to know himself to understand the universe. "Know thyself, presume not God to scan/ The proper study of mankind is man", said Alexander Pope. What is the true nature of this self, this soul, this atman? The elusive, evanescent and esoteric nature of the atman is much more mysterious to unravel than the invisible atom, the fundamental building block of the physical world. The Svetasvatara Upanishad clearly elucidates the ethereal nature of this self: "That incarnate Self, according to his own qualities, assumes many shapes, coarse or subtle, and having himself caused his union with them, he is seen as another and another, through the qualities of his acts, and through the qualities of his body".

When you probe the psychological depths of your being, when you try and fathom the innermost recesses of this mysterious selfness that pervades your every thought, word and deed, nay even your very life, you intuitively glimpse the indivisible umbilical oneness of the self, the atman, with the universal self, the Brahmn. As the Upanishads explain: "He is the one God, hidden in all beings, all-pervading, the self within all beings". From the depths of the divine despair of modern physics, you catch a fleeting glimmer of the same indivisible oneness of consciousness and physical reality.

The Lotus of a Thousand Petals

C S Shah

EVEN AFTER extensive study, we are unable to understand or predict the course of evolution. Bound by sense perception, we continue to view progress materialistically. Simplicity, renunciation and discrimination are necessary preconditions to transcend genetic limitations to that state where reality or consciousness is expressed in its full glory.

Some wonder why we cannot let nature take its own course of evolving this 'better' human being. No monkey or ape made any conscious attempt to become a man; it happened naturally. Evolution created a brain structure with an intelligence that enables us to control and guide our own evolution. Such evolution may bring about changes in the brain structure by adding one or more lobes to the brain, or developing new connections in the cerebral cortex. The brain can develop new connections to control centres of lust, hunger, sensory perception, autonomic nervous system, and so on. With this, every activity of body and mind is suspended to a stage where limiting adjutants are no more active, and consciousness is perceived as it really is: universal, unlimited, and free. This is *nirvikalpa samadhi,* or the domain of the thousand-petalled lotus, in Tantra terminology.

Some new centres could evolve in the brain that would control the present-day frontal lobe. According to modern medicine, the brain has the capacity to continuously change its structure, even its function, throughout a lifetime. This plasticity allows the brain to respond to environmental changes or to changes within the organism. The brain is altered also by hormones and other chemicals produced by the brain in response to injury, drugs, or stimulation by *japa* or meditation.

The adult brain retains the capacity to compensate for injury or neuron loss by changing its structure. The change is most likely to be in the number, or efficiency, of connections between neurons. Mechanisms controlling plasticity include not only those factors that directly change synapses or create new ones but also mechanisms which change the supporting cast of synapses between nerve cells.

The required energy will be made available by preventing wastage from external sense pleasures. The arrangement and quality of the brain will determine its capacity to express consciousness like a mirror. As one reflexively removes the hand from the flame, evolved persons abjure any thought that could trigger a feeling of possession.

With the development of the neo-cortex in human beings, which was a leap over monkeys and apes, language, art, music and mathematics entered the human consciousness. Similarly, this new cortical development will add qualities of universal love, brotherhood, renunciation and discrimination to future human consciousness. Human qualities are employed towards great progress in science and technology. Similarly, the new intelligence will make it possible where, with renunciation and discrimination, it would be quite natural to live in a state of mystic meditation and in altered states of consciousness.

You are the Centre of the Universe

Sadhu Vishwamurtidas

CIENTISTS SAY the universe is expanding in all directions as a four-dimensional space-time continuum. Space-time itself is expanding. Therefore, there can be no fixed background or in-built coordinate system against which to chart the ballooning cosmos and extrapolate even a hypothetical central point of origin. From a more pragmatic perspective, every living person is the centre of the universe, since for each person the universe exists only because he or she observes it.

The spokes of the great cosmic cartwheel emerge from you and merge back into you. You are the centre wherever you are, wherever you go. But what are we at our very core? We are obviously much more than just our physical hands and legs, for if a person's limbs are amputated, his or her thinking ability will still remain whole. Above all his activities, which are common with other animals, man is a thinking animal. "The most powerful computer", say scientists John Barrow and Frank Tipler, "has a storage capacity and information processing rate between 10 and 1,000 times less than that of a human being".

Even the least intelligent of human beings possess an information processing capacity 10 times greater than that of a Cray II computer. The IBM computer Deep Blue which defeated Gary Kasparov, regarded as probably the greatest chess player of all time, could perform an amazing 300 million computations a second. It is obvious that Mr Kasparov was not using his brain's full capacity. If even an average human being was to use all of his or her information processing capacity, Deep Blue would be a long way off from defeating him or her and, of course, far removed from defeating the brightest of human beings.

Mere information processing is not enough for divine knowledge. Self-awareness or consciousness is a pre-requisite. Not only is the human being over-endowed with information processing capacity, he or she also possesses consciousness. Why? The answer is clear. The purpose of human life is to search for the Ultimate Truth. But which truth? The truth behind the culmination of all truths; the truth behind every word, concept or dream that may or may not be listed in the dictionaries and encyclopaedias of the world; the truth of everything, including ourselves.

If an ordinary man could only see the five elements of consciousness as void; the four physical elements as not constituting an 'I'; the real Mind as formless and neither coming nor going; his nature as something neither commencing at his birth nor perishing at his death, but as whole and motionless in its very depths; his Mind and environmental objects as one: if he could really accomplish this, he would receive enlightenment in a flash. So said Huang Po, the Chinese philosopher.

"The Self is Brahma, the Self is Vishnu, the Self is Indra, the Self is Shiva, the Self is all this universe. Nothing exists except the Self", said Adi Sankaracharya. If we do not utilise this special ability to contemplate and understand ultimate truths, it means we have lived lives parallel to that of the other animals in the galaxy.

Nataraja Reveals Cosmic Secrets

Sharada Srinivasan

RITJOF CAPRA catapulted the dancing Nataraja of Chidambaram, Tamil Nadu, into a modern-day scientific icon when he euphorically stated in his book, *The Tao of Physics,* that "the dancing Shiva is the dancing universe, the ceaseless flow of energy going through an infinite variety of patterns that melt into one another". Did creators of the image actually have a scientific comprehension? Texts such as *Naisadhiyacharita* describe the scattering of stars by Shiva's dance, while the *Vadnagar Prasasti* speaks of Shiva playing with planets as if they were crystal balls.

An examination of the symbolism in Chidambaram shows that the ancient seers' revelations encompass concepts that are at once mystical and scientific. *Chit* is consciousness and *ambaram* is the cosmos. So a literal translation of 'Chidambaram' would be 'cosmic consciousness'. The shrine architecturally and conceptually links cosmic realms with inner consciousness through Shiva's *anandatandava* or dance of bliss, where he is described by the Tamil poet Umapati as *sachchidananda;* that is, 'being, consciousness and bliss'.

The Chit Sabha or the 'Hall of Consciousness' in Chidambaram is the only shrine where the Nataraja icon is worshipped in the sanctum. In all other Shiva temples it is the *lingam* that is worshipped. Shiva, as *lingodbhavamurti,* is the infinite cosmic pillar whose beginning and end could not be fathomed (somewhat like the mysterious pillar in the sci-fi classic *2001: A Space Odyssey* by Arthur C Clarke, of which it was said: "My god, it's full of stars!"). Instead, inside the Chit Sabha, by the side of the Nataraja bronze, is the enigmatic *chidambara rahasyam* or the secret revelation of Chidambaram, wherein Shiva is worshipped as the formless *akasa lingam* represented, aptly, by a curtained empty space. The curtain represents the formless manifestation of Sivakami or Shakti, primordial feminine energy who inspires and witnesses Shiva's cosmic dance. This presages an intuitive understanding of concepts such as wave-particle duality of quantum physics, with matter and energy as sides of the same coin.

The *Tatvaryastava stotra* describes Shiva as sky-clad and Chidambaram as the spot where he is both the universal dancer and the witness of his own dance, who creates and removes *maya.* Not only is Shiva's dance cosmic, but Shiva can also be identified with the sentient universe as well as the consciousness within, which creates and destroys notions of reality. These ideas hint at quantum mechanical paradoxes such as observer-created reality inherent to Heisenberg's Uncertainty Principle. They also bring to mind ideas of 'quantum consciousness' and 'the infinite brain' theorised by physicist Roger Penrose in his book *The Emperor's New Mind.* Indeed, the profound concepts symbolised by the Chidambaram temple are a humbling reminder of our sheer insignificance and transience in the gigantic universe that we, so often self-indulgently and haughtily, inhabit.

Towards a Theory of Everything

K M Gupta

HE FIRST major breakthrough in science was the reduction of the material world into about a hundred elements. Then these elements were reduced to a few particles. The many forces were reduced to many faces of electro-magnetic force, and all kinds of radiation, from light to gamma rays, were reduced to electromagnetic waves of different wavelengths and frequency. Finally the basic features of the entire universe were reduced to space, time, matter, electromagnetism or energy, and gravitation. Einstein reduced it further. In the Special Theory of Relativity he hit upon the interchangeability of matter and energy ($E = mc^2$), and in the General Theory of Relativity he propounded the indivisibility of the space-time continuum.

Thus the whole universe was distilled down into time-space, electromagnetism or matter-energy, and gravitation. In the Relativity Theory, Einstein reduced gravitation into a metric property of the space-time continuum. In his Unified Field Theory, his last, he reduced electromagnetism to just another metric property of the T-S continuum. So, at the end of the reductionist process, what was left of the universe? Just the time-space continuum with its two-fold (three-fold, if electricity and magnetism are counted separate) metric properties. This is the point where Einstein left theoretical physics.

In the 50 years after Einstein and his UFT, theoretical physics has not made an inch of substantial progress. That is not because physicists were lax, but because there was nowhere to progress. Where do you progress from an abstract space-time continuum which can't be distilled any further? This was the point at which science should have been able to arrive at a final Grand Unified Theory or a Theory of Everything (ToE).

But it didn't. Why? I believe the mental paradigm of the scientists came in the way, something that I don't want to go into here.

To put it briefly: At least for the present, it is hard for the western mind to make the necessary paradigm shift to arrive at a ToE. Had it not been so, Einstein himself could have pronounced it, as he had arrived at it already without realising it. It is less hard for an Indian to have the necessary mental paradigm. I had arrived at ToE a quarter of a century back, but incredible as it may seem, I couldn't find my way to put it across to the world. Here I set out the prototype of the ultimate ToE which can only be paraphrased, expanded and explicated, but cannot be challenged substantially. I mean, what is said here can be said in other words and in more words, but all that is to be said will be what is said here.

1. Elements make all.
2. Particles make elements.
3. Energy makes particles.
4. The content of the world is matter-energy.
5. Electro-magnetism makes energy.
6. Matter-energy happens in the time-space continuum.
7. Electro-magnetism and gravitation make the three dimensions that make space.

8. Electro-magnetism constitutes the cosmic 'length' and 'breadth', and gravitation the cosmic 'height': Space is the lay of electro-magneto-gravitation.

9. The interplay of the three metric dimensions of space, electro-magnetism and gravitation, makes matter-energy.

10. The order of events makes time, the fourth dimension.

11. Consciousness and space are not different from each other, just as matter-energy and space-time are not different from each other. Consciousness and space are respectively the interior and exterior of the same substance.

12. Consciousness-space by the interaction of its metric properties creates the universe.

13. Consciousness-space is a continuum without borders, without an outside, and as it is, the entire spectrum of being falls within the c-s continuum as it has not and cannot have an outside.

14. Since all things that fall within space are its products, by the interaction of its metric properties, and they are sustained and reabsorbed by the same space, a God is not and cannot be.

15. If there is and can be a God, it is and can only be the c-s continuum which makes, keeps and takes back all.

16. The four-dimensional space-time-consciousness continuum is God or Nature.

17. No second God is or can be.

18. The God of a religion is the First Father or Primogenitor of his original race/nation.

19. A religion is just the catharsis of its original race/nation. Gods, scriptures, prophets and places of worship are adjuncts of racial identity.

20. Revelation doesn't and can't filter except through a medium, and when it filters through a medium it shapes to the mould of the medium. Revelation descends only as crafted and qualified by the medium, never in its original purity.

21. Pure Revelation is met only on the other side of the medium of senses and mind, and at maximum entropy.

22. The separation of the electro-magneto-gravitational fields that make the metric dimensions of space is temporary. They were one basic primordial field in the beginning, and they will be that in the end at maximum entropy.

23. Maximum entropy is the terminus ad quem and terminus a quo of the universe: the zero degree of being.

24. The being or state at maximum entropy, at ZDB, is Reality, and its evolution and revolution from ZDB to ZDB in a cycle is Appearance.

25. The four-dimensional space-time-consciousness continuum is Appearance, Phenomenon.

26. The Unified Field of the electro-magneto-gravitational fields, the ZDB, is Reality, Noumenon.

27. The f-d-s-t-c-c is metric, 3-D; the UF is the Sub-metric, Zero-D.

28. The UF is the Supreme Being. The Ultimate God. The Absolute Idea.

29. The f-d-s-t-c-c is the Executive God and the UF is the Absolute God.

30. Phenomenal being is the geometry of the f-d-s-t-c-c.

31. The f-d-s-t-c-c geometry is the ultimate superior spirit, the most radiant beauty, cosmic intelligence, Providence, the Almighty, and all. This metricdom dissolves in the Submetric at maximum entropy.

32. Life is the metrication of the Submetric by means of the three metric dimensions.

33. Mind is the electrification of brain. When the brain is electrified the fired neurons form into modules which are 'pictures'. Magnetism and gravitation join electricity to make brain's pictography 3-D.

34. Electricity, magnetism and gravitation produce the super ego, ego and id in humans, and thus make the individual self out of the Cosmic self.

35. When the electro-magneto-gravitational fields come together into the Unified Field at maximum entropy, all beings attain salvation.

36. Individual beings can attain salvation prior to maximum entropy by working up the Unified Field in the brain by way of arresting the constantly shifting modulations.

Happiness is Not Simply a Passing State of Mind

Ananda Wood

APPINESS FOR most of us is a state of mind which alternates with an opposite state, 'unhappiness'. To be unhappy is to feel at odds with one's circumstances. To be happy is to feel one with 'hap', the happenings that take place in one's experience. Does this mean that happiness is just a warm, gooey feeling of sentimental pleasure which must necessarily give way to cold, hard facts of pain in a hostile world?

Literally, happiness is the shared principle common to all happenings in the physical and mental world. In this literal sense, it is what Aristotle called "the unmoved mover". It is the common principle of motivation that inspires all acts and happenings. It is that for which all acts are done. The Taittriya Upanishad says: "It is just this essential savour that is spontaneous and natural. It's only when one reaches this essential savour that one comes to happiness. For what could be alive at all if there were not this happiness at the background of all space and time, pervading the entire world?" How can we reconcile these two views of happiness? How can happiness be, on the one hand, a passing state of sentimental mind, and on the other hand, the continuing ground of all motivation?

When an object is desired, the desiring mind is dissatisfied. It feels insufficient in itself, and seeks some object that is thought to be outside. This is the state of 'duality' where experience seems divided into two. This divided state is unhappiness. When a desired object is attained, the desiring mind comes temporarily to rest, so that its divisions are dissolved. This is a state of non-duality: where experience no longer seems divided, because the knower is at one with what is known. Where dissatisfied desire has given way to a non-dual state of fulfilment, we experience happiness. In this non-dual state of happiness, there is only undivided consciousness, entirely self-contained, unmixed with any alien object that is known outside.

The source of happiness in this non-dual state cannot be the desired object, for the mind soon gets fed up with this particular object and starts agitating for something else. The moment that the mind rises up, the state of happiness has passed; so it cannot be from the risen mind that happiness appears. All happiness must come from underlying consciousness: which continues at the background of experience, while the mind changes from one state of experience to another. In this ground of consciousness, there are no alien objects. It is pure consciousness, entirely self-contained. It is just this that seems obscured, in all our minds' unhappiness. It is the ground of happiness from which all acts and happenings arise: the ground we cannot help but seek. As it is put in the Brihadaranyaka Upanishad (4.3.32): "The fluctuating ocean of the many-seeming world turns out to be one single seer, beyond duality....This is one's final state. This is one's final happiness. All other things that have but come to be, subsist upon only a measure of this happiness".

A Technology for Inner Growth

Raja M

NE DAY, the confused people of Kalama in north-west India asked the Buddha: "So many preachers come to us with their beliefs. Each says what they teach is the truth. Who do we believe?" The Buddha's answer is extraordinary in the history of religion. "Believe not anything just because it is said by your elders, the wise, the enlightened ones or the Buddhas. Accept as truth only what you find, through your direct experience, that which is beneficial and good for all, harmful to none".

The *Kalama Sutta* explains that the Buddha focused on the experiential wisdom that each individual must earn for himself. "The enlightened can only show the Path. It is for you to walk on it", he often said. That emphasis on self-dependence and wisdom gained from direct experience is the essence of vipassana, the technique to experience the quintessence of the Buddha's teaching.

Vipassana does not have a dogma, gurudom; nor is it a cult pointing to Heaven's Gate. It has been termed a 'technology for inner development'. This technique of self-observation is now being practised in more than 90 countries. It is particularly popular with people of science. IIT Delhi has regular vipassana courses conducted within its campus. Fritjof Capra would be pleased.

The Pali word 'vipassana' means 'to see it as it is' minus the delusions and illusions that cloud intellectual exercises. Also, judging from the people who take the 10-day residential vipassana courses, it is the meeting point of religions. They are even being held in Christian seminaries; and last winter, a group of students from Iran came to Dhamma Giri, the main vipassana centre at Igatpuri, near Mumbai.

Vipassana begins with bodily sensations. "The deepest region of the mind is constantly in touch with our body sensations", says Dr Raman Khosla, a Pune-based neuro-psychiatrist and an authorised vipassana teacher. "Vipassana purifies the mind by objectively observing these body sensations, without craving for the pleasant or showing an aversion for the unpleasant".

That hard-earned equanimity begins to change the mind's deep-seated conditioning for negative behaviour. With the penetrating insight of a purer mind, vipassana explodes the Great Delusion. The vipassana student realises that we are constantly reacting to the bodily sensations that arise from contact with the world: our habit pattern of blind reaction, not the outside world, is responsible for our misery. The vipassana student understands this *anicca vijya:* the experiential understanding of *anicca* or constant change, which is cosmic law. The student also experiences the *asava,* or biochemical flow of subatomic particles as subtle sensations. There is just an arising and a passing away. Using one's own body as a laboratory and one's mind as an observing instrument, the vipassana student experiences the fundamental truth of nature as it is, not as we would like it to be. The delusion of the ego begins to crumble. One begins to experience real happiness, and not the fickle, fake 'high' of euphoria.

Finding Purpose in the Flow

Nergis Dalal

N HIS book, *Flow: The Psychology of Happiness,* Mihaly Csikszentmihalyi claims that decades of research on the positive aspects of human experience have proved that what makes any experience satisfying is a state of mind in which attention is totally concentrated. The self feels effortlessly free. Emotional problems disappear and one's abilities are at their peak. A state of transcendence or flow has been achieved. This is the 'autotelic experience', in which the experience is not a means to a reward, but is its own end and reward.

In an autotelic state, concentration is so complete that there is no attention left over to think of anything irrelevant. Painters, writers, musicians or chess players can be so absorbed in their creative efforts that time is completely distorted or ceases to exist. The same exalted state can be experienced by engineers, doctors, scientists, soldiers, athletes and mountain-climbers, even by technicians working in a factory.

The difference is not between one kind of activity and another, but between the degrees of experiential intensity. All of us are free to use our limited attention, after all, either by focusing it intentionally or by diffusing it in random movements. The shape and content of our lives depends on how our attention has been used. As Saint-Beuve wrote: "I am only fulfilled when, pen in hand, I sit in the silence of my room".

The human nervous system is so complex that a person can make himself happy or miserable, regardless of what is happening outside of himself, simply by changing his consciousness. What we think, feel, see and desire is information that we can manipulate and use. Consciousness can be thought of as intentionally ordered information. Too many of us end up feeling that we have wasted our lives.

So how then can we live joyfully and creatively in an indifferent universe? The only way to do this is to control consciousness and restructure it. Whatever we do should itself actively be the reward. Autotelic personalities are strongly directed towards purpose, where energy is not constricted by thoughts of the self. The Taoist scholar Chuang Tzu observed that the right way to live was to flow spontaneously, without hoping for rewards, yet moving with total commitment. This flow is characterised by a feeling that one's skills are adequate to cope with challenges in a goal-oriented system, which, along the way, provides clues to how one is performing.

"The autotelic self transforms potentially entropic experience into flow by setting clear goals, becoming immersed in the activity, concentrating on what is happening and learning to enjoy immediate experiences", writes Csikszentmihalyi. The autotelic personality does not wish to dominate the environment. It finds a way to live harmoniously with and within it. People who are successful generally enjoy what they are doing: self-registered goals, when concentrated upon to the limit, produce a flow in which new skills can be developed, psychic energy increased and actions are integrated into a unified purpose: this is what we mean when we speak of 'a meaning to life'.

Liberating Yourself from the Web of Desire

S H Venkatramani

OW CAN you curb your desires? In what manner should you control and channelise them? Better still, how do you redirect your desires in such a way that the energy which they generate can give you enduring happiness? These are questions that have intrigued the human mind ever since man, as a sentient being, began to wander the face of the earth.

Why does desire worry us? Because the harder we try to escape it, the more we become tangled in it. The satisfaction of one desire spawns more, and so on in an endless series of cravings and occasional fulfilments. Early Christianity taught man to renounce worldly possessions, the principal objects of human desire. Gospels of Matthew and Luke say: "Do not lay up for yourselves treasures on earth...but lay up for yourselves treasures in heaven...For where your treasure is, there will your heart be also". Saint Catherine of Genoa says poetically: "We must not wish anything other than what happens from moment to moment, all the while, however, exercising ourselves in goodness". These teachings spring from the idea that Jesus expressed in the celebrated saying: "Blessed are you poor for yours is the kingdom of God".

The feeling of a desire, the feeling of a need is, however, primarily mental. Even a physical need is not a need unless it is felt in the mind. Simplicity is also of the mind. Material possessions may make for the satisfaction of physical desires, but the craving for them is of the mind. Self-denial may deprive that craving of satisfaction, but it does not prevent that desire from springing up in the mind. You can transcend desire, not by controlling it, not by suppressing it, not by trying to will it away, but by letting it be, by being passively aware of it.

The attempt to control or suppress desire will only cause internal tension, creating two dissonant voices within you. Just be 'choicelessly aware' of desire, as Jiddu Krishnamurti suggests. Look at it as a bud trying to flower, a spring trying to bubble and well up in your mind. You will derive a great spiritual strength from that uninterfering observance. It is easier to renounce the choicest material possessions than to give up the hold of fond memories, lovingly cherished ideas, tenderly nurtured concepts and beliefs steadfastly clung to. The self, *jivatma,* hangs on to them desperately, and derives its sense of identity from them. It is only when you give up this sense of identity, not by an act of will, but by becoming aware of it and transcending it, when you become poor in mind and spirit, as Eckhart used to say, that you will directly perceive the Divine, the *paramatma,* in all things. Eckhart writes: "A man should be so poor that he is not and has not a place for God to act in". In that state of intimate poverty, God will become the man himself.

Learning to Live The Spiritual Way

Shashi Prabha

MONG THE advertisements one reads every day are those which say: 'Learn Yoga in 10 easy lessons', 'Meditation for the stressed-out', 'Learn to breathe scientifically', as well as notices for lectures on a meaningful life. Training is imparted as in professional job-oriented courses. It's amazing to learn that one has to attend classes with exorbitant fees to learn activities that are at the core of the natural development of the human mind and body, and which need to be imbibed from childhood itself.

This indicates that there is a dire need for reviving the principles governing traditional patterns of life and education, where the discipline of body and mind and the true values of life were given first priority. In the competitive world of today, textual and career-based knowledge is given preference. In the mad race for monetary rewards, comforts and luxuries, which have no *lakshman rekhas,* we have forgotten the true goals of human life. People crave for a quick buck or money more than their requirements; the negative effects of which lead to stress and frustration.

Values have deteriorated so much that criminal gangs boast of receiving resumes from youngsters desirous of joining their outfits. It's frightening to see the extent to which we are being driven by desire. Undoubtedly, money is required for survival. Those living in slums can't, by any stretch of the imagination, be considered happy. However, one must be aware as to where one's priorities lie and to live within one's means. Lao Tse, a Chinese monk, said: "He who knows that enough is enough will always have enough". The world has enough resources to meet the basic needs of all human beings. But there is not enough to satisfy their greed.

Almost 2,600 years ago, the Sakya king of Kapilavastu, Suddhodana, could not entice his son, Siddhartha, to live a luxurious and worldly life. Exchanging his royal attire for a sadhu's garb, Siddhartha walked out alone in search of truth. Gautama Buddha, as came to be called, advised his followers thus: "Your property will remain when you die. Your friends and relatives will follow you up to your grave. But only your good and bad actions which you have done during your lifetime will accompany you beyond the grave". His eight-fold path is followed to this day by millions who wish to lead a more complete life.

Centuries later, Guru Nanak advised his followers against materialism: *Sadho, yeh tan mithia jano/ Ya bheetar jo Ram basat hain sacho tahi pehchano* (Consider this body false. The only truth is Ram, who resides within). He even beseeches God not to grant him riches because they may take him away from the path of love for the Lord. However, people often cite children as a reason for accumulating wealth, to which the poet-philosopher Kahlil Gibran replies: "Your children are not your children./ They are the sons and daughters of life's longing for itself./ They come through you but not from you,/ And though they are with you, yet they belong not to you". So wouldn't it be far more sensible to seek refuge in the Lord?

The Modern Man Must Relax and Meditate

Yogacharya Shri Anandji

S THE world spinning too fast? Are tensions tearing you apart? These are the kind of questions asked of those suffering from hypertension, which unfortunately is a consequence of present-day lifestyles. A remedy suggested is meditation, which often does not provide desired results. The reasons can be found in Patanjali's *Yoga Sutras*. In his attempt to evolve a complete approach to yoga, Patanjali realised that there were cleansing processes for the body and the ever wandering mind. These processes are short-changed in today's jet-age meditation.

These days, there is often confusion between relaxation and meditation. According to Patanjali, a tense person cannot meditate. He has to relax first. Patanjali goes on to argue that both body and mind can be disturbing factors in meditation, unless one follows prescribed methods to cleanse and control them. He thus calls human beings body-mind complexes. As long as one's body is aching and the mind is wandering, one cannot meditate. Therefore, *yama* and *niyama* are the first and second stages in his eight-fold path. These are meant to achieve the clairvoyance of mind before one goes further to achieve physical control through the third stage, *asanas,* where physical well-being and fitness is established. Thereafter, an attempt is made to control the brea-thing through *pranayama,* since breathing reflects one's state of mind.

After achieving mental, physical and breath control, the next step was to control the senses, which could be a major distraction and create hindrances in one's ambition to meditate. Patanjali prescribes *pratyahara* or control of the senses as a next step which can make one incredibly strong, like the shell of a tortoise which gets tough on withdrawal of its five limbs. Incidentally, the senses are also five. Having established control of the senses, one can very easily pour all senses in the desired direction, which Patanjali calls *dharana* or concentration. When concentration matures, one can identify the self as the subject or the object as the case may be, when one is able to review the subject without being involved in it. When there is a close proximity with the subject, it is termed *dhyana*, which is meditation.

This continued effort of regular meditation can further culminate into *samadhi,* when the everlasting bliss or *sat-chit-anand* is experienced. It can be experienced all here and in this world with the help of Patanjali's *astang yoga.* It is the most ideal and realistic form of scientific evolution according to Swami Vivekananda, which can be attempted or practised by any individual. This can be done without running away from society. Hence, the need for an average individual experiencing stress and undergoing tensions is to adapt to a disciplined life and make a conscious effort to relax. So, a conscious attempt at relaxation is the best short cut for modern human beings, and meditation can further help evolve one's spiritual vistas. Thus a tense person under great anxiety cannot meditate, unless s/he first learns to unlearn and unwind.

Bliss as the State Beyond Happiness

Vijay T Salve

NO LIVING being is free from stress. Advances in science and technology have not made life easy but have in fact added more stress. No wonder stress induced diseases like hypertension, coronary artery diseases, and many psychosomatic diseases are on the rise. Stress mostly results out of the inability of an individual to accept the non-existence of 'imaginary idealism'. Modern science has been able to reason and solve problems of humankind to some extent. But the 'randomness of occurrence' has limited science. Each individual, every phenomenon, is unique in itself. As a medical man, I have experienced this randomness in the sense that in spite of best efforts, diseases do not get cured, they become variable, and patients die in the best of hospitals. The big 'why' cannot be answered every time and we tend to land up in the infinite loop of 'why and how', which ultimately leads to frustration. Psychologist Carl Jung said: "Theories based on experience are essentially statistical, in that they formulate an 'ideal average' which abolishes all exceptions on either ends of the scale and replaces them by imaginary means. This mean is quite valid, though it may not exist in reality. Ultimate truth is the goal of science and this cannot be reached by our limited conscious experience".

In here comes the ultimate and supreme power, God, the only conceivably absolute entity. By realising this fact one can break the infinite chain of unsolved queries. The limited human intellect cannot answer all questions and has to rely on the Supreme Lord. As Jung said: "The rupture between knowledge and factor is a symptom of split consciousness, which is a characteristic of the mental disorder of modern society". Knowing the true nature of the self is an essential aspect in this context. The 'Inner Self' is not one's own body mind thoughts, but it is that entity which is much beyond all this. In the Bhagavad Gita, it is said that one who conquers himself and his own self is a friend to himself, but to the unconquered 'self', this self appears like an external enemy. The *Ashtavakra Samhita* puts it differently: "Have faith my son, have faith. Never confuse yourself in this, you are knowledge itself, you are lord, you are self, much beyond, nature".

By knowing the true nature of 'Inner Self', giving up false ego, one can definitely experience freedom from the psychic pattern of desire, frustration and depression. The technique of self-observation was described by the Buddha. One can just observe one's own thoughts and not necessarily act on them. The source of unhappiness in most instances is either past experience or future anticipation. One has to realise that the past has already happened and cannot be changed by any means and the future cannot be predicted. Living in the present is an essential key to happiness and a stress-free life. Discarding all prejudices, ideologies, presumptions and assumptions, living in the present moment and giving the credit of the final results to the Almighty, one can definitely experience bliss — a state beyond happiness.

Learn to Let Go, Adapt to Change

Anant G Nadkarni

ODAY, DEALING with change is perceived as a huge challenge. Employees are increasingly having to grapple with changes in the workplace. The number of people striving to learn more and grow is increasing by leaps and bounds. Most of us are fairly quick at learning, at cultivating new tastes and fashions. Yet, our first reaction to change is always tinged with suspicion and caution, and in some cases, resistance.

In this context, it would be useful to recollect words of wisdom from our scriptures: lead me from death to immortality. And also a prayer from school: "It is in dying that we shall rise to eternal life". Both these hold the promise of immortality and eternal life; but on one clear condition: one has to first 'die' in order to attain immortality or eternity. In other words, adapting to change involves some amount of give and take. You have to let go of something to gain something else.

At a recently-held convention for heads of companies and professionals, one participant was asked to remove his shoes into which a second person stepped. The second person asked whether he could remove his own shoes before getting into the other person's shoes. At which, the faculty said: "In all forms of change there has to be a letting go of your shoes first". At another point the chairman of a large corporation said that he would like to see his conglomerate on the forefront of whatever business they did, by remaining in the present moment and shedding off the past. In one sentence he made it clear that the future does not necessarily come out of the past.

As part of company philosophy, a leading company encourages its managers not to talk about yesterday's accolades. Dr Wayne W Dyer in *Your Erroneous Zones* and *Your Sacred Self* suggests that the difficulty in 'letting go' of something comes from a kind of 'benefit' or 'pay-off' one has found for being in the same state of existence consciously or unconsciously. Dr Dyer helps us identify and deal with pay-offs at the bottom of resistance.

In the Bhagavad Gita, Arjuna compares the mind to the wind and wants to know how to control it. Krishna says that the mind can be cultivated gradually through dispassion. A clear significance is attached to letting go of an old habit in order to acquire a new one. At an organisational level, those managing change could identify the key shifts required and establish pay-offs at the deepest reasonable level as to why employees by and large want the status quo. On the basis of this pattern, employees could be encouraged to focus on their pay-offs so that they get motivated to change to a faster track, towards a better future.

As children, most of us have abundant curiosity, creativity and exploratory abilities. Along the way, certain circumstances create pay-offs, putting the brakes on and we begin to prefer stability and certainty and as a result we cling to the status quo, and our ability to change stiffens. On letting go, Albert Einstein said that only the insane can expect radically different outcomes by doing the same thing over and over again.

Uses of Spirituality at the Workplace

R Venkatesan

DOES THE recent interest exhibited in non-fiction titles such as *The Soul of Business, A Spiritual Audit of Corporate America, The Stirring of Soul in the Workplace* among others in the US point to the possible evolution of the 'enlightened' corporate sector? Do Indian managers, born in a land that has offered yoga and meditation to the world have the first-mover advantage? International research on stress has found that while Swedish executives experience least stress, executives from the US, UK and Germany are able to manage stress effectively unlike their counterparts in Japan, Singapore, Brazil, Egypt, South Africa and Nigeria. Both *Newsweek* and *Time* recently devoted articles to stress busters, their common theme being that chronic stress is harmful to both employees and employers and the solution lies in ancient Indian practices of yoga and meditation. Yoga as union between mind and body is seen to offer solutions that physical workouts cannot offer.

The recent work of Danah Zohar on spiritual intelligence, John Kay on implicit trust relations within and outside the firm, and Avinash K Dixit on strategic thinking point out future directions for the corporate sector. Zohar refers to spiritual intelligence, a form of creative thinking concerned as much with rule making as rule breaking, as the basic foundation for an effective EQ (emotional quotient) and IQ. She says that SQ could be explained in terms of the lotus model with its centre and six petals, corresponding to the seven *chakras* described in *kundalini yoga*. According to Kay, the essence of a firm is defined by the totality of relationships among, first, its stakeholders and, second, between itself and other firms. Dixit mentions that unlike a traditional firm which tries to hold rather than share information, a progressive and enlightened firm makes sharing its dominant strategy.

According to *Time's* article on yoga, "enlightenment and good health require a proper balance between the seven *chakras*, apart from a free flow of the life force which, in turn, is acquired through the awakening of dormant *kundalini* energy". The Indian philosophical tradition attributes perception to the mind, conceptualisation to the intellect and illumination to the self. Further, they speak of an ascent from intellect through meditation. Integration of the inner self with the cosmic spirit, otherwise referred to as self-realisation, is considered the route to highest knowledge. In other words, spirituality at the workplace is considered necessary not only in terms of managing stress but also as an aid in reaching higher levels of consciousness.

Mata Nirmala Devi, founder of Sahaja Yoga, says: "En masse inner transformation of human beings by self-realisation is the reality now. Everyone can now become aware of the absolute truth and reality through Sahaja Yoga. Sahaja Yoga is the spontaneous union of individual consciousness with the all-pervading power through the awakening of the residual power of the *kundalini* which lies dormant within all human beings". Perhaps it is time for Indian corporates to draw upon the great traditions of India's ancient spiritual heritage.

A Resort Within the Mind, all Your Own

Aruna Jethwani

AUGHT UP in a sea of turbulence? Stressed out? You will have to learn some tricks. One is to create a holiday resort of your own. A space in the mind, heart, psyche, which would be an oasis of peace. A perfect place where the strength of equilibrium, power of positivism, and oneness with the great mystery are all yours. Creating this resort requires years of effort, positive thoughts, erasing of the ego and wiping off one's past. It needs the support of your dear ones, of pilgrimages to energy fields, and faith. Once this resort is ready, whenever there is turmoil, all that you have to do is turn inwards, let your hair down in your inner niche and relax.

How does one really start building one's inner resort? The First Step: Take a mental flight to the most beautiful landscape you can remember. Relish it. Being subject to the law of increasing returns, the more such flights you take, the more peaceful you become. The Second Step: A minute's prayer every day will sow seeds of faith. Choose a prayer which is an experience to you. In due course, faith will bloom and flourish, covering the mind's space with fruits of good deeds and blossoms of bliss.

The Third Step: A three-minute meditation every day will show you the route which passes through the holiday resort. A three-minute meditation? Yes, three minutes are sufficient to unload the mental stress and bring relief to the core self. What kind of meditation? The simplest one. The one that makes you surrender everything to the Higher Power and helps you accept everything as the 'best' solution. Meditation of Breath, meditation of your *Isht Dev*, meditation of Space, meditation on the third eye, or mere Silence. This gets rid of all mental garbage. Allow it to escape.

The Fourth Step: Align yourself with nature, just for a minute. It is that link road to your resort which brings equanimity, peace, and harmony. An excellent flyover to your destination. How does one align with nature? Whisper to a plant, embrace a tree, speak to the stars, sing to the sun and enjoy their company. The Fifth Step: Create a happy memory album. Recollecting one good incident or one happy moment of life every day will make a good collection of happy moments. If and when you are bored at the holiday resort you can go through your memory album and feel refreshed. Happy memory albums are not escapism. It is a mere affirmation of the happiness you have had. The Sixth Step: Increase the level of subtle energy within. What if your holiday resort plunges into darkness because of electricity failure? You have to tap different sources of energy. Learn a technique of increasing your energy levels such as deep breathing, *pranayam, mantras (aum* or the *adi mantras)* or *mudras* (there are more than a thousand). Choose the technique your subtle body accepts easily.

Will this holiday resort within work? Well, try it. It has worked for many, why not for you?

Conquering the Fear of Death

Muthusamy Varadarajan

HERE IS a story in which a woman wailed before the Buddha at the loss of her only child. The Enlightened One asked her to search for a home that Death had not visited, and then return to him for a miracle. The end of the story is obvious.

The one certain thing in life is death. With the certainty of death goes the uncertainty of time and place, manner and circumstance. The Hindu believes that one evolves through many births until one is born to the coveted human state. Having been so privileged, he has to conduct himself in such a manner that he will not need to be born again. The Christian believes he goes to sleep in the Lord and will rise, with all the others, when the call to reawakening sounds on the Day of Judgment. He beseeches the Lord to bless him, as James Agee puts it in *A Death in the Family,* so that "we shower forth Thy praise, not only with our lips, but in our lives, by giving up our selves to Thy service and by walking before Thee in holiness and righteousness all our days". The Muslim holds that on the Day of Reckoning, *roz-e-kayamat,* all the dead will be called to render account.

Man believes death, in this life, is final. It signals the inevitable close of an evanescent chapter. Knowing this, and knowing that death is inescapable, our philosophy teaches us not to seek escape from death, but to conquer the fear of death. For it is this dread of the unknown that destroys man. He has, therefore, to be constantly reminded (in Shankara's words): *Punarapi jananam punarapi maranam punarapi janani jataro sayanam,* that is, life is the cycle of taking birth, dying, sleeping in the mother's womb awaiting release. Through all this, one must take the name of Govinda, for not all the riches of grammar and literature will help when one lies dying: as Shankara exhorts, in his *Bhaja Govindam:* "Reflect on the secret, fundamental truth. Then life would not have been in vain, nor death fearsome".

The ways of seeking and (hopefully) finding this secret truth are varied and geared to the *manovritti* or disposition of each human being. The point is that it is only the relentless inquiry into the Self, based on the persistent query that Bhagwan Ramana Maharshi phrased as 'Who am I?' that can illuminate the mind and liberate it. As the *Vishnu Sahasranama* suggests, it is the chanting of the thousand names of Vishnu, the preserver and sustainer of the universe, that can relieve one from the dread of birth, death, old age and disease. When the inquiry into the Self, in whatever manner it is carried out, reveals the truth, then one becomes a *sthithaprajna,* one of steadfast mind, to whom desire and frustration, joy and sorrow, success and failure are the same. This is the teaching of the Bhagavad Gita. It is from this state of mind, also, that one can pose the challenge that St Paul did in his first Epistle to the Corinthians: "O Death, where is thy sting? O grave, where thy victory?"

Wrestling with the Dark Mystery of Death

Ramadas Rao

HANKS TO science, we are now slowly beginning to grasp some of the complex processes that go into the creation of life; but death, and what happens after death, remains an impenetrable mystery. What man does not know, he fears. The celebrated poet John Keats, who was consumed by tuberculosis, expressed this in the deeply moving sonnet, *When I Have Fears That I May Cease To Be*. To Keats, as to many thinkers, death is extinction, an abyss into which life disappears. He writes: "...then on the shore/ Of the wide world I stand alone, and think/ Till love and fame to nothingness do sink".

In many periods and cultures, however, there has also flourished a philosophical tradition which has rejected fear and trained the piercing beam of the intellect on the enigma of death. This tradition is best embodied in those thinkers whose understanding of death permitted them to radically transform the accepted conception of life that prevailed in their times. It was the sight of a dead body, among other signposts of misery that threw the mind of Siddhartha into turmoil and set him on a quest for enlightenment. It is true that as the Buddha, he did not really dwell on death; but then, having accepted it as inevitable, he could speculate all the more profoundly on life and the liberation of humankind from its overwhelming burden of suffering.

It is in the Upanishads, composed nearly 3,000 years ago, that one finds the intellect truly grappling with death, soaring above ritualism to scale unparalleled heights of speculation. The philosophers of this age faced death not with trepidation, but with burning curiosity. Wrestling with this great mystery, these philosophers propounded the concept of the self or soul, the atman, as an immortal entity separate from the body. In the following passage from the Katha Upanishad, the atman is described thus: "The intelligent self is neither born nor does it die. It did not originate from anything, nor did anything originate from it. It is birthless, eternal, undecaying and ancient. It is not injured even when the body is killed".

From this concept of the soul followed the theory of rebirth, elaborated in terms of karma. According to Upanishadic philosophers, the soul flits from body to body, the level of existence in each birth being determined by actions in the previous birth until the being attains complete realisation of the inner self. Once this goal has been achieved by a mind free from desires and attachments, the self "is not born again". By holding that the self is immortal, Upanishadic philosophers attempted to transcend the chilling finality of death.

Born of a spirit of inquiry, the theory of the immortality of the soul and the concepts of karma and rebirth continue to deeply influence thinkers both in the East and the West. Echoes are found in the works of German philosopher Arthur Schopenhauer (1788-1860): "What sleep is for the individual, death is for the 'will'... Through the sleep of death it reappears fitted out with another intellect as a new being..."

Waiting Upon
the Lord of Death

Lata Jagtiani

EADING JOHN Donne's poem *Death be not proud,* we were starry-eyed at Donne's audacity in taking on death, the great leveller. Kings and paupers, criminals and law-abiding citizens, men and women, have all feared the final call. It is death that brings down the curtain on our familiar life and ushers us to the unknown. Fear accompanies death and shapes our future choices. It is one of the strongest motivating forces in the world so long as it is not an agent for cowardly behaviour. To be paralysed in life, to become depressed and to be afraid of failure are indications of fear working in our lives as a deterrent force, and not as a constructive one.

One is reminded of the words Aurangzeb wrote to his son Azam a few days before he died: "I came alone and I go as a stranger. I do not know who I am, nor what I have been doing. I have not been the protector and guardian of the empire. Life, so valuable, has been squandered in vain. I fear for my salvation, I fear my punishment. I believe in God's bounty and mercy, but I am afraid because of what I have done". To his other son, Kam Baksh, he wrote: "Every torment I have inflicted, every sin I have committed, every wrong I have done, I carry the consequences with me".

On the other hand, we have the poise and equanimity of Ramana Maharshi and Ramakrishna Paramahansa, both of whom suffered the ravages of cancer, yet kept calm and continued to stay relaxed despite the agony. They did not opt for suicide as Adolf Hitler did. Instead, they accepted the inevitable with dignity because their lives had been blameless. There is no denying the fact that they suffered physically but their minds, hearts and souls remained calm and at peace. Goodness and a life devoted to the right path appear to offer us the chance to face death with calm. There appears to be an almost causal relationship between a life devoted to goodness and a death without mental agony. Although physical pain cannot be avoided, the sage surely has no regrets and no fears, and that undoubtedly helps alleviate a great deal of pain.

One would do well to remember Ramana Maharshi's advice: "Whatever is done lovingly, with righteous purity and peace of mind, is a good action. Everything which is done with the stain of desire and with agitation filling the mind is classified as a bad action. Do not perform any good action through bad means thinking it is sufficient if it bears good fruit". The secret of defeating death appears to be encapsulated in this story: Once a sage was narrating the battle in the Bhagavad Gita in which the Lord urges the devotee to plunge into the thick of battle, while maintaining a peaceful heart at the lotus feet of the Lord. The disciple asked the sage: "How can I achieve that?" The sage replied: "Decide to be satisfied with any results your efforts may bring".

The Mind's Conquest of Pain & Suffering

Anjali Singh

SUFFERING IS a healer. Its occurrence in the life of a person need not necessarily be negative. Sorrow is the outcome of the negative tendencies in one's subconscious finding their way into the open. If dealt with, not only does suffering equalise our past actions, it actually cleanses us at an unconscious level within and makes us aware of our futile attachments, which cause the sorrow in the first place. All sorrow in the mind is caused by some kind of attachment or dependence on something or someone, an event or happening that is not fulfillingour expectations. If we use the phase of suffering in our life to evaluate our relationship with the world, it can become means for a total change in us.

The thought pattern during suffering hinges around the thought 'I am unhappy'. One's personality gets totally identified with one's emotional layer. The outermost layer is the physical structure, the body. Subtler than that is the mental layer, the mind, which entertains varied emotions of love, hate, jealousy, compassion. Subtler than that is the intellectual layer, where the intellect makes decisions, gets ideas and holds convictions. When we are unhappy we tend to stay wrapped in the emotional layer, holding on to the idea that 'I am the sufferer'. If we can stand apart and watch the unhappy thoughts as a disinterested witness, the thought pattern changes from 'I am unhappy' to 'these are unhappy thoughts'. The fact is that I can observe my body, I can also observe my emotions and ideas. One disassociates the 'I' from the unhappiness because one has shifted one's identification from the sufferer to the witness of the sufferer.

How long will the thoughts remain unhappy without the cooperation of 'I'? It is the mind that suffers, not I. The 'I' has become a witness. There is a strange happiness even in watching our unhappy minds. One need not try and remove those thoughts, one should just watch them without classifying them as good or bad and let them come out of our subconscious, just as fizz comes out of a soda bottle when the cap is released.

When suffering comes in our life, we can use this chance to raise ourselves to a higher level. Swami Chinmayananda says: "Lunacy, drunkenness, neuroses, spells of hypnotism are some of the examples wherein the existing thought pattern suddenly gets shocked and tumbles to fall into a different pattern, and the individual behaves as though he is not himself. Misused, it becomes the modern political method of indoctrination. Rightly used, it can unshackle the human personality from the chain of attachments and misconceptions to rediscover its divine, blissful status". If we do not make the effort to get out of the state it will be used by others to influence our way of thinking and behaving and our dependence will continue. If we make the effort, there is no way of not succeeding. The choice is ours.

A Majestic Way to Face the Inevitable

Amrit Gangar

 T THE time of writing this, an 85-year-old Jain woman has entered the 29th day of fasting. For the past many days, she has even stopped taking water, leave alone food. And she is still conscious. She is visited by Jain nuns several times a day, who recite sacred texts to her. There is a feeling of joy around, soulful joy; death is no longer a spectre but its being happily invited in absolute agreement and equanimity.

Why has the old woman been fasting so rigorously? "She pondered for a long time before taking the decision of meeting death at will, in complete peace. She does not have worldly attachments nor does she possess anything material, except the clothes she wears", her son tells me. I look at the fasting woman's face and find it without any anxiety. What a majestic way to face death.

Sallekhana is facing death voluntarily, either by an ascetic or by a lay Jain. This vow is normally taken when one is nearing her/his end and when normal life according to Jain religion is not possible due to old age, or incurable disease. It is done through subjugation of all passions, abandonment of worldly attachments, by gradually abstaining from food and water, and by simultaneous meditation on the real nature of the Self until the soul parts from the body. The basic concept underlying the vow is that the human being, who is the master of his own destiny, should face death in such a way as to prevent influx of new karmas and liberate the soul from bondage of karmas that may be clinging to it.

"Isn't it suicide?" someone asks me impatiently. I immediately refer him to a book, *Sallekhana is not Suicide,* by Justice T K Tukol, in which he explains: "Suicide is killing oneself by means employed by one. Every living being has a fondness for its body and takes care of it by adopting such methods or modes as are necessary to keep it in sound health, free from illness or any form of suffering. Suicide is normally a misfortune of one's own making. A victim of suicide is either a victim of his mental weakness or of external circumstances which he is not able to circumvent".

Justice Tukol firmly believes that *sallekhana* is not suicide since none of the psychological and sociological aspects found in the negative act of suicide are found in it. "The sole intention of the person adopting the vow is preceded by purification of the mind. Contrary to the suicidal intention, there is no desire to put an end to life immediately by some violent or objectionable means. There is no question of escaping from any shame, frustration or emotional excitement. There is no intention to harm oneself or any member of one's own family".

There are many historical and archaeological references especially in southern India to *sallekhana*. There were a large number of Jain acharyas and munis who flourished in the South. The history of Jainism attests the popularity of the practice of *sallekhana* or fasting unto death, that is part of the unique Jain art of living or non-living.

Learning to Live With the Call of Yama

Pravin Shanker Mehta

N THE Mahabharata, the exiled Pandavas stop at a lake to drink water. A *yaksha* appears and asks them to answer his questions, one of which is, what is the biggest surprise in the world? Yudhisthira replies that people die all the time, yet those who are living, desire permanent life. What could be a bigger surprise? Why do we cling to life? Even a person suffering from a painful, terminal disease might exclaim that he wants to die, but deep within his heart the desire to live remains rooted firmly.

Krishna says in the Bhagavad Gita that death is inevitable for one who is born and one who dies must be reborn. The latter part of the statement appears anomalous. If we take life to be a line then it begins with birth and ends with death. A chain of such lines goes on forming in accordance with the law of karma. But there is also a line which, though begins with birth, goes on to infinity, which precludes the possibility of another succeeding line to be formed. There are cases when a soul, having snapped off all ties of attachments and desires that are the cause of births and deaths, attains salvation.

To explain this seeming anomaly it is necessary to analyse 'death'. What is called death is the casting away of the body by the soul only to re-enter another body at some point in future, just as a snake sheds its outer skin for renewal. Thus, it is not the final departure of the soul from the world but only a state of transition required for acquiring a new body. Such a soul leaves the world encumbered by an astral body, *sukshma shareera,* which according to Osho is one's built-in programme comprising the gist of all acts done, acts desired and contemplated but not done. These encumbrances necessitate the seeking of another body by the soul. But an emancipated soul can jump out of this circle to become one with God. Admittedly this happens in the rarest of rare cases. Nevertheless, it does happen.

This state of deliverance from the cycle of birth and death is beyond the five senses, beyond mind, beyond space and time, as Christ has said: "There shall be time no longer". Hence, only certain references have been made to this state by sages. It is the *param dham* from where there is no return (Gita, 8-21). Upanishads refer to it as eternal existence, consciousness and bliss, *sat-chit-ananda.* The Buddha calls it *nirvana.* To Ramana Maharshi, it is the egoless state where the self comes into its own, as the ego vanishes completely. Osho calls it *mahamrityu,* where the individual identity merges into universal existence.

The term 'death' is not applicable to the demises of such a person as he is said to have transcended or jumped beyond death. Thus the supposed anomaly in the assertion regarding inevitability of rebirth after death is, in fact, no anomaly, if the reality of death is properly understood.

Life is Beautiful, Don't End It

Sudhamahi Regunathan

T IS sheer desperation that pushes some to contemplate ending their lives. Several persons actually do it. However, opting out of life is not the solution. While many texts extol the value of life, the epic Ramayana, simulating situations of extreme despair, has quite a few instances where one or more characters mull over whether or not to take this extreme step. The counsel forms the storyline: if the said character had taken his or her life, the story of the Ramayana would not be what it is and good would never have conquered evil.

When Hanuman goes to Lanka looking for Sita, he searches high and low, but nowhere is he able to find Vaidehi. Desperate, he reproaches himself: "What will happen if I go back and tell them I have not been able to find Vaidehi? Rama will not be able to bear it, he may fall dead immediately. On seeing this, Lakshman will not be able to live a second longer. If they perish Sugriva, my king, too, will perish. If Sugriva gives up his life, so will Tara and Angada. If our beloved chief dies, the whole monkey race will self-destruct".

Hanuman began considering different ways of ending his own life. That Hanuman, who is known for his strength, valour and courage too could hit such an all-time low, is comforting to the not-so-strong mortals. Hanuman's alternatives begin with lighting a raging fire and entering it. Or starving and letting the crows and birds of prey eat up his body. Or, jumping into the waters and drowning. Valmiki describes all these options in such a beautiful manner that you can feel Hanuman's joy in the thought that his problems will finally come to an end. But then, argues Hanuman, the way to prosperity has never been through despair. Motivating himself, he rises with renewed energy and finds Sita in Ashok Vatika soon afterwards.

When he finds Sita, he discovers that she, too, was considering the option of taking her life. Rama had not, till now, found her. She wondered if Rama had lost interest in her. She felt she deserved this punishment. Yet, she wonders: "How is it that my heart indeed is still in one piece? Having been struck by such a thunderbolt, it should have by now shattered into a thousand bits. Is it made of granite?" So she decides to commit suicide. "It is not at all sinful to do so", she assures herself, for the alternative is to face Ravana's advances and maybe even cruelty.

She too wonders how to execute this action. She decides to use her braids, the only instrument available, to hang herself. But the exercise of despairing gives her new strength. A sudden spurt of hope saves her that instant. Hanuman who is observing all this, so fresh from a similar predicament himself, sees the foolishness of such an act. In his reflection is the counsel. He realises the futility of his, Rama's and the monkey army's efforts if Sita should kill herself. Hanuman assures her that her husband is ever thinking of her, she has only to be patient. For it is in her wait that her husband's courage would be attested: the cause for which she wants to die is the cause for which she should live.

Embracing the Beautiful
and the Terrible

Rajni Bakshi

 OW LONG can I expect to live? a man asked Dr Ernest Borges in 1960. "About six months", replied the cancer specialist. Hearing this, the afflicted man laughed. "I am thinking", he told the doctor, "of King Parikshit, who was told that he had seven more days to live. I have no empire to take care of and you have given me six months. I am a rich man!" He returned to his small-town home to die, quietly at prayer, among his family and friends. Yet, for most of us, the dread of suffering stands firmly at the doorstep of Tata Memorial Hospital. The cancer hospital is a unique concentration of pain under one roof.

The fear of agony clouds most faces in the corridors of the hospital's outpatient department. The doctors and nurses stand out in their matter-of-fact calm and work-as-usual briskness. It is simultaneously the location of concentrated prayer and defiant courage. Prayer is not merely folded hands and *japa*. All untiring action to relieve suffering is also prayer, be it the labour of a doctor or of a ward-boy.

This relation is an entry-point. Here is an opportunity to sift faith from mere convictions. It is easy to see the Lord in a laughing child. But when the same child is undergoing painful therapy for cancer, it is difficult to accept this as yet another facet of the Lord's creation. Why? Perhaps it is because we resist embracing the terrible. Mahendranath Gupta, the chronicler of Sri Ramakrishna Paramahansa, once stood before the image of the goddess Kali at Dakshineshwar. He observed: "In one aspect She is terrible, and in another She is the ever-affectionate Mother of Her devotees. The two ideals are harmonised in Her. She is compassionate and affectionate. It is also true that She is terrible, the 'Consort of Death'."

Ramakrishna died of an excruciating throat cancer. When disciples and devotees asked him to pray to the Divine Mother for relief from pain, he said: "I should like to see it cured, but it is still there. Everything depends on the sweet will of the Divine Mother". The learned Pandit Shashadhar Tarkachudamani pointed out to Sri Ramakrishna that perfect souls like him have to merely concentrate their mind on the affected part to cure it. Sri Ramakrishna's answer was instantaneous: "You are a scholar and yet you make such a senseless proposal! I have given my mind once and for all to God. How is it possible for me to take it away and concentrate it upon this cage of rotten flesh and blood?"

But what of us less evolved mortals who are not able to give our mind "once and for all to God"? For some, like the humanitarian Dr Borges, a daily battle with the suffering of others is itself a *sadhana*. Others, like the man who happily compared himself to Parikshit, are saved by a life-long striving to keep their mind on the Divine. For them, there is no horror in the prospect of leaving this body, or even in the inevitability of pain. For the rest of us, such lives stand as beacons in the dark.

All for the Love of God

M N Chatterjee

N MEDIAEVAL India, the focus of spiritual attention shifted to a new concept of divinity, less abstract, less epic and more ardent. The Krishna cult that sprang up in the Gangetic valley marked this transformation. Centred on Krishna's romantic exploits, this movement emphasised a loving and lovable aspect of Vishnu. The self-abandonment of the gopis in Krishna's love symbolised the height of spiritual bliss. Jayadeva's *Gitagovinda*, written in the 12th century, stands out as a unique poem in which expression is given to the complexities of divine and human love through Krishna's love for Radha and her deep longing for him.

The *Gitagovinda* is an elaboration of the fleeting pangs of the senses, alternating with the momentary pleasure arising out of separation and union. The glorification of *Krishna-lila* (divine play) in the *Bhagvat Purana* was thus moulded into a literary masterpiece. If Jayadeva achieved a harmonious blend of the mystical and the mundane, the sacred and the sacrilegious, Vidyapati, in the same tradition, brought the leitmotif of divine love to a wider audience. He wrote his love songs in Maithili. While retaining the underlying spirit of classical Sanskrit poetry (he also wrote in Sanskrit), Vidyapati enjoyed mass appeal.

Radha is a complex character in Vidyapati's songs, and her yearning for the Lord is uninhibited by social conventions. Though this has been widely interpreted as the soul's craving for union with the Infinite, many critics are disinclined to read mystical meanings in Vidyapati's love lyrics. Should Vidyapati's poetry be judged as a love poem disguised as a mystical ode, or a mystical ode in the language of love? These ideas are not mutually exclusive. The steady assimilation of Maithili into mediaeval Bengali produced a hybrid known as Braja-buli, which served as a new poetic diction for Vidyapati's songs in Bengal's Vaishnav circles. Vidyapati's poetry is also the inspiration behind some of Tagore's poems, particularly those titled *Bhanu Singher padavali* (The Anthology of Poems of Bhanu Singh).

A notable contemporary of Vidyapati was Chandidas. The spiritual fervour of his devotional lyrics on the Radha-Krishna theme cast an enchanting spell on Chaitanyadeva. Chandidas believed in salvation through love of God, based on the earthly passion for a human, sublimated to a higher plane. He became a household name in many parts of eastern India because of his songs, popularly known as *Krishna-kirtan*. Classified under different sections dealing with various phases in the lives of Radha and Krishna, the songs are suitably interspersed with elucidatory remarks by the singers to contextualise the spiritual message for different occasions and periods.

The corpus of *bhakti* lore, enriched by generations of devotional poets and mystics, gave impetus to a new form of religious expression, the *kirtan:* group singing, at times accompanied by a dance of surrender to ecstatic joy. The old socio-ritualistic order gave way to a new order of saint-singers, an order that disregarded casteism and acknowledged the equality of all before the loving Lord.

The Sufis are Animated by a Holy Love

Asghar Ali Engineer

ASAWWUF, OR mysticism, has been an important stream within Islam. Representing the inward and esoteric side of Islam, it emphasises spirituality rather than ritual: It has become known to the world principally through Sufis, also called 'friends of God'. Muhiyudiin Ibn Arabi, the great Sufi saint, founded the doctrine of *wahdat al-wujud,* oneness of being, that considered all created beings as manifestations of God. Ibn Arabi would say: "My heart is a mosque, a church, a synagogue and a temple".

Self-abnegation is the hallmark of Sufis: Their ultimate aim is *fana fi'llah* (annihilation in God). For central to Sufism is the love of God, manifested at one level through compassion for His creatures. Sufyan al-Thauri, another great Sufi saint, would say: "If I give bread to the dog, he keeps watch over me so that I can pray. If I give it to my wife and child, they hold me back from my devotions". Among women saints the universally revered Rabi'a al-Adawiyya was a Sufi par excellence. The Sufis practised complete equality between the sexes: In this connection, Fariduddin Attar notes that the Sufis value women as much as they do men because they believe in the Unity of God. "In this Unity", he asks, "what remains of the existence of 'I' or 'thou'? So how can 'man' or 'woman' continue to be?"

The scholar Margaret Smith observes that "the Sufis themselves give to a woman the first place among the earliest Muslim mystics and have chosen her to represent the first development of mysticism in Islam". The reference is to Fatima, the Prophet's daughter, who is venerated as the first Qutb or spiritual head of the Sufi fellowship. Attar, Rabi'a's biographer, extols her as "that one set apart in the seclusion of holiness, that woman veiled with the veil of religious sincerity, that one on fire with love and longing, that one enamoured of the desire to approach her Lord and be consumed in His glory, that woman who lost herself in union with the Divine, that one accepted by men as a second spotless Mary". Renowned Sufis as Hawan Basri, Malik Dinar, Sufyan al-Thauri and Shaqiq Balkhi visited her in her isolated hermitage; at other times, she would withdraw into the wilderness: "A broken pitcher, out of which she drank and made ritual ablutions, an old reed mat, and a brick which she occasionally used as a pillow, were her only belongings".

Rabi'a never approved of selfish love of God: Love cannot and should not be reducible to a set of motives. To Al-Thauri, she said: "I have not served God from fear of Hell, for I should be like a wretched hireling, if I did it from fear; nor for love of Paradise, for I should be a bad servant if I served for the sake of what was given. But I have served God only for the love of Him and desire for Him". Commenting on the philosophy of divine love that Rabi'a embodied, Margaret Smith writes: "She teaches, first, that this love must shut out all others than the Beloved. The Saint must rise above the claims of the senses and allow neither pleasure nor pain to disturb his contemplation of the Divine".

The Return of the Love God

Devdutt Pattanaik

HE HARIVAMSA describes him as the son of Vishnu, the preserver, and Lakshmi, the provider. The Atharva Veda exalts him as the Supreme God, "he who was born first, whom neither gods, ancestors nor men have equaled". He enticed Shiva into the embrace of Shakti and helped generate life in the womb of love. He is Kama, lord of desire, who revealed to man and woman the wonders of life, infusing bodies with passion, hearts with inspiration, transforming all into lovers.

Kama, like the Graeco-Roman Eros, was a charming God who used a sugarcane bow to shoot love-arrows. Only the unfortunate were spared his wounds. Vasanta, the spring-god, was Kama's inseparable companion. And so as winter mists parted, a series of festivals known as Kamotsava, Madanotsava and Vasantotsava were celebrated to welcome the love-god. Vivid descriptions of these festivals can be found in classical Sanskrit works like Harsha's *Ratnavali,* Rajashekhara's *Karpuramanjari* and Kalidasa's *Malavikagnimitram.* Kama was a catalyst to Nature's fertility, worshipped by women who sought husbands and children. An offshoot of his role as procreator was the development of the cult of pleasure. For, with damsels of desire, came the muses of music, poetry, dance and wine. His consorts were Rati, mistress of erotic arts, and Priti, goddess of longing. It was only a question of time before Kama earned the ire of the sages.

The Buddha saw Kama as Mara, the demon who brought suffering, an emotion also reflected in the wrath of Shiva, the cosmic ascetic, who burnt Kama with his third eye. But neither could wipe Kama out completely. For though a dangerous obstacle on the path of salvation, the love-god was necessary for life. The tension between the austere hermit and the amorous nymph, the *rishi* and the *apsara*, forms the plot of many Indian tales. These tales are a literary expression of the primal struggle between the demands of the body and the needs of the soul.

At one point, a solution was reached. Kama was allowed to exist, but without that receptacle of sensuality, the body. He became Ananga, the bodiless one. But this did not appeal to the masses. Kama needed to be redefined; love had to have a form acceptable to the artist and the ascetic. It was found in Krishna. As the beloved of Radha, the delight of Madhuvana, Krishna with his winsome smile, beauty and charming ways, radiates the essence of the love-god. In Krishna's flute one discovers the new love-bow, in his music are the darts of desire. But unlike Kama, Krishna is not the obstacle to salvation. Passion for Krishna is the rope to liberation. Through Krishna, *kama* becomes *prema,* a passionate romance with the divine that promises eternal ecstasy, not transient orgasm. Krishna supersedes Kama to become Madana-Mohana, 'he who can charm Cupid'. Holi, the last of the spring festivals, has gradually lost its sexual overtones. Water is still thrown to calm the fires of passion, the colour red still fills the air to remind us of earth's bursting desire but with Krishna dancing on the horizon, the frolic is now infused with the promise of divine union.

Kroh Grasps the Magic of Detachment

Raja M

T'S A mysterious word, Kroh, School Boy said. And the most misunderstood. Love? Detachment, School Boy said. There's a new Anti-Detachment Club in the Village. They wear blindfolds and cling to each other, Kroh, School Boy chuckled. That's expressing love for one another, they think. Kroh remembered Kahlil the Prophet: "Like two strings of a lute...like the pillars of a temple stand apart... for the cypress and the oak cannot grow in each other's shadow". Ronaldo the Rabbit calls it the 'I' factor, School Boy said. It's the ego, the delusion of 'I'. So the Club translated loving someone to wanting someone, badly. And to be wanted by someone, badly. You actually only love your own wants and desires, Ronaldo the Rabbit, the Village policeman, had warned Club members once. You're actually in love with yourself. They chased him away.

Ronaldo saw enough in his jailhouse to separate love from lust, passion from compassion. One, the product of the I factor. The other came with a progressively pure I-less mind. To truly love someone you have to see them as they are. And for that, one needs to be detached from the ego I and its endless likes and dislikes. Simple logic. So why are they so terrified of detachment, School Boy? Kroh asked. They misunder-stand detachment to mean distance or indifference, School Boy said. They think its letting go. They don't realise they let go only their own delusions and cravings that create barriers between them and the world.

School Boy watched the sun set beyond the Blue Mountains. Lamplights in the Village and his homework beckoned. He remembered his Physics class. They studied some Quantum Mechanics today. At the ultimate level, children, the Physics Master said, matter is substanceless. The solidity of your body is only an apparent reality. At the actual level it arises and passes away, a trillion times a second. A super-scientist called Gautama the Buddha had experienced that truth. Quantum physicists are getting there, School Boy heard, slowly unravelling the strange mysteries of the subatomic world. Here, at the level of ultimate truth, beings are not attached to each other. Yet they communicate. What one particle experiences, the other feels. Their ephemeral bodies don't touch, yet they are partners in the cosmic bio-dance. Always arising, always passing away, for, as Heraclitus the Greek sang, change is the only constant.

To see that change, one has to be detached, Kroh, School Boy said. The ego has to shrink. Kroh saw cooking fires dance in the Village. To see more of the other, one has to see less of the self. And beyond the delusion that one wants the other. For when one wants, one cannot give. In that lay the magic of detachment, Kroh realised. To be actually close to another, the ego has to be away. Then, there is a deeper communion of true love, beyond clinging to mere decaying flesh, bones and blood. Which is why true love needs true detachment, Kroh the curious crow scrawled in his diary. The Anti-Detachment Club doesn't know the freedom of love, yet. They know only the bonds of misery.

Outside Living and Dying

Ayesha Irani

TODAY IS a day for splendid drunkenness. And yet, no calendar commemorates this day: September 30, the birth anniversary of that great mystic poet, Mevlana Jelaluddin Rumi. Perhaps, after all: "This is not a day for asking questions/ Not a day on any calendar". For: "Spring, and everything outside is growing,/ even the tall cypress tree./ We must not leave this place./ Around the lip of the cup we share, these words,/ My Life Is Not Mine./ If someone were to play music, it would have to be very sweet./ We're drinking wine, but not through lips./ We're sleeping it off, but not in bed./ Rub the cup across your forehead./ This day is outside living and dying".

Jelaluddin was born in the first decade of the turbulent 13th century. He became an eminent theologian. His academic sobriety lasted till he was 37, when a profound spiritual experience transformed his life. It was an extraordinary meeting with a wild, wandering mystic of Tabriz: Shams, the Sun, who had travelled across West Asia in search of "someone who could endure his company". His intuition led him to the unsuspecting Rumi. From the moment they met, Rumi was a changed man. The man who once looked down upon poetry began to mouth nothing but verse: "Love has taken away my practices/ and filled me with poetry...I used to be respectable and chaste and stable/ but who can stand in this strong wind and remember those things?" Shams and Rumi were lost in *sohbet,* spiritual communication until jealousies tore them apart. Shams fled to Damascus, only to be tracked down and murdered by Rumi's son Allaedin. Rumi's life was shrouded by the loss of the Friend. He was left ever-searching.

Rumi called his collection of odes and quatrains *Mathnawi: The Work of Shams of Tabriz.* The *Mathnawi* is peppered with jokes, anecdotes and lewd references. In a manner reminiscent of the Tantric masters, especially Ramakrishna, Rumi talks of taming oneself by channelling desire to the Divine, but never by shaming sexuality. The stories of the lustful Caliph, the gourd-crafting maid, the scholar who took his first sip of wine make you collapse with laughter, and when the laughter dies down, you feel the wisdom. Rumi's verse sweeps across us, now leonine and fierce, now self-derisive, taunting, now severe, now delicate yet, through it all, the unswerving *zikr,* remembrance of the Friend. His aesthetic soars to supra-aesthetic heights; breaking the bounds of narrowness, it races towards *fana,* that annihilating moment in which the candle becomes "nothing but a tongue of light", all vestiges of I-ness burnt down.

What Mahaprabhu Chaitanya did for the Bhakti movement in India, Rumi did for Sufism. Dynamic meditation in the form of *kirtana* or 'the turn' is the dance of surrender. Both invite the devotee to use the entire self in the praise of the Infinite, beginning with the sense organs and limbs and then moving inwards. So, as Rumi would say: "Start walking towards Shams". No matter if you've not learnt how to walk, you can dance. Today is a good day to begin.

A Widening Circle of Love

Michael McGhee

OU ARE sitting quite still and upright, aware of your body, and also of your mind. You are invited to look upon yourself with *metta* or loving-kindness. It is an unexpected invitation, since you may be accustomed to thinking well of yourself already, or you may consider yourself fit only for self-loathing. But neither of these familiar attitudes displays the perspective of *metta,* since both exemplify the mental poison of 'comparison', whereas *metta* simply regards you in your humanity, as a being capable of joy and sorrow. To see yourself under that description is to have a new thought, which is also the focus of an unexpected feeling only to be found with such a thought, one of *mudita* or sympathetic joy towards one who flourishes, of *karuna* towards one who suffers. But how can I feel such things towards myself?

I know what it is to suffer, but what it is to flourish? A bell rings, and you hear yourself quietly invited to extend this *metta* towards a good friend. Affection and warmth spring up, but the invitation is to a modification even of these spontaneous feelings. You are to see them as exemplifying the human condition, as another being who suffers and strives. Indeed you catch glimpses of them in this identity as you imagine their presence, you even see yourself in this way for a moment as you recall some common experience. It is suggested that you hold the friend's image before your mind and allow yourself to be filled with the feeling discovered in the thought of them as a human being, but soon you feel the gravitational pull of egocentric preoccupations, which you see for a moment only as a form of suffering. And there you have seen yourself under the aspect of what it is to be a human being, the movement backwards and forwards between a kind of oppressive constriction and an expansion of being.

But you are told to expect these distractions of self-enclosure, and gently but firmly you turn your attention back to *metta bhavana.* The bell rings again and you come to the third stage, that of the neutral person, with whom you have no strong relationship. So it is a little more difficult to hold the image of them in your mind, to summon the feeling that belongs only to that thought, of a human being also caught as well as you between the difficulty and the splendour of life, the feeling of *mudita* or *karuna* according to their state, real or imaginary.

The bell rings, and the fourth stage is announced, to develop loving-kindness towards an enemy. Again it is the same task, to see them not against yourself but in their humanity, so that hatred perhaps starts to turn into compassion. Finally, you are to turn *metta* to each of these persons, yourself, the friend, the neutral person, the enemy, thence to be spread to an ever-widening circle of sentient beings... and so the practice ends. Your eyes slowly open, and you think: Can this practice have no bearing on your attitudes, on your dealings with fellow beings, or with yourself?

Celebrating Death, Not Mourning It

Yousuf Saeed

BOUT 16 days after Id-ul-fitr, many Muslims and non-Muslims in and around Delhi take part in the Satrahvin Sharif, literally 'Holy Seventeenth'. This is the Urs or death anniversary of Hazrat Amir Khusro, companion of the 12th century sufi Nizamuddin Auliya. Thousands of people throng their twin *durgahs* and offer flowers, *chadars* and sweets, or just sit listening to ecstatic qawwalis. There is also *charaghan,* illumination with lamps, everyone makes merry in a colourful fete, which goes on for three to four days.

One might ask as to why someone's death is celebrated. According to Khwaja Hasan Sani of Dargah Nizamuddin, death for a sufi is a final step to the soul's communion with God, a wedding with the divine, hence the celebration. The Arabic word *uroos* from which Urs is taken literally means a wedding. There may be thousands of saints in Indian subcontinent whose tombs become centre of such occasions at least once every year, yet the legend of Amir Khusro and Nizamuddin Auliya is special. Khusro, according to popular belief, was a steadfast sufi and the favourite disciple of Nizamuddin Auliya. However, contemporary scholars know him as a court poet who successfully managed to appease more than seven rulers of the Delhi Sultanate with his charming poetry. A devotee visiting the tomb, who may not be aware of this reality, continues to respect Khusro as a saint of no lesser degree than Nizamuddin Auliya himself, and requests him to mediate between him (the devotee) and God. As an Amir, noble, in the court, Khusro may have indulged in all sorts of material pursuits, but only in his pir's Khaneqah did he find real love and an atmosphere for the evolution of his creative and spiritual faculties.

The death of the two was also a peculiar event. When Nizamuddin breathed his last, Khusro was away in Bengal on Mohammad Tughlaq's royal mission. On seeing his pir's grave he is supposed to have read the following Hindi doha impromptu: *Gori sovay sej pay, mukh par daray kes/ Chal Khusro ghar aapnay, saanjh bhaee chahu des* (The maiden rests on the bed/ her face covered with hair;/ let us Khusro, return home now/ the dark settles in four corners of the world). Khusro's condition started deteriorating and within six months, he died, rather his love met ultimate consummation. This incidence and the above couplet are remembered as the highest point in Khusro's relationship with Nizamuddin and also probably the reason for their becoming a combined legend.

Interestingly, there are many other *dohas* and songs ascribed to Khusro, especially the *Babul* sung in North India at the departure of the daughter on her wedding, also sung by qawwals in the *dargah.* For instance: *Bahut rahi babul ghar dulhan chal tere pi ne bulaee/ Khusro chali sasurarl sajni, sang nahin koi jaee* (You have stayed in your father's home too long/ come, your beloved is calling now/ dear Khusro, you have to go to your in-laws alone; no friends will accompany you now).

Make Music with Love and Knowledge

M N Chatterjee

THE ESSENCE of Chaitanya's philosophy of love is: "Be humbler than grass, more forbearing than the tree. The tree does not complain, even if cut at the root; it does not ask for a drop of water even if it dries up. It gives freely its flowers and fruits without expecting any return. A Vaishnav should be respectful to others and not be proud, because Krishna is present in every soul". Chaitanya was born in 1485 at Navadvip, a cultural and religious centre, in Bengal. He was known as Nimai and by age 16, he had mastered Sanskrit, logic and rhetoric.

It was Nimai's visit to Gaya for his father's funeral that proved to be a turning point. In a Vishnu temple he was seized by ecstasy as he gazed at the deity. He became a God-intoxicated *bhakta* who chanted 'Krishna, Krishna' unceasingly and frequently burst into tears in his anxiety to meet Krishna. His fervid devotion found expression in *sankirtan,* chanting of hymns, accompanied by dancing in abandon.

The chant of 'Krishna, Krishna' has become integral to Vaishnava bhakti in eastern India, echoes of which reverberate even today. The magnetic appeal of Chaitanya's spiritual personality and the simplicity of his message soon attracted followers irrespective of caste, creed or religion. He laid the foundation of a bhakti cult based on universal love. When barely 25, he felt an irresistible urge to take to ascetic life, as absolute surrender to his Lord. Leaving behind his mother, wife Vishnupriya and the entire Navadvip in tears, he met Kesava Bharati, a monk of the Bharati sect of Sankaracharya, and Nimai became Krishna Chaitanya. He went to Orissa and spent most of his life in Puri thereafter. According to Ramakrishna Paramahansa, Chaitanya used to experience three moods. In the innermost mood he would be lost in samadhi, unconscious of the outer world. In the semi-conscious mood he would dance in ecstasy without being able to talk. In the conscious state he would sing of the glories of the Lord.

Having lost all contact with the world and sense of 'you and me' during samadhi, he was one with God and realised the truth of non-dualism. But coming back to the normal state, he became a dualist; he was a lover of God and God was the beloved, the two being separate entities though deeply involved. He wanted 'to taste the sweetness of sugar, and not become sugar'. He was against the rigours of a doctrinaire approach and found essential harmony between love and knowledge.

Chaitanya's teachings, marked by an intensity of passion, moved the people for whom religion had degenerated into sordid adherence to customs and superstitions. His egalitarian philosophy was mass-based, bringing into its fold the demoniac and the angelic alike, the rich and the poor, the Brahmins and the 'untouchables', all sanctified by the Krishna mantra. The cardinal principle of Chaitanya's mystical theology is that Krishna is the acme of divinity. It is through ardent bhakti that one can reach the supreme state where one can identify emotionally with Radha and achieve union with Krishna.

Love as an Antidote to Negative Energy

Valson Thampu

TWO AFFIRMATIONS are common to all religions: peace and love. In Christianity, Jesus, who came to reveal God's love for man, is also the prince of peace. Almost all Hindu prayers end with 'Om Shanti'. Islam, as the name indicates, is a religion of peace. Jainism and Buddhism take the commitment to peace to exalted heights. Valorous opposition to forces of evil in Sikhism stems from a commitment to peace and justice as a measure of its moral vitality. How do resources of love become the logic of peace? To understand this, we have to understand love spiritually. Love is the cementing force between people. At the macro-level, hate aggravates alienation between nations and provokes war and large-scale cruelty. When love dries up in religion, it succumbs to communalism and degenerates into an instrument of alienation.

In the mind, love becomes passion for truth and a refusal to be enslaved by untruth. Ideologies of violence wield untruth as a weapon. Justice is the essence of dharma, that which is under girds and sustains a society. Dharma is synonymous with peace. Peace is not merely the absence of war or conflict. It is a state of comprehensive well-being as indicated by the Jewish concept of Shalom. Love in the soul finds expression as compassion. The life of Ashoka proves that compassion eradicates war-mongering. As a people abjure compassion in their culture and outlook, they acquire a taste for conflict and cruelty. Craving for war robs peace of its attractiveness in their eyes. Where there is love there is willingness, even eagerness, to serve. The erosion of love cripples the spirit of service. Work is sacred; but its sanctity can be experienced only in an ambience of love. Service is an acknowledgement of our belonging together and is a statement of our attitude to others.

It is impossible to create a culture of peace without nurturing in people a capacity and commitment to love. This is the spiritual standpoint. The worldly assumption, in contrast, holds that peace results from the balance of terror. By this logic, the invincibility of wars leads to peace. When the nations of the world know that there are no victors in wars, peace will prevail in the world. However, the millions of lives lost since World War II and the many conflicts that continue to ravage peoples in the Afro-Asian nations disprove this assumption. That is why peace remains an interlude between wars, and not a stable condition for human life and well-being.

The Indian contribution to the discourse of peace must focus on the spiritual foundations of the culture of peace. Peace cannot be pursued as a goal in itself, it is a holistic phenomenon. It can be realised only if all its coordinates, relationship, truth, justice, compassion, service and development, are nurtured and affirmed. This calls for a paradigm shift from the culture of power to the culture of love. Hence the spiritual correlation between the culture of peace and the culture of love.

Rediscovering the Ideal of Seva for Our Times

Michael Lobo

N ANCIENT India, service or seva had a religious significance and embraced a wide range of human activity. The gods, the fields and animals, community and household were all objects of seva. The Hindu ideal of seva also obliged one moved by compassion to give alms to the poor. Yet only a detached form of compassion found place in higher reaches of Vedantic philosophy, which proclaimed the individual's karmic isolation, the aloneness of his quest for salvation. For the *sevak*, the right attitude towards the recipient of his service was disinterestedness.

Similarly, the Buddhist belief in interdependence of all life evolved another perspective on service through the Bodhisattva ideal, the being who deferred his nirvana in order to serve others. Santideva, the Buddhist master, expressed the Bodhisattva's vow as: "I would be a protector of the unprotected/ a guide to wayfarers/ a ship, a dyke, a bridge for them that seek the further shore/ a lamp for them who need a lamp/ a bed for them that need a bed/ a slave for all who need a slave". In later Vaishnavite Bhakti, seva became an element of devotion. It formed the basis of Sikhism and finally, of Gandhi's philosophy. Guru Nanak articulated this understanding: "Recluse, hero, celibate or sanyasi, none will earn merit without devoted service". For Ramakrishna and Vivekananda, seva was contained in the Vedantic idea of oneness of all life implicit in Krishna's command in the Bhagavad Gita: "Worship me in all beings". For Ramakrishna, it was service that lay at the basis of right conduct; indeed, service was God-realisation: "He who sees Shiva in the poor, in the weak, in the diseased, really worships Shiva".

In no religion, however, is charity the basis of the creed as in Christianity. The phenomenon of God becoming man, expiating humankind's sins through suffering and death, the supreme seva, is the keystone of Christian faith and the inspiration of the Christian idea of service. When Jesus knelt down to wash his followers' feet at the Last Supper, he committed them to love and service. "I am among you as a servant" was the kernel of his teaching. "Love your neighbour as yourself" is a command of social service. "Love one another as I have loved you" is a command of religious perfection. "Love one another as I love the Father and the Father loves me" is seva as mystical experience.

Mahatma Gandhi, an outspoken reformer of the Hindu practice of seva, gave it a practical and political direction. He envisaged a society based on mutual aid, in which serving would give way to sharing, each member contributing according to his or her ability. Sharing of wealth would also mean sharing of poverty. Gandhi's views continue to be relevant in this fast-moving age, when the modern state has ensured that taxes provide services, and there seems to be no motivation for seva. It is against this backdrop that all religions must address the difficult task of presenting the sacral and selfless character of seva: the act of reaching out to others which is really the visible form of the unity of all mankind as children of God.

The Purity of Giving

Ranjit Hoskote

OU GIVE but little when you give of your possessions. It is when you give of yourself that you truly give, says Kahlil Gibran in *The Prophet*. It is somewhat ironic that we wait for an annual pretext, like Diwali or Christmas, to express feelings of happiness, regard and sharing through an outward token. Should we express these feelings through goods whose value lies more in their worth as products? And is it not possible that, all too often, beneath the sincere level of affection, the giver is actuated by another motive? If custom sanctions the spurious sense of occasion, it is because social interplay demands the creation and periodic reinforcement of a mutually assured regard among superiors and subordinates, clients and patrons.

This process creates a network of relationships, in which individuals are bound to a wheel of obligations and expectations. This mechanism forces individuals into reciprocal action. It places them under the yoke of gratitude: a claim that can be activated as a favour returned. This is what anthropologists term the gift-exchange economy: an economic institution that governed the dealings of humankind at an earlier stage of development, in which two groups established a relationship by giving gifts and continued it through the regular, ceremonial exchange of gifts.

The value of a gift is defined by the intention that lies behind it. In the Bhagavad Gita (VII, 20-22), Krishna analyses the act of giving in terms of the three gunas, the attributes that define the nature of all things. "A gift is pure, of the essence of sattva, when it is given from the heart to the right person at the right time, and when we expect nothing in return". He adds a caveat: "But when a gift is given in the expectation of something in return, or for the sake of a future reward, or when it is given unwillingly, the gift is of the essence of *rajas*, impure". Krishna rounds off his counsel by warning against a gift that emerges from *tamas*: "A gift given to the wrong person at the wrong time and in the wrong place, or a gift which does not come from the heart and is given with proud contempt, is a gift of darkness". What is elucidated is an ethic of appropriateness and dignity. A gift is contaminated if it is informed by a hunger for recognition, a self-congratulatory arrogance; or if it is extended as an act of patronage intended to buy oneself a place in history, or to bribe one's way to prestige. If Krishna's reflections should offer the giver pause, they also hint at a course of action for the taker.

Refusing a gift that is tainted by negative motivation is not a mark of churlishness, but of concern. It testifies to sensitivity on the refuser's part towards his own spiritual health and that of the giver. Indeed, this refusal is a gift of liberation. It releases both giver and taker from a limiting transaction; it illustrates Gibran's suggestion that "there are those who give and know not pain in giving, nor do they seek joy, nor give with mindfulness of virtue; they give as in yonder valley the myrtle breathes its fragrance into space".

A Mongoose Teaches a King a Lesson

Ramadas Rao

LL YOUR charity does not measure up to the ounce of flour given away by a poor Brahmin, who, though he was starving, fed his guest". These words were spoken to the virtuous Pandava emperor Yudhisthira, not by a sage glowing with wisdom, but by a mongoose. The mongoose began to roll on the ground in Yudhisthira's court, and the assembly noticed that one of its flanks was pure gold. Yudhisthira and his brothers had just finished the Ashwamedha yajna. An enormous amount of wealth had been given away to the needy and a sense of 'goodness' suffused the Pandavas.

But just as the flames of the sacred fire had died down, the mongoose appeared. Turning to the emperor, he narrated the story of a Brahmin who lived in abject poverty. A meal was so scarce that the family would eat once in three days. One day, as the family who had scraped together a morsel each, sat down to eat, a weary traveller came by. Though faint with hunger, the Brahmin offered him his share of food. But the guest was still hungry so the Brahmin's wife gave away her morsel. When this too proved insufficient, the son and the daughter-in-law gave up their morsels too. "When I rolled on the ground", concluded the mongoose, "the crumbs left there turned one of my flanks to gold. Since then, I have visited royal sacrifices where kings have given away vast sums in charity, to see if I could turn my other flank to gold as well, but in vain. Having heard of Yudhisthira's virtue, I came here with great hope. But, again, in vain".

This episode from the Mahabharata clearly indicates that giving away possessions acquired through honest means constitutes the highest form of charity. A shining example of *tyaga* or sacrifice, it ranks far above *dana* or the giving away of amassed wealth. Thus, says Vyasa in the Mahabharata, it is not the quantity that one gives away but the sincerity and the circumstances under which a charitable deed is performed, that wins the approval of the gods.

This litmus test holds good for the present, with its scramble for publicising 'good' deeds performed with wealth acquired through all sorts of means. These, like the charitable deeds performed at Yudhisthira's yajna, fall short of genuine sacrifice. The yajna did not come up to the mongoose's expectations, despite being performed by the most virtuous king of that age, because it grew out of the flaunting of might and wealth. Then, as now, we perform yajnas and pujas without grasping their significance.

Towards the end of the epic age, even as the deeds of great warriors had begun to be sung as ballads, there was a current of thought which deplored the wastefulness, the hubris and the slaughter of animals in sacrifice — this would ultimately give rise to the great pacifist religions of Buddhism and Jainism. The episode of the mongoose is a reminder to those who perform rituals without realising their true spirit.

True Religion Lies in Selfless Service

M N Chatterjee

AMAKRISHNA PARAMAHANSA remarked upon meeting reformer Ishwarchandra Vidyasagar that he had come to an ocean of learning. "At the confluence of the oceans of learning and compassion stands a *siddhapurusha,* who has attained Divine grace", said the mystic. "How can I be a *siddha* without *sadhana?*" asked Vidyasagar. Ramakrishna looked at the motley gathering in the house, which included students, a child widow and a social outcast, waiting for succour. "You selflessly serve others", said the sage of Dakshineshwar. "The so-called holy men strive for their own salvation. If you are not a *siddha,* who is?"

Vidyasagar was born to a poor, orthodox Brahmin family of Bersingha village in 1820. It was an age when child marriage was the norm, widow remarriage was prohibited, polygamy was common and women's education was taboo. The plight of widows moved Vidyasagar deeply. As a social reformer, he denounced child marriage; supported widow remarriage and advocated women's education. To counter his bitter orthodox adversaries, he relied on the interpretation of scriptures like the Parashara Samhita. Though trained as a traditional pandit, Vidyasagar was quick to assimilate western liberal thought. His keen interest in the rationalist theological discourse drew him to the Brahmo Samaj and its Society for the Propagation of Truth. He used its journal, the *Tattvabodhini Patrika* to articulate his strong views against the compulsory celibacy of widows. His imaginative reformist campaigns were marked by the missionary zeal of a radical modernist. On the horse-drawn carriages of schoolgirls, he inscribed lines of the Manu Samhita declaring that a daughter should be educated like a son.

As Special Inspector of Schools, Vidyasagar set up 35 schools for girls in Bengal and played an active role in establishing what became the first women's college in Calcutta. As principal of the Sanskrit College, he removed all caste restrictions on admission. His tireless campaigns bore fruit in 1856, when widow remarriage was recognised by law. Soon after, he set a personal example by blessing the marriage of his son to a widow.

Realising that most of the injustices of Indian society were caused by the lack of social awareness and moral perspective, the scholar-activist reinterpreted traditional religious concepts. In *Sabdamanjari,* his incomplete dictionary, he rendered the complex Sanskrit term 'dharma' to mean 'virtue, righteousness, duty, quality, justice, religion', in that order. He held that it was quite possible for a householder to lead a religiously meaningful life through the practice of dharma; it was not necessary to renounce the world.

Vidyasagar was never explicit about his religious views: he had no time for polemic. While this has led some people to brand him an atheist or agnostic, there are many who believe that his true religion was *paropkar,* the selfless service of others. It would be pertinent here to recall Swami Vivekananda's words: "To be pure and unselfish, to be good and do good to others... that is the whole of religion".

The True Measure of Wealth is Giving

Namita Devidayal

IWALI CAME and went with a feeble bang. Yet, most Hindus performed the Lakshmi puja in their homes and workplaces with fervour. Pandits scuttled from house to house peddling faith-flavoured incense sticks. Even those otherwise given to scepticism propitiated the goddess of wealth, hoping that trade would pick up or at least the share bazaar would swing back along the prosperity curve. The ever-elusive Lakshmi remains discreetly silent, though. Perhaps she waits for her followers to realise the long-abandoned mantra: that wealth is measured not by how much you have, but how much you give.

In the past, the act of giving was assigned to the king or the *annadata*. He was a trustee for his wealth, which belonged to everyone and to no one. This is reiterated throughout the scriptures, beginning with the Rig Veda, which speaks of a man who does not share his food as a sinner. In the Mahabharata, Bhishma warns Yudhisthira that a king is doomed if even one person goes hungry in his kingdom. Krishna speaks to Arjuna on the cycle of mutual dependence initiated by Brahmn: "Those who partake of the leftovers of the yajna, those who eat after having offered all others and all of nature are the virtuous".

In a democracy, the people are the 'kings'. Consequently, the act of giving, of ensuring that all those around you share a basic minimum level of comfort, now rests in the hands of we the people. Giving is not merely about dashing off a cheque to your favourite charity or sponsoring an annual meal for the poor. Remember the parable about Jesus, who observed two people entering a temple. The first, a rich merchant, made an offering of a hundred gold coins. The second, a poor old woman, put down two mites. Which of the two, Jesus asked his gathered disciples, made the bigger offering? Obviously the merchant, right? Wrong. It was the woman. For, while the merchant gave out of what he had to spare, the old woman gave up something she could ill afford to sacrifice.

Giving is about giving of yourself. It could take the form of contributing time or offering a skill. With a lawyer, it may mean taking on that pro bono case. A doctor could set aside a few hours for free consultation. A businessman, instead of whining about the rapid increase in urban crime, could easily take on the responsibility of educating underprivileged children and helping them discover alternative options to crime. Someone who is concerned about environmental pollution could simply begin to plant trees in her neighbourhood.

The act of giving is well-entrenched in our residual memories and merely has to be resuscitated. We should, this New Year, pray not for riches, but for enrichment through values such as these. As long as we hold Narayan, a metaphor for noble thought, right action, the capacity to give and share, or however else one chooses to define godliness, close to our hearts, his beloved Lakshmi will inevitably be by his side.

Money as the Sign of a Divine Force

Vinod Dhawan

AMAKRISHNA PARAMAHANSA had great aversion to money. One day, Vivekananda came to Dakshineshwar and found that Ramakrishna was away. He suddenly felt a desire to test the genuineness of Ramakrishna's often expressed contempt for money. So he hid a rupee under Ramakrishna's mattress. Soon, Ramakrishna returned. No sooner had he touched the bed than he recoiled, as if he felt physical pain. Ramakrishna asked a temple attendant to examine the bed. The rupee was discovered, and Vivekananda explained what he had done. Ramakrishna fully approved of the test.

J Krishnamurti was once going for his customary evening walk. On the way some urchins were playing marbles. On seeing the meticulously dressed Krishnamurti, one of them begged him for money. Krishnamurti told him that he never carried money. But seeing the child disappointed, he offered to play marbles with him. The boy accepted the offer and both sat down on their haunches for a serious contest. JK took to the sport so eagerly that he uttered shouts and whoops of delight. He would crouch in the same way as his rival and then jump up to alter his position to take better aim. Next day, when starting for his evening walk, JK filled his pockets with coins. These he offered to the urchin. But the boy refused to accept the money. Instead, he said: "Let us play marbles!"

When Sri Aurobindo returned to India after studying in England, he took up job as professor of English in the Baroda College. He would empty on a tray the lumpsum of three months' pay and would not bother to keep money in a safe box, neither did he keep accounts. Anybody was welcome to take away money from the tray. Asked why he did so, Aurobindo would reply: "Well, it is proof that we are living in the midst of honest and good people. It is God who keeps account for me. He gives me as much as I want and keeps the rest to Himself. At any rate, He doesn't keep me in want, then why should I worry?"

Later, as the sage of Pondicherry, Aurobindo decried the ascetic approach to money. He said money is the visible sign of a universal force. In its origin and its true action it belongs to the Divine. But like other powers of the Divine it is delegated here and, in the ignorance of the lower Nature, can be usurped by the ego or held by Asuric influences and perverted to their purpose. To proclaim poverty as the only spiritual condition is an error, he said. It leaves the power in the hands of the hostile forces. To reconquer it for the Divine, to whom it belongs, is the supramental way. "You must neither turn with an ascetic shrinking from the money power, the means it gives and the objects it brings, nor cherish a *rajasic* attachment to them or a spirit of enslaving self-indulgence in their gratifications. Regard wealth simply as a power to be won back for the Mother and placed at her service". He emphasised: "If you are free from the money taint but without any ascetic withdrawal, you will have a greater power to command the money for Divine work".

The Ascetic Offers a Pound of His Flesh

Amrit Gangar

A T THE edge of the Rann of Kutch is the Pachchhmai range of hills whose 1,525-feet high black hills, or Karo Dungar, are the highest in Kutch. These mysterious hills hide several unique legends in their womb. Atop Karo Dungar is a tiny temple. There is nothing picturesque about it. No statue of any deity but footprints engraved in marble. As the sun sets, you find the temple priest shouting '*long, long*' holding a vessel full of a sweetmeat made of wheat flour and jaggery. As his words echo back from the range of mountains, you see hordes of four-legged animals rushing towards him to consume the food. They are jackals, old denizens of the hills. The food is actually prasad offered to Pachchhmai Pir by human devotees. The priest offers the remaining portion to jackals twice a day, every day.

As you try to deconstruct the word long you discover the legend of a unique ascetic. Long is a distortion of '*lo ang*' which means 'take my limb or flesh'. As the legend goes, many years ago an ascetic came to the black hills to meditate. Kutch was gripped in a terrible drought then and human beings as well as animals were dying of hunger. One day, an old jackal passed by the meditating ascetic. He thought the ascetic was dead and began to eat his body. But as the animal went closer to the ascetic's body, he fell down for some mysterious reason. Dropping the idea of eating the ascetic's body, the animal found it wise to lie down there doing nothing.

When the ascetic came back to consciousness, he very compassionately thought of the animal's misery. Immediately, he cut off a portion of his body and threw at the hungry animal, repeating the words "lo ang, lo ang". This is how he saved the animal from hunger. For his life-saving noble work for all living beings around, the local people revered him as Pachchhmai Pir. Centuries have gone by but his legend is alive and being enacted by the priest of the shrine on the black hills of Kutch. Generally, the sodhas of Kuran village on the plains are the regular devotees of the pir and they offer 'prasad' at the shrine.

According to the popular belief, if animals eat up or accept the food, it means the pir was pleased with the human devotees offering their oblation to him. If not, it would mean that they would have to do it again until the animals accept the food. In other words, the devotee would always look up to the animals with awe in order to please the pir and fulfil her/his wish. Rarely do the animals disappoint the humans. Not only that after consuming the food they go back to their hilly holes and thank the food-giver with a strange cacophony. The black hills resonate the sounds against the sky creating a deep mysterious feeling. And you can see the black hills through the darkness of night only through the sparkling stars in the humbling sky.

Worship God Through Community Service

Shaheen P Ansari

NE FRIDAY afternoon, on his way to offer the *namaz* at a mosque, a friend found an accident victim lying unattended on the road. As he hesitated over what to do a few more passers-by joined him. Reasoning that the injured person will now be taken care of, he continued towards the mosque. But that day, no matter how hard he prayed, peace eluded him. He agonised over whether he could remain indifferent to a fellow human being's suffering while making fervent attempts to serve God through prayer?

The practice of religion guides us to this supreme vision. But often, we mistake the guideposts for the destination. It is then that prayers become mere empty words, rituals become mere routines and the soul becomes a slave of habit. Nizamuddin Auliya, the sufi saint of Delhi, used to say that rituals are like spices in a cauldron; the real thing is the 'meat'. If there is no meat, there can be no stew and the spices are of no use. Renunciation of worldliness can be likened to the 'meat' in the cauldron. It means to live in the world, dedicating your life to the service of God by giving what you have to those who need it more. When Muinuddin Chishti of Ajmer was asked to explain the highest form of devotion which endeared man to God, he said: "Develop river-like generosity, sun-like bounty and earth-like hospitality".

In the eyes of God no spiritual exercise, no penitence, no prayer, no vigil has greater significance than removing the misery of fellow human beings, bringing consolation to distressed hearts, and helping the downtrodden. For the Sufis service to mankind is the highest form of worship. It is prayer in action. It is love of God that finds its most exalted expression in the service of fellow beings. It is also a love that knows no boundary. Nizamuddin Auliya mentions the story of Abraham. The Prophet never took his meals without a guest. One day he found himself with a polytheist. He hesitated in giving food to this man till Divine admonition came to him: "Abraham! How is it that we can give life to this man yet you cannot give him food?" The message is clear: A traveller of the Path transcends all barriers of cult or race, caste or gender, language or geography in helping his fellow creatures.

Violence only begets more violence. Nizamuddin Auliya used to say that if a man places a thorn in your way and you place another thorn in his way, there will be thorns everywhere. It is only acts of forgiveness and unbiased love which can break this vicious circle. We live in a world torn by conflict and violence, destruction and despair. The world is replete with desolate hearts that are parched with fear and distrust, envy and hatred. The Sufis' message of the heart is a call to unearth the streams of love buried in our hearts. These waters can make gardens of peace bloom once again.

Springsteen Keeps the Faith

Girish Shahane

OM SAID: "Wherever there's a cop beating a guy, wherever a hungry newborn baby cries, where there's a fight against the blood and hatred in the air, look for me, Ma, and I'll be there". Bruce Springsteen sang: "Where there's somebody fighting for a place to stand, for a decent job or a helping hand, where there's somebody struggling to be free, look in their eyes Ma and you'll see me".

This is Bruce Springsteen's homage to America's greatest fictional working-class hero, Tom Joad, the protagonist of John Steinbeck's *The Grapes of Wrath*. Joad's last words are based on a politically-oriented belief which asserts that all souls are part of a larger Oversoul. There is a special presence behind Joad, which provides a metaphysical charge to his lyrics and is traceable through Steinbeck to the Upanishads. An interesting story of cultural dissemination underlies this apparently incongruous coupling of pop music with Vedanta. The Upanishads remained arcane knowledge for 2,000 years, available only to Brahmins who were uninterested in any kind of give-and-take among cultures. This changed with the Mughals, particularly Akbar, who was interested in synthesising religions.

Akbar's great-grandson, Dara Shikoh, commissioned in 1656 a translation of the Upanishads into Persian. His French doctor, Francois Bernier, obtained a copy of the *Oupnekhat,* the Persian translation, and took it to Paris. A century later, another Frenchman, Abraham Hyacinth Anquetil-Duperron travelled in Asia; learnt some Sanskrit and much Persian, and translated the *Oupnekhat* into French. In 1803, Alexander Hamilton, who was proficient in Sanskrit, and stopped by in France. The Napoleonic wars broke out, leaving him stranded. He was, however, allowed to catalogue Sanskrit manuscripts at the French national library and teach Sanskrit. A German scholar, Friedrich Schlegel, attended Hamilton's lectures and began teaching Sanskrit in Germany, thus inaugurating the German fascination with India. Philosopher Arthur Schopenhauer read Anquetil-Duperron's translations of the *Oupnekhat,* and said they had been the solace of his life.

German idealism provided the metaphysical basis of mid-19th century New England renaissance in the US. American transcendentalists, Emerson in particular, took up the German enthusiasm for Indian philosophy, expressing it in poems like 'Brahma'. Emerson's concept of the Oversoul, borrowed from his reading of the Upanishads and the Bhagavad Gita, was given a political angle by John Steinbeck writing in the shadow of the Great Depression. And through Bruce Springsteen continues this cultural transmission initiated by Akbar and Dara Shikoh, brought to Europe by a French doctor, given a new twist by the outbreak of a war, and then nurtured by German poets and philosophers, taken over by the intellectuals of a young nation and in one strand, leading to a theology of social liberation. This excavated history shows that it is communication which enriches cultures, not a hankering after purity and a fixation upon the past.

Existence is a Test of Reality

Rajgopal Nidamboor

MADHVACHARYA, EXPONENT of the *dvaita* school of Vedanta, was an uncompromising dualist. The cornerstone of his conviction was a belief in the basic difference between God and individual souls. As he set out to refute the non-dualistic credo of Shankaracharya (who believed the individual self to be a mere phenomenon and the absolute spirit, Brahmn, to be the only reality), Madhva also strongly rejected the Hindu theory of maya, illusion. To know a thing, he said, is to know it as distinct from all others. He maintained that the mere fact that things are transient and ever-changing does not mean that they are not real. For this reason, Madhva held the view that every new relation modifies a substance to a greater or lesser extent. Departing from orthodox Hinduism in a number of ways, Madhva offered concepts of heaven and hell, with the third alternative of a Hindu purgatory, where rebirth or transmigration of souls took place. He, therefore, glorified the difference between soul and God, between soul and soul, between soul and matter, between God and matter, and between matter and matter.

Madhva gave no credence to the idea that creation had been produced from nothingness. Real creation, in his view, means an eternal dependence of matter and souls on God. God's will, Madhva reckoned, is the sustaining principle for humanity. Reality of God is of independent nature, with human souls being dependent on it. The real, he held, is present in the mind of God as a systemic repertoire: it holds even those realities that are beyond human perception and conception.

This metaphysical understanding implies that all acts of consciousness by the dependent selves are finally dependent on God's will. Madhva taught that an eternal and indissoluble relationship of boundless object and bounded reflection, of *bimba pratibimba bhava*, connects the infinite and the finite. Brahmn, the infinite, was the source of all reality, consciousness and activity. Madhva's doctrine is a philosophical touchstone intended to explain and bring about a rapprochement between the presence of evil with the notion of divine perfection.

To "how can evil exist unchallenged in a universe created by God?", Madhva suggested, according to Madhva scholar B N K Sharma: "If there is a possibility of moral and social paragons, it is equally possible to hold that there may be persons who act on the motto, 'Evil, be thou my good', and such Satanic conduct could only merit eternal misery."

"Existence", Madhva taught, "is a test of reality". His theme song, finally, was that actual existence at some place and some time in the world is a sufficient test to separate the real from the unreal. Similarly, the possibilities of bondage in the world and release from the world are also real; and it is devotion to God alone that can pave the way to release, since divine grace is the one requirement for salvation.

I Don't Care, I'm Agnostic

Dilip D'souza

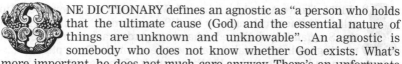 NE DICTIONARY defines an agnostic as "a person who holds that the ultimate cause (God) and the essential nature of things are unknown and unknowable". An agnostic is somebody who does not know whether God exists. What's more important, he does not much care anyway. There's an unfortunate element of frivolity here. Not being either a believer or a non-believer is one thing, but not to even care about it? Is the agnostic that uninterested? Is it at all commendable that he sit swinging his legs uncaringly on the fence, particularly on a question of such profundity? For me, the answer is unequivocal: Yes.

Being agnostic puts your life squarely where it belongs: in your hands. You have to take responsibility for every action. In contrast, it may be religion's greatest weakness that it pushes you to give up responsibility. That is why religion has so much misery and bigotry to answer for. Those things can always be blamed on somebody else. God, sometimes. The rest of the world, other times. But me, even if only for being blind to the misery? Almost never.

"It's God's will", some will say. "He works in inscrutable ways, don't you know?" Christianity argues that suffering is cleansing of sin. This is supposed to explain everything from a horrible disaster, needless deaths, to crippling poverty. It forces convoluted ethical compromise. Bertrand Russell wrote: "No man who believes that all is for the best in this suffering world can keep his ethical values unimpaired, since he always has to find excuses for pain and misery". In finding those excuses, we also persuade ourselves that we cannot do much about miseries we can address. After all, if God planned for millions to live in poverty, well, we mortals can hardly fight that, can we?

This attitude engenders an acceptance where there should be outrage. When an external, sacred entity is the reason for life's obstacles, I am off the hook. Not only do I not need to feel outraged, I don't need to feel any responsibility. Preordained things happen to me: I have nocontrol over them. It doesn't need a stretch of imagination to see that this profound renunciation of responsibility explains much that is wrong around us.

Agnosticism addresses helplessness in the most direct way: by telling you to leave God alone. When you don't care whether God exists or not, you are left with no choice but to grapple with problems yourself. That turns out to be the only way they ever get solved. In fact, grabbing responsibility with both hands turns out to be the best reason of all for agnosticism. There's nothing remotely frivolous about that. Beginning a 1948 radio debate with a Father Copleston, Bertrand Russell pronounced himself an agnostic. Copleston then asked him: "Would you agree with me that the problem of God is a problem of great importance?" Russell replied: "Roughly speaking, yes". Or: It may be important, certainly, but is it really important enough? Those three words, it seems to me, capture the essence of being agnostic.

Life Ends, Survival Begins

Chief Seattle

N 1851, Native American tribes of Washington were 'persuaded' to sell their ancestral lands to the US government. Seattle, chief of the Suquamish, delivered what is regarded as one of the most moving environmentalist statements ever made. Excerpts:

How can you buy or sell the sky, the warmth of the land? If we do not own the freshness of the air and the sparkle of the water, how can you buy them? We are part of the earth and it is part of us. So, when the Great Chief in Washington sends word that he wishes to buy our land, he asks much of us. For this land is sacred to us. This shining water that moves in the streams and rivers is the blood of our ancestors.

We know that the white man does not understand our ways. One portion of land is the same to him as the next, for he is a stranger who comes in the night and takes from the land whatever he needs. The earth is not his brother, but his enemy, and when he has conquered it, he moves on. He leaves his fathers' graves behind, and he does not care. He treats his mother, the earth, and his brother, the sky, as things to be bought, plundered, sold like sheep or bright beads. His appetite will devour the earth and leave behind only a desert...The air is precious to the red man, for all things share the same breath: the beast, the tree, the man. The white man does not seem to notice the air he breathes. But if we sell you our land, you must remember that the air shares its spirit with all the life it supports. And if we sell you land, you must keep it apart and sacred, as a place where even the white man can go to taste the wind that is sweetened by the meadow's flowers.

The white man must treat the beasts of this land as his brothers. I am a savage and I do not understand any other way. I have seen a thousand rotting buffaloes on the prairie, left by the white man who shot them from a passing train. If all the beasts were gone, man would die from a great loneliness of spirit. For whatever happens to the beasts, soon happens to man. All things are connected. If men spit upon the ground, they spit upon themselves. This we know: The earth does not belong to man; man belongs to the earth. Man did not weave the web of life: he is merely a strand in it.

God gave you dominion over this land and over the red man. That destiny is a mystery to us, for we do not understand a future when the buffalo are slaughtered, wild horses tamed, secret corners of the forest heavy with scent of many men, and the view of the ripe hills blotted by wires. Where is the thicket? Gone. Where is the eagle? Gone. The end of living and the beginning of survival.

The Perils of Imitation

Peggy Mohan

NDIAN VISITORS wandering into Hindu temples in Trinidad are in for a cultural shock. In Trinidad, Hindus who didn't convert to Christianity have picked up something of Christian worship. A Hindu temple in Trinidad looks like a church. There is a stage with an altar, and benches, or 'pews', for a large congregation. But strangest of all is the service itself. On the stage there is a pundit performing a *havan*. Sitting on the pews, is a full congregation singing *bhajan* after *bhajan*, on their own. Here is one process by which a very organic, very diverse religion begins to contradict itself as it takes on the outward look of a monolith built around a *samaj*, large concrete places of mass worship, and an abstract Paramatma.

There is something about modern Christianity that impresses and challenges the Hindu fanatic. Because of the view that Christianity is a fierce and macho religion whose followers rule the present-day world. This, despite the gentler face in the form of baby Jesus and the message of 'turning the other cheek'. Christian cathedrals are built to overawe and intimidate. Church choirs are trained to blend their voices, even as they sing in parts or counterpoint, into a single complex harmony. Coordination, control, certainty, size: modern capitalism seems only an offshoot of the Protestant Reformation.

It is this macho face of Christianity that bedevils Hindu fanatics. Like those unhappy men who mutely suffer humiliation in office and go home to build back their pride by beating their wives, our Hindu fanatic is a creature in deep distress. And so he begins to transform Hinduism itself into the sort of martial force that matches the ugliest face of Christian fundamentalism.

Oh yes, Hinduism is indeed in danger. But not from the ones who converted away from Hinduism. It is the very body of Hinduism that stands threatened as it gets 'cleansed' of those features that have no place in the violent, homogenised, macho world of today! Love and friendship are wonderful. But admiration is positively lethal, carrying as it does all the longing, anxiety and despair of people who love themselves too little. John Lennon was killed by one of his own fans. Admiration isn't really about good feelings. It is what you are reduced to feeling for those you can only watch from afar, waiting, waiting for them to come down to earth, unprotected. And sooner or later some of them will cross your path, without the mantle of protection. And like lambs to the slaughter, they will pay the price for all the pent-up bitterness you have been hiding behind a helpless smile.

These are complex emotions at work: not hate, not indifference, not love, but terrifying when they suddenly erupt into force. And so a new generation has come of age, which is actually ashamed of the empathy and wisdom of the old strands of Hinduism; and, to face the western juggernaut, they feel compelled to remake themselves in a new image, a (dare we say) Protestant Hindu image. And people like me are left to mourn, a second time, another loss of an earlier world of grace.

Superkid Calvin and His Instant God

Abhijit Majumder

AILING DOWN a hillside on an out-of-control sled, Calvin, our 'Generation Next' superhero, remarks: "I hate waiting. I like to have everything immediately". Hobbes, the tiger, noticing that they are about to plunge off a cliff, wonders whether they ought to anticipate death. "I don't know why I bother trying to have discussions with you". Calvin responds. "You are always so morbid".

Through the six-year-old Calvin, Bill Watterson's *Calvin and Hobbes* has been serving epiphanies on the breakfast table for years. Readers have followed Calvin as he saunters with his walking-talking stuffed tiger past the timeless swaying of trees in the forest, or while he abandons himself to the gruesome side of his ambition with his wish-gun, the 'transmogrifier'. The mischievous boy is named after the stern Protestant theologian of Geneva, John Calvin; the jolly but sensible tiger is named after the utilitarian philosopher Thomas Hobbes. Calvin's relationship with the Divine is one of bargain. At Christmas, he knows he must be good for the presents. But, he wonders, can he be thought good if he has been good only to get the presents? "All I'm saying is that I can be bribed", he asks. "Is that good enough, or do I have to be good in my heart and spirit?" But this brief insight vanishes and strategy takes over. "Okay", he asks, "so how good do I have to act?"

In his adventures, Calvin is repeatedly reduced to a failed quasi-Nietzschean hero: malevolently superhuman in ambition, pathetic and lovable in failure. He wouldn't spare a wink before entering into a deal with the Devil. And while he thinks his command over the history of the stegosaurs and the brontosaurs will bring him fame and immortality, he fumbles with spelling and arithmetic and ends up with a D-minus-minus. Face-to-face, God scares Calvin with sharp insights into his own all-engulfing loneliness. At the end of a star-gazing session with Hobbes, the boy gets bristle-hair in sudden awe of their ghostly solitude on earth.

The tiger is symbolically a stuffed one, impotent to the normal eye, coming alive as a guide and companion only in the imagination and essentially in solitude, as a source of balance to Calvin the child, whose manic innocence leads him to revel in the annihilation of snowmen as a prelude to spring. Calvin's companionship with the comforting Hobbes is an assurance that imagination is man's only guide in a spiritual void. The stuffed tiger unfailingly tempers Calvin's improbable longings with a pinch of common sense, counters his dereliction with the nudge of duty.

Ironically, thoughts of time and death become Calvin's learning moments: he wonders, for instance, what the woods would be like when he and Hobbes are no longer there, but his bonsai super-consciousness keeps him steeped in spiritual dormancy. Like many of us, he is trying to keep things from jetting out of his hands to allow his learning to evolve into knowledge, or his cleverness to mature into wisdom.

A Cheeky Letter from Me to My Dear God

Bhavana Pankaj

MY dear God,

I was very little when I first heard of you. My mother said: "You are God's miracle". My baby heart merely saw the tenderness in her eye. My years in a Hindu family were filled with your stories. The entire world was your creation, I was told. You, the cosmic dancer, and the universe, your eternal dance. I wanted to see you. Hear you. Hear a bird sing, they said. Or the wind whistle. See a flower bloom, they said. Or a star twinkle. For starters, said mother: "Love all and be loved yourself. Give your all so you are never wanting. Be kind and the world's compassion will fill you. You will see Him then".

The child's heart believed all. I grew up in faith. Got on with life. And the innocent toothless smile was lost in the furrows of hope and despair. The world wasn't all about stars and flowers. It was about power. Of pelf, politics, polemics. I had read in school of your promise that the meek shall inherit the earth. I saw, instead, the powerful hijack the earth. I heard them wage wars in your name and slaughter your creation. Tyrants, thinkers, theologists, politicians, scientists, ideologists. They came in as many garbs as you had names. They chained you to the temple and pulled down the mosque. Fettered you to a mosque and marauded a temple.

I saw the magic of your stories turn black as they butchered innocent people in selfish wars. Consigned widows to the funeral pyres of their husbands. Killed little girls in the womb of life. Damned the rivers and fuelled the forests. I wondered if you, the Dancer, were bored now. Disinterested now. Why else would you do little about tyrants snuffing out lives in gas chambers? Or when fanatics pumped bullets into the hearts of saints? And the end? Well, the bird still sings. But I don't hear you in the song. Will you break your silence and speak to me? I want to hear no one else but you. Hear from no one else but you. Will you return to me my baby smile, the eye that sees, the ear that hears, the heart that knows? Will you give me the trust and the patience that someday, somewhere, you will? And I will too?

I know things are not all that bad. Can't be. Remember how the Jewish mystic Baal Shem prayed: "Lord, you need me just as much as I need you. If you did not exist, whom would I pray to? If I did not exist, who would do the praying?" It is possible that I speak out of turn. But here is another chance for you to forgive me. If that sounds cheeky, know that fun and innocence are quite alive and kicking. Know also that I would like to see you grin and bear it as much as you would like to tweak my ear after you've wiped all my tears. How about a date, dear God, in 2000 AC?

Yours forever...

PS: AC here stands for Always Current.

Spiritual Mosaic of the Two Hemispheres

Janina Gomes

MANY PEOPLE have tried to bridge the gap between the East and West. Bede Griffiths, an English Benedictine monk, was one of them. A seeker of truth, he came to India in 1955 and assisted in the founding of the Kurisumala ashram, a Syrian Christian monastery in Kerala, before joining the Saccidananda ashram in Shantivanam, Tamil Nadu. He joined two Frenchmen in the Saccidananda ashram, Jules Mochanin and Henri Le Saux, in attempting to find in India a Christian community following the customs of a Hindu ashram and adapting itself to Hindu ways of life and thought. This was long before the movement for dialogue with other religions in the Catholic Church found universal acceptance and the concept of enculturation came to be accepted.

Bede Griffiths was most struck by what he calls the greatest discovery of Indian thought: discovery of the atman, which is the ground of personal being and which is one with Brahmn, universal being. In his *Return to the Centre*, he wrote that the way to truth was not of progress, but that change or metanoia were a return to the source, what the Chinese call the 'uncarved block'. He found in his personal search for the truth that humility, simplicity and purity of heart in Indian spirituality led to a knowledge of the Centre.

As a sanyasi, he felt he was called to go beyond all religion, human institution, scripture and creed, till he came to that which they signified. He felt this did not call for a rejection of his own religion, but rather was a going beyond the signs to reach what was signified. He also found that his experiences of the beauty and mystery of nature and the religious experience it mediated, which was expressed in the writings of romantic poets in the West like Wordsworth, Shelley and Keats, was the common faith of India for countless centuries. Griffiths made a deep study of the Vedas and Hindu scriptures and felt the Catholic Church in India needed to adapt its organisation to Indian instead of Roman models. He believed the Catholic Church in India had to learn to see its own Semitic tradition with all its unique value in the light of the Oriental tradition, and to learn what Hinduism, Buddhism, Taoism and Confucianism had to teach it, so that there was a meeting point between East and West.

In his book *Marriage of East and West* he stressed that the future of the world lay in Asia, Africa and Latin America. While this did not mean a rejection of the values of western democracy and science, it meant that the rationalist mind of the West had to be balanced by the intuitive, receptive power of the East. Moved by the extraordinary sacredness which is attached to every created thing in India, Bede Griffiths realised that though the truth is one, it has many faces and manifests in different religions and traditions. While each religion should hold to its fundamental truth, it should also expose the tradition of other aspects of truth. His was a rare spiritual quest for a marriage between East and West which he exemplified in his own life.

Sitting on God's Front Porch

Eugene Cernan

OW DID I feel on the moon, where I spent three earth days on the Apollo 17 mission? That's nearly 75 hours, a good 2,50,000 miles away from what was my reality. The earth kept drawing my gaze away from the moon's bleak surface, and reality felt like a hallucination. I reflected on the rare privilege of standing on the moon and looking back at the only known place in the universe that contained life.

I've always believed in God. When I went to the moon on Apollo 10 is when I first realised that there must be a Creator of the universe. Because when you go that far away, you begin to see earth in all its beauty. You watch it rotate on its axis. It doesn't tumble through. The logic, purpose is almost beyond your comprehension. It is surrounded by three-dimensional blackness: the endlessness, infinity of space and time. I'm not sure that I understand that, but I can tell you that it exists; I saw it with my own eyes. A picture doesn't do it, you've got to see it.

There must be a Creator, who stands far above all religions. When I went back to the moon on Apollo 17, I had a chance to literally challenge that theory. And it came back loud and clear. On the moon, you have no choice but to believe in a Creator. If you can let your imagination wander, it's almost like sitting on God's front porch, looking back home at the earth. It's a very humbling experience. Did all this distract me from my work? Not really, but you keep wanting to steal a look at earth and everything around you. I think, I'm only here for three days, so I'm trying to drink in as much of it as possible. You can literally hide the earth with the palm of your hand, or even a thumb. It's so dramatic. And the earth is four times the size of the moon. Like a Christmas tree ornament, sitting out there in space.

On my first space mission, on Gemini 9, I floated right along with the spacecraft; I was its satellite, attached to it by an 'umbilical cord'. I almost didn't live through it; it was a close brush with death. Looking back, I'm now getting to be more philosophical than technical. There's a spiritual aspect to all this. The space vehicle orbiting the earth was travelling at 18,000 miles an hour. And there I was, orbiting the earth along with it, at the same speed. You begin to look back and feel different, spiritually and philosophically. My watch, set to earth time, was my window to reality in my life: not the moon, but my life back on earth. The moon was a temporary dream. But this watch window kept me in touch with my real life: it was my wireless umbilical. Time takes on a whole new meaning out there: without beginning, without end. How do you measure time in infinite terms? It has no meaning. Time is relative. You realise you're moving through time, not just space.

(As told to Narayani Ganesh)

Cartesian Thoughts on Hindu Stone Gods

Francois Gautier

ROUGHT UP on Logic and Cartesian Reason, from Descartes French philosopher, mathematician and physicist, who in his *Discourse of the Method* elaborated a system whereby doubt is used to analyse any unknown phenomenon, we westerners are taught to believe only what we can see and to have faith only in what we experience. Those whose parents have Marxist leanings are also injected with a dose of atheism: to disbelieve in the unnatural, the supernatural, the religious, and generally what is invisible to the eye. This is why many of us when we come to India, have difficulty with the way Hindus adore gods in statues. How in heaven can there be any divine presence in a piece of stone?

Yet, a few westerners, instead of rejecting outright this 'pagan' habit that Hindus have had for millennia, have tried to analyse it, using the very Cartesian logic with which we are endowed, thanks to our rigorous education. One such person was Alexandra David-Neel, writer, explorer, spiritualist, and the first western woman to have explored Tibet. In her 1951 book, *India as I saw it,* she remarks: "The energy which the Hindus project on the idol is not totally immaterial. The existence, real or not, of the deity has no importance, what matters is the accumulation of the psychic forces in the statue, a function similar to a car battery. The adoration of devotees charges the statues. Once fully charged, one can draw energy out of it, because like a battery, the statue will not get empty if one continues to charge it with prayers". She concludes: "It is thus that an idol which has been adored for centuries by believers is now charged with considerable energy due to the repetition of incalculable acts of devotion". Her wrapping up of the subject is simple: Gods are thus created by the energy emitted by the faith in their existence.

Will this rather 'scientific' explanation of idol worship be sufficient to convince disbelievers? This reminds one of the story of Bruno Philip, ex-correspondent in India of *Le Monde*. Like any good Frenchman, he tended to disbelieve in supernatural stories. When he heard that Ganesh was drinking milk a few years back, he went to the nearest temple with a smirk on his face. But lo, he saw the God actually drinking the milk. However, when he telephoned *Le Monde* in Paris, he was told that he must have drunk too much the night before! But then, Bruno could have told his disbelieving boss in Paris that all religions, however Cartesian they are, have their share of beliefs in the supernatural and unscientific. Is it more rational or Cartesian (than worshipping stone idols) to think, for instance, as Catholics do, that Mary conceived a child while a virgin, or that Christ came back from the dead and ascended physically to heaven (and not in his subtle body, which is more likely), or that Jesus multiplied breads and cured incurable people? Even today, American preachers who come to India carry advertisements in newspapers promising whoever comes to their rallies will not only encounter God, but also witness miracles.

Descartes must be shaking his head in heaven.

The Good News About Communal Harmony

Farida Khanam

OING BY media reports alone one would get the distinct impression that our country is plagued by communal tension and disharmony. The truth, however, is that in India 99 per cent of people live together quite peaceably. A mere glance at our festivals, functions, educational centres, shopping centres will suffice to show that this is a fact. A telling anecdote would indicate why the media gives a different picture. In a Hindi BBC bulletin last year, a letter was read out from a listener in Mauritius. He pointed out that though Mauritius had a large number of people whose mother-tongue was Hindi, and he regularly listened to the BBC's Hindi programmes, he never heard anything about Mauritius. The BBC correspondent remarked, laughingly, that in Mauritius there was only good news and, since the motto of the media was 'good news is no news', bad news had to be created if Mauritius was to be covered.

On December 6, 1992, when the Babri masjid was demolished, the news reached every city and village. But there are about five lakh mosques, large and small, functioning all the year round, with people saying their prayers there without this ever forming a part of the media coverage. It is not surprising then that the average Muslim knows and talks more about the Babri mosque than the one he visits daily. Some years ago the Rajiv Gandhi Foundation conducted a comprehensive survey on communal riots in the country after 1947. It revealed that most riots had taken place in urban centres and not in villages. As we all know, about 85 per cent of our population lives in villages. This means that the riots affected at most 15 per cent of the population.

For instance, Hindu processions go along streets without any tension. Another important development, the broadbased movement for self-improvement of Muslims in education and the job market, has gone unreported. We have heard so much about bias and discrimination but now the circumstances have changed considerably. Muslims have greatly benefited from the democratic and secular set-up of the country, which has enabled them to make tremendous progress. But the media seldom covers such constructive activities.

Again, owing to the open policies of the government, Muslims are making visible progress in the economic field. For instance, the richest person in the country, Azim Premji of Bangalore, is an Indian Muslim. During my recent visit to Bangalore, a Hindu businessman remarked that New Bangalore is a gift from Azim Bhai. Everywhere, be it in private or communal life, Hindus and Muslims go hand in hand, complementing each other, sharing their joys and sorrows, joining together in festivities and functions, be it Iftar, Eid, Muharram or Diwali. Indeed, barring a few stray incidents, they have lived together for centuries in perfect amity. The Partition did, of course, cause a great rift, but now both communities seem to have realised that our destiny is one. Only by accepting this, and by sharing everything with one another, can we make progress, not only individually, but also as a nation.

Multiple Ways of Seeing Things

Daisaku Ikeda

CULTURAL DIFFERENCES translate into other ways of looking at the world where deep bonds of trust are established. All too often, however, such differences are the cause of conflict. At 32, historian Arnold Toynbee visited Turkey to study the Greco-Turkish War. Guided by St Augustine's injunction: *Audi alteram partem,* hear the other side, he first observed conditions from the Greek side, then the Turkish. He placed particular emphasis on listening to the side that was "more in danger of not being given a fair hearing". Witnessing the suffering of Turkish refugees, he was outraged that these atrocities went completely unreported in the West. Writing facts exactly as he saw them, he wired these to the *Manchester Guardian.* The editor courageously published the full text of Toynbee's reports.

Because for centuries Turks were portrayed as uncivilised savages and horrors of the 1915 Armenian Massacre by the Ottoman Turks were still fresh in people's memories, the newspaper was attacked for publishing articles sympathetic to the "unspeakable Turk". But the paper's admirable stance of refusing to bend to what Toynbee saw as prejudice against Turks shines to this day. The article made a deep impression on the Turks. They were astonished that a young Englishman had visited a Turkish refugee camp, impartially recorded what he had seen, and that a British newspaper had published it. It was the first time that their side of the story was conveyed to the world.

Toynbee knew it was wrong to stereotype people. He had to get to know the people. Putting this conviction into practice, he made friends with Turks and learnt the language. "When one becomes personally acquainted with a fellow human being, of whatever religion, nationality, or race, one cannot fail to recognise that he is human like oneself", he said. Viewing things from a western perspective does not necessarily provide the true picture. There is an African view of the world, a Middle Eastern and Latin American one, and one seen by ethnic minorities. Information is often tailored to fit preconceived notions and stereotypes. In wartime, we repeatedly air scenes of 'our side' coming under attack-scenes of the hellish misery inflicted on the citizens of the other country are rarely broadcast.

Dialogue that creates peace with others must first start with an open and earnest 'inner dialogue'. It is vital to ask ourselves: Do I accept without question the images provided to me? Ceasing to introspect, we become self-righteous and dogmatic and discourse becomes a one-way street: Unable to hear others, real dialogue becomes impossible.

We need to awaken to a common consciousness. This is not found in some distant place or on a computer screen. It lies in our hearts, in our ability to share the pain of our fellow human beings. It is the spirit that says: "As long as you are suffering, whoever you are and whatever your suffering may be, I suffer also".

What's Become of the Guru?

Kedar Kamat

HE WORD 'guru' is derived from the Sanskrit roots *gu* signifying ignorance and *ru* implying remover. Thus a guru does not give so much as removes. If you are in the grip of illusions, for instance, a true guru helps you emerge from it by arousing the powers of discrimination that are latent within your own consciousness. So that he helps you to uncover your own intrinsic nature rather than imposing a doctrine upon you. The guru acts in the conviction that nothing can be your own that was not yours already. Just as a person is not enriched by a loan so too a person is not truly enlightened by a second-hand enlightenment.

Today, gurus of all shades and persuasions abound in the world; those who shop in this supermarket of spiritual wares ought to be careful and not fall into the clutches of a charlatan who promises to transform them, no matter what their own nature and inclinations. The true guru is one who fathoms the depth, or shallowness, of the pupil before beginning to teach. The traditional *guru-shishya* relationship had particular importance in ancient India, when students would grow up under the canopy of their guru: as a member of the *gurukul,* or teacher's family, the student would derive a multi-dimensional education.

Beyond providing formal education, the guru imparted an ethical perspective: the importance of guiding values was emphasised, and the teacher in ancient India would undoubtedly point his disciple to ultimate knowledge, of the cosmic principle which the Upanishads exalt as Brahmn. Such is the importance of the guru as a guide through the perilous ways of life that even such divine incarnations as Rama and Krishna are shown, in the epics, to have flourished under the guidance of their gurus Vishwamitra and Sandipani.

In modern times, however, the role of the guru and of the *gurukul* system of education has been substantially bypassed. It seems as though this ancient approach to learning has become redundant in a materialistic age. While the emphasis in former times was on helping students fulfil their potentialities and develop their consciousness,the education system has a new mandate today: to train students to survive and succeed in a cut-throat environment in which professional advancement and material aggrandisement are the only recognised emblems of success. The teacher, like everyone else, takes his or her place in an assembly-line system of production, in which knowledge too is a commodity.

Education is no longer a process of evolution; it has become a trade in fact-lists and score-sheets, in which a short-term memory that is orientated towards the examination is prized over the development of a long-term ability to reflect upon oneself, others and the world. Rather than attending to individual needs, teachers today seem driven by the need to send yet another batch of ill-formed students on their way into the literacy statistics. In such an ethos, the guru is no longer a dispeller of darkness; s/he has, tragically, joined the forces of ignorance.

Muhammad Taught
a Gospel of Compassion

Asghar Ali Engineer

HE PROPHET of Islam, Muhammad bin Abdullah, was born in 570 AD. He was brought up in Mecca by his grandfather, Abdul Muttalib, in dire poverty. Mecca was no ordinary city. For the Arabs, it was twice blessed: a great centre of pilgrimage (the House of Allah, the Ka'aba was situated in it). It was also an important international centre of commerce. Trade caravans passed through it; and with them came new influences.

Tribal bonds were being dissolved. Profits from trade were either reinvested or spent on conspicuous consumption: private property, unknown in tribal society, produced the malaise of greed among the newly rich Meccans. The poor were neglected. Even though he had done well as a trader himself, he began to reflect on the crisis of his age in the cave of Hira, outside Mecca. It was here that he began to receive the revelations which he was soon to proclaim to the world.

The Islamic teachings, which were revealed to the Prophet, laid great emphasis on justice and equality. The earlier revelations exhort the faithful to care for the poor and needy. In fact, *zakat*, the poll tax made obligatory for all Muslims, is required to be spent on the weaker sections of society. Islam's condemnation of hoarded wealth and its prohibition of usury should also be seen in this perspective: the rich Arabs of the Prophet's time would lend money to the poor at exorbitant rates of interest, causing untold misery. Islam was greatly concerned with the imperatives of social justice. The Qur'an says: "Have you seen him who belies religion? That is the one who is rough to the orphan, and does not urge the feeding of the needy".

Compassion is integral to din or religion: one who is harsh to the needy negates religion entirely. The Prophet taught that it is more meritorious to feed a hungry person than to pray all night long. Throughout his life, he was distinguished by this sensitivity to suffering: indeed, he was renowned as 'Rahmatun lil'alamin', mercy of the worlds. The Prophet always exhorted his followers to treat their slaves and servants as members of their family. He made Bilal Habshi, his liberated black slave, a summoner to prayer: the greatest of honours.

When the Prophet migrated to Medina, he drew up a pact with followers of other religions to live in harmony and with dignity. When a Christian delegation came to meet him, he insisted that they pray according to their custom inside the mosque. The Qur'an also lays down that Muslims should show equal respect to all the prophets Allah has sent to different nations.

Declaring that there is no coercion in religion, the Qur'an says: "Abuse not those whom they call upon besides Allah, lest, exceeding limits, they abuse Allah through ignorance" (6:109). It is also said: "And everyone has a direction to which He turns (himself), so vie with one another in good deeds" (2:148). Thus the basic emphasis of the Qur'an is on pluralism, on what it calls *istibaq bi'l kharyat*: excelling one another in good deeds and not competing in ways of worshipping.

Pausing on Threshold of the Sacred

Vithal C Nadkarni

HE SAMADHI of Jnanadeva in Alandi marks the place where the 21-year-old sage-poet entombed himself 700 years ago. It is considered a living monument by his followers, who form the Warkari sect of Maharashtra. An ineffable sense of the master's presence fills the place. And there is the mystery of what may lie beneath the tomb's rock-lined parapet. One is led, for instance, to wonder whether the master, enraptured in eternal samadhi, is seated in *siddhasana*? Or is he seated in the lotus position, as tradition maintains, on a deerskin covered with *tulsi* and *bel* leaves? Surely the original copy of the *Bhavartha-dipika*, his Marathi commentary on the Bhagavad Gita, lies open in front of him?

According to Jnanadeva's contemporary, Namdev, Jnanadeva ceremonially entered the crypt. As he sat in his *asana*, wearing *tulsi* garlands, he folded his hands three times and finally closed his eyes in what is described by his devotees as the fearsome *bhima-mudra,* the departure of the sun from their lives. Stories about the shrine abound. One recalls, for instance, being shown a hole in the tiled temple flooring, stoppered with wood, believed to communicate directly with the samadhi' vault. One sees people prostrating themselves near it, to get a whiff of the blessed air supposedly emanating from the samadhi. An equally striking tale is about a 'golden' peepal tree believed to have sprung directly from Jnanadeva's wooden armrest.

By the time of Sant Eknath, however, the roots of this bodhi tree had reportedly grown so luxuriant that one of them pressed against the master's throat. The master's distress was communicated to Eknath in a dream over three nights. Eknath is then believed to have entered the samadhi with a machete, to clear away the roots and relieve the master. He is also said to have sat for three nights in the samadhi, immersed in communion with Jnanadeva; in the course of which, he received instructions about interpolations in the *Bhavartha-dipika*. Eknath then carried out the first major revision of Jnanadeva's masterwork. The story may well be a mythicised rationalisation of the later saint's great purification and enlightenment.

Some years ago, a German firm offered to introduce an endoscopic camera into the samadhi to photograph it. There was a public outcry. What the foreign researchers failed to realise is that the samadhi is not a dry pharaonic mausoleum, to be opened without invoking feelings of sacrilege. It is a monument cherished by a tradition that is vibrantly alive and cannot be expected to tolerate an intrusion, however well-meaning, into its most hallowed shrine. Indeed, the Warkari cult continues to flourish today because of inspired choices that the master made. Like Chakradhar, founder of Mahanubhava, another protestant sect of Maharashtra, Jnanadeva insisted on using Marathi rather than Sanskrit. Writing in a simple idiom, Jnanadeva at once opened jealously guarded secrets of religious thought to common people. His lilting, immortal poetry wrought rest of the magic.

Surrendering to the Master's Grace

Lata Khubchandani

HE BLIND was given the lamp, and yet his darkness was not removed. What is the use of teaching one who has not purified the body? This verse was composed by Dadu Dayal, a 16th-century mystic who is often overshadowed by relatively better known masters of the time like Kabir and Jnanesvara. But Dadu's devotional poetry is a rich source of consolation and enlightenment: It outlines a pathway to freedom from the cycle of birth and death.

"Great ascetics have fallen under the onslaught of the mind; gods and men have been ruined, even Brahma, Vishnu and Shiva... Dadu has found a snake-charmer in his guru. He alone has removed all poison from the mind". The path that Dadu advocated is based on the power of the Word, celebrated in various religious traditions as the holy name, the logos, *shabda* or *bang-e-aasmani*. The mind can slowly but surely be brought under control through the concentrated repetition of the holy names given by the master. It learns, at first, to establish that its actions are monitored by the senses: this awareness helps it develop distaste for sense pleasures, and the initiate begins relishing the repetition.

There is an awareness of a different kind of power: of letting the senses be, not controlling or suppressing them, but merely becoming aware of them. This allows the meditator power to let his senses occupy their rightful place without letting them control his actions. Psychologists have explained this by observing that when you let a thing be, it lets you be; but when you resist it, it rebounds. Difficult as the practice is, at its heart lies a simplicity. For on this path, what often seems like abortive effort is in reality a surmounting of well-identified obstacles. The initiate can take heart from the realisation that there are no failures on the path of the benevolent, guiding master. He cannot judge what is failure or success — he must practise what has been taught to him and leave the rest to the master. Learning to leave things to the master is an active act of faith which is the source of love for the guru. Surprisingly, on this path, unlike others, the greatest virtue that a disciple can possess is not love for the guru, but obedience. The disciple must at all times obey the master: because, while love may still be an illusion, it is only on the scale of obedience that the initiate can measure his progress on the right track: "The fickle mind wanders in the four directions. Bind it with the instructions of the guru... Then it will be united with the Supreme Lord, O Dadu".

Obviously on this path, all external means of worship are considered a mockery; the disciple can free himself of every superstition, every belief in ritual, and life becomes very simple indeed. As Dadu sings: "As long as the Master is not found, doubts cannot be dispelled. He alone extricates man from all bondage. He reveals the God within; Only then does man attain the highest goal, O Dadu".

A Glimpse of the Unknown in Known

Kailash Vajpeyi

HE WORLD is in a mess/ And blind with sin and woe/ You show a man the truth/ And he becomes your foe. These lines from Kabir are relevant even today, when we are celebrating his 600th birth anniversary. Kabir is one of the most controversial saint poets of India. Both his birth and death are shrouded in mystery. Who was Kabir? A devotee, a saint, a rebel, a mystic or perhaps a God intoxicated seer. Where was he born? In Varanasi or in Magahar? Which community did he really belong to? As per Rev Westcott, he was born in the year 1440 AD, but according to a couplet popular among his followers he was born in the year 1455 Vikrami. According to a legend Kabir was born of a Brahmin widow who abandoned her baby under mysterious circumstances. The newborn was picked up by a childless weaver couple, Neeru and Neema. Kabir in his couplets, often refers to himself as a Muslim-weaver but never forgets Rama whom he worshipped by choice.

Varanasi, since time immemorial, has been an important centre of various sects, including Yogis, Shaivites, Vaishnavas, Shakts, Tantriks, Buddhists, Jainas and Sufis. Kabir came in contact with many of them. Some think that he was initiated by Guru Ramanand while others mention the name of Taqi Mir. However, in his search for truth he questioned the ritualistic approach of most of the dogmatic sects of his time. Truth is the essence of existence that can be glimpsed in deep meditation. Kabir has expressed the dilemma of a seeker who wanted to know the real reality behind the apparent reality. For Kabir, who was a hypersensitive poet, no ideology, no system of thought was free from the stupidity of its followers. That is why he wrote: "To whom should I be generous?/ To whom be less than kind/ The elephant and the insect/ Both come from God's own mind".

Kabir was a rebel poet who protested against all orthodoxy. The tragedy with Kabir was that he had seen a glimpse of the unknown in known, formless in form and emptiness of the whole. But at the same time he also had to deal with a number of dogmatic commentators with their arrested thinking. That is why his poetry has a rough and rugged quality. Because of his bitter commentary on the hollowness of organised religion he was hounded by Muslim and Hindu leaders alike.

Kabir's abstract utterances have their roots in Shankar's non-dualism. Whereas his agony and unconditional love of the unknown has its moorings in Sufism. In the history of human experience, Sufism surpasses all levels of known sensitivity. The Sufis comprehend 'Al Haqq' (Truth) as meant to be lived and not spoken of. If Kabir's creative ecstasy is comparable to the drunken man's state than no sober critic is in any position to truly appreciate the depth and range of his poetry. Hazari Prasad Dwivedi who interpreted Kabir for the modern reader says: "Kabir was never understood properly during his own times. Nobody ever bothered to find out as to how and why and for whom he wept".

A Faith That Sings

Narayani Ganesh

NEARLY 400 years ago, Guru Arjan Dev, fifth guru of the Sikhs walked into the River Ravi never to return. He had put an end to his persecution and to the agony of his sympathisers. But not before leaving behind a rich legacy. The first among martyred gurus, Arjan Dev canonised the philosophy of Sikhism by systematising it, closely exploring and weaving in music with religion and philosophy, which took final shape in the Guru Granth Sahib. By setting the contents to music, the fifth guru has immortalised the spiritual insight of a religion steeped in secularism and community service. He collected verses, oral and written, of previous gurus from all parts of the country. After sifting the authentic from the apocryphal, these verses were set to musical notations based on 30 ragas. The compositions (*shabads*) of the gurus in order of succession were given first place, followed by poetic forms like *ashtapadis* and *vars*. After each guru's composition, the same raga was extended to the bhakta's pieces in a similar format. Nearly 6,000 hymns were, thus, put in order including those of the first five gurus and about 15 saints from diverse castes, occupations and regions.

Guru Granth Sahib has been likened to a vessel of amrit, nectar of wisdom, of not only gurus, but of others as well who were known for their devotional music and spiritual evolvement. Hence we also find the poems of devotion of people's poets like Kabir the weaver, Namdev the seamster, Ravidas the tanner and those from other faiths like Farid. The highlight of the Guru Granth Sahib is the Japji of Guru Nanak followed by Guru Arjan Dev's elegant and simple Sukhmani (Psalm of Bliss). When the Guru Granth Sahib assumed finite shape, it was formally installed in the inner sanctuary of the Harmandir Sahib at Amritsar, also built at the instance of Guru Arjan Dev, now famous as the Golden Temple. The words uttered during this ceremony were: "He Himself hath succoured His saints in their work; He Himself hath come to see their task fulfiled, Blessed is the earth, blessed the tank; Blessed is the tank with amrit filled. Amrit overfloweth the tank; He hath the task completed". When the Suchcha Padshah or the True King (Guru Arjan Dev) got the Harmandir built over the water tank, he provided for four doors facing four directions to symbolise universality. It was also to signify free access to members of any caste, creed or sect. He said: "My faith is for the peoples of all castes and creeds from whichever direction they come and to whichever direction they bow".

The guru will however be most remembered for closely linking music with Sikh religion, with which the Guru Granth Sahib has assumed a divine form, pleasing to the finer senses. Guru Arjan Dev can be credited with infusing art into Sikhism: a huge canvas of profound but simply articulated thoughts set to lilting musical notations in the classical tradition, confident enough of its substance to allow room for inclusion of folk music as well. The canvas includes not only Punjabi but also Persian, Urdu, Brijbhasha and Sanskrit, flavoured liberally with overtones of Islam, Hindu and Sufi mysticism.

Treading the Path of Serene Virtue

Damodar Prabhu

CONTEMPORARY of Confucius and the Buddha, Lao Tzu founded the rather unusual philosophy of living known as Taoism. Lines like these tell of his depth, commonsense and humanity: "The sage accumulates nothing/ Having used what he had for others,/ He has even more./ Therefore, the way of Heaven is to benefit/ And not cause harm;/ The way of man is to act on behalf/ Of Others and not compete with them".

One of Lao Tzu's best known sayings is: "And when your constant virtue is complete/ You'll return to the state of uncarved wood.../ When uncarved wood is cut up, it's turned/ into vessels/ Truly, great carving is done without splitting up". In China, two diametrically opposed philosophies of life coexisted almost amicably: Taoism and Confucianism. While Taoism, according to Lin Yutang "gives philosophic sanction to whatever is idle, freedom-loving, poetic and maverick in the human soul", Confucianism has "only a practical sense of proportion". Full of dos and don'ts, the schoolmasterish Confucian teaching is a briefing for an ideal social order that aims for high morality and righteousness.

But what is Tao really? To Lao Tzu, it is the Way, the name for the ultimate primordial reality that gave rise to the universe. Like a great womb, the Way is empty but holds the seeds of all things; after giving them birth, it remains in them in some subtle form as a dynamic power that inwardly pushes each thing to grow and develop in accord with its true nature. Another analogy given for the Tao is that of an untended, uncultivated field, in which in the right season all growth happens as though on its own. The field does nothing, yet nothing is left undone.

Lao Tzu says that a truly virtuous person is unaware and unconcerned that others think of him or her as virtuous: "The highest virtue is not virtuous, therefore it truly has virtue. The lowest virtue never loses sight of its virtue, therefore it has no true virtue. Therefore, when the great Way is rejected, it is then we have the virtues of humanity and righteousness. When knowledge and wisdom appear, it is then that there is great hypocrisy. And when the country is in chaos and confusion, it is then there are virtuous officials". Lao Tzu is very contemporary in tone and mood, especially in his views on the polity, on corrupt politicians and administrators who excel at moral pliancy. The bane of humanity has always been its sense of competition, with the stress, unhappiness and conflict it generates. Lao Tzu's advice is to avoid these and lead a long, peaceful and fruitful life. He invokes the image of the sage, not the saint, often.

According to the Tao, each of us has two beings within: the great one and the lesser one. If we take the hand of the great one, it will lead us to greatness; the lesser one's hand will lead to lesser things. The choice is ours to make, and it is a crucial one; we must remember that the Taoist sage, though he may seem to be outside us, often speaks from within our soul.

A Voice from the Valley

Raj K Dhar

T IS poignant irony that the Kashmir Valley, long known as 'Rishivaer' or Garden of Rishis, has been in the throes of terrorist violence for almost a decade now. The Valley has borne holy men and women who preached a humane belief in the uniform treatment of people of different faiths, and a conviction that there was a single God beyond sectarian divisions. True mystics as they were, their sayings, mostly in verse, emphasise ecumenical thinking. It was in the Valley that Muslim ascetics established the Rishi order, notwithstanding the fact that the concept of a rishi is alien to Islam. On the other hand, Hindu saints did not shy away from associating with Muslim sages. The common goal of both was the realisation of the self.

One such saint was Lal Ded. Born to a Brahmin family in Pampore near Srinagar, this 14th-century saint was drawn towards spirituality from a young age. She did not believe in idol worship, sacrifices and rituals nor did she discriminate between Hindu and Muslim or rich and poor. In one of her sayings, called *vaakh*, she says: "Shiva is everywhere, don't discriminate between Hindus and Muslims. If you are intelligent, realise yourself: that will introduce you to God". Spiritual awakening brought by the knowledge imparted to her by her guru Siddha Shrikanth had freed her of all bonds. Since her guru taught her the ultimate Truth, she sings, she began to wander around clad in nothing (because clothes had lost their importance, as self-realisation became her sole objective in life). "I gave up lying and deceiving and taught myself to see the Absolute in everyone", she says. "Now I accept food from whoever offers it to me (be that person a Hindu or Muslim)".

There are some anecdotes popular in Kashmir about Lal Ded's association with Sayyid Ali Hamadani and Sheikh Noorudin Noorani (Nund Rishi, the founder of the Rishi order). It is said that when Nund Rishi was born, he refused to suckle his mother. Lal Ded went to his house and said to the infant: "If you were not ashamed of coming into the world, why do you fight shy of drinking your mother's milk?" Nund Rishi, on hearing her words, started suckling his mother's breast.

Lal Ded rebelled against the prevalent Brahminical orthodoxy and questioned the practices and rituals performed by Hindus. Kashmiri Brahmins, most of them Shaivites, are non-vegetarian. Lal Ded did not approve of this and upbraided a Brahmin who was taking a sheep to the butcher's: "This animal hides your shame and gives you warmth, it eats grass and drinks water. Should you make a meal of it?"

Lal Ded was an ascetic of a very high order, a yogini, a *majnuni aqila* (madwoman in love of God), a Rabia Sania (a second Rabia). Her sayings will never date. She is as relevant today as she was 600 years ago. It makes one weep that some among the people who call her Lal Moj (Mother Lal), people who constantly have her *vaakh* on their lips, have lost respect for her memory. They have forgotten the spiritual and ecumenical legacy bequeathed to them by their saints, and plunged the Valley into a bloodbath.

Travelling Many Roads to the Infinite

N S Chandramouli

T WAS in the course of his practice of Islam that the 19th century contemplative Ramakrishna Paramahansa of Dakshineshwar had one of his remarkable visions: "I was meditating under the banyan tree when I was shown a Mussalman. He came to me with rice in an earthen plate. The Mother (Kali) showed me that there exists only One and not two. It is Satchidananda alone that has taken various forms; He alone has become the world and its living beings". Ramakrishna was initiated into Islamic practice by a devout Sufi Govinda Rai. He repeated the holy name of Allah and recited the *namaz;* the Hindu mode of thought vanished from his mind during this period, which culminated in his vision. As his disciple Mahendra observed: "The mighty river of Islam also led him back to the Ocean of the Absolute".

Ramakrishna's life is unique in the annals of religious experience. Although born to an orthodox Brahmin family of Kamarpukur in Bengal and trained as a priest, he practised a wide catholicity of religious expression. He advocated the positive acceptance of other faiths and resolved the dilemma of religious plurality by direct experience. Realising that all religions are paths leading to the same goal, he said: "He who is called Krishna is also Shiva and the primal Shakti; and it is He again who is called Jesus and Allah. There is only one Rama and He has a thousand names".

Eight years after his beatific vision of Allah in 1866, Ramakrishna became seized with the desire to grasp the inner truth of Christianity. Possessed by the thought of Jesus Christ, he was walking in the garden of his devotee Jadu Mallick's house at Dakshineshwar when he saw a luminous figure approaching him. As the figure drew nearer, he heard within himself a cry of recognition: "Jesus, the great Yogi, the loving Son of God, one with the Father, who gave his heart's blood and put up with endless torture in order to deliver men from sorrow and misery". The figure of Jesus embraced Ramakrishna and merged in him. In this way, Ramakrishna realised his identity with Christ as he had already realised his identity with Kali, Rama, Hanuman, Radha, Krishna and Allah. After this epiphany, he lost all consciousness of the world and entered samadhi or deep communion with the Infinite. The savant Romain Rolland said: "It is because Ramakrishna more fully than any other man... realised in himself the total unity of the river of God, open to all rivers and all streams, that I have given him my love".

By communing with God through the path of Islamic mysticism, Ramakrishna showed a new way of transcending religious barriers. It was in this spirit that his disciple Vivekananda wrote: "Practical Advaitism, which looks upon and behaves to all mankind as one's own soul, was never developed among the Hindus universally. I am firmly persuaded that without the help of practical Islam, theories of Vedantism, however fine and wonderful they may be, are entirely valueless to the vast mass of mankind. For our own motherland, a junction of the two systems Hinduism and Islam is the only hope".

Discovering the 'I' in Sixty Minutes

Seema Burman

S I boarded the train to Kanyakumari a friend pleaded: "You must go to Ramana Maharshi's ashram". When the train stopped at Villupuram, I got down hesitantly. Guidance came in the form of Providence. It was easy to spot Ramana Maharshi's ashram: there were numerous peacocks, monkeys, squirrels, dogs and cats. Cycling towards the ashram at the crack of dawn were Australians, Italians, French, Japanese, Americans, British and others. What brought them here? "The simple teachings of Bhagvan Ramana Maharshi", whispers Mani, Maharshi's nephew.

At 16, Venkataraman (Ramana's given name) experienced self-realisation. Sitting in a room he felt as if he were dying. Later, he recounted: "This body is dead. It will be carried stiff to the burning ground and there be burnt and reduced to ashes. But with the death of body, am 'I' dead? Is this body 'I'? This body is silent and inert. But I feel the full force of my personality and even the sound 'I' within myself, apart from the body. So 'I' am a spirit, a thing transcending the body. The material body dies, but the spirit transcending it cannot be touched by death. I am therefore the deathless spirit. All this was not a mere intellectual process, but flashed before me vividly as living truth, something that I perceived immediately, without any argument almost. 'I' was something real; the only real thing in that state, and all the conscious activity that was connected with my body was centred on that. Then 'I' or my 'self' was holding the focus of attention by a powerful fascination from that time forwards. Fear of death had vanished once and forever. Absorption in the self has continued from that moment right up to this time".

In an hour he became a fully realised soul. He left home and went to live in Arunachala mountain. Many came to him for achieving Cosmic Consciousness and Maharshi told them: "You are already That, only the veil of ignorance has to be removed. You are already Real, you are not going to realise anything new. Your effort must be directed towards removing ignorance by enquiry". The Maharshi explained that to know the Truth, you need not undergo rigorous learning. He was against *mauna* or silence for though it certainly gave powers, it did nothing to reveal the Self. *Sanyas* was unnecessary. He advocated living in the world as necessary for *sadhana*. If one could do this, that is, be in the world yet not of the world, one had achieved a high state of detachment.

Maharshi's piercing look established a bond between him and the seeker and put them on the path of active thought: "Who am I?" and changed their mind. Mind and thought were the same, he maintained. The secret of a clear mind lies in whether we are attached to our actions or not. Wasn't a guru necessary for the less fortunate? The sage explained that a guru is none other than the Self of the disciple. When the Self is realised there is neither guru nor disciple. A guru's duty was to awaken the ignorant to the fact that what they perceived was unreal and the only Reality was their Being.

God is where the Pathmaker is Breaking Stones

M N Chatterjee

AGORE'S MEDITATIONS on God, man and nature, especially those collected in his *Gitanjali* echo the Vedantic perception of the Infinite. God makes Himself known to us, Tagore suggests, through the beauty of creation. "My poet's vanity dies in shame before Thy sight, O Master Poet", he sang. And, speaking as he did of God as the 'Master Poet', he called his religion the poet's religion, conceived not through knowledge but through vision. Tagore's religious ideas were eclectic: his religious life, according to him, proceeded along the same mysterious line of growth as his poetic life; the two were wedded to each other and informed his writings with a unity of expression.

Tagore was a true exponent of the reformist age and the milieu into which he was born (his father, Debendranath, had attempted to develop a monotheistic religion based on the Upanishads). But the individualist in Tagore refused to be swayed by any kind of institutionalised creed: he believed that contact with the Infinite could be established only through independent exploration. The attainment of self-realisation was to him too personal a quest to be bound by collective dogma.

Inspired by the limitless sky, with its implication of an endless Beyond, he confessed himself a follower on the path of the Vedic seers: he delighted in the intimate companionship of the clouds, the storm, the rain and the river. But he was not content with a mere description of what he observed; there was a yearning to go beyond physical phenomena to identify their hidden spirit. Tagore believed at first that an unknown principle was at work behind all creation; his early religious ideas suggest a pantheistic conception of the Divine. But he was far from satisfied, because there could not be a personal association with an impersonal force. He quested on for a God who could be conceived in a tangible personality. Tagore took a clue from the bauls, the wandering devotional singers of Bengal who sing of the divinity of man and of love for all. And so the Infinite merged with the finite in humanity. Tagore saw the universal significance of truth under its individual aspect, and found his religion: the religion of Man. He said in *Gitanjali*: "Whom do you worship in this lonely dark corner of a temple with doors all shut? Open your eyes and see your God is not before you!...He is where the tiller is tilling the hard ground and where the pathmaker is breaking stones..."

A man's religion, according to Tagore, does not consist of blind beliefs; rather, it is a man's 'innermost truth', a creative force, a life-sense which is an extra awareness, greater than his material sense. The ancient precept 'Know thyself' has its own import. But, Tagore felt, 'be known to others' could be an equally vital concept. And there is no limit to this unfolding of the inner self. In his own words: "If there is any philosophy of religion in me and I leave a wrong impression of its true nature, then I shall be doing the greatest injustice to myself and to others...it is important that its value and utility are rightly assessed".

The Tale of a Sorcerer's Apprentice

Nergis Dalal

N 1960, Carlos Castaneda, then an anthropology student at the University of California went to Arizona to study the medicinal properties of local plants. There, he met a Yaqui Indian called Don Juan Matos, a man highly skilled in the gathering and use of medicinal and psychotropic plants. He was also a *brujo* or sorcerer: in the language of his tradition, a 'man of power'. Don Juan agreed to teach Castaneda what he knew, but not for money. All he wanted was Castaneda's undivided attention. The result of this apprenticeship was the book, *The Teachings of Don Juan,* which, to the astonishment of Castaneda's agent and publishers, became an instant bestseller. Over the years, many have claimed Don Juan was an invention. But as author Peter Matthiessen said: "If this were so, then spurious ethnology becomes a great work of the imagination; whether borrowed or not, the teachings ring true".

Castaneda subsequently wrote about his apprenticeship in *A Separate Reality, Journey to Ixtlan* and *Tales of Power* that were all best-sellers and brought their author an enormous cult following. But Castaneda remained invisible, for 30 years. He was never photographed, never appeared on TV, never took part in promotional tours, never gave interviews. When *Time* did a cover story on him, the cover picture turned out to be a fake. Following the publication of his ninth book, *The Art of Dreaming,* Castaneda suddenly surfaced. Explaining his appearance, Castaneda said he felt impelled to show others that, with the help of masters like Don Juan, we can all see beyond life's surface realities to a state he described as 'the second attention'.

To a sorcerer the universe is essentially a matrix of energy, each strand containing worlds as real as ours. When a person has learned to see instead of merely look; and when he has stopped his 'internal dialogue', his perception of reality springs from direct experience. He becomes another kind of being, rocks dance, winds blow out of clear skies and people can change form at will. Don Juan told Castaneda early in their relationship that the seeker could accomplish absolutely nothing until he had learned to stop his internal dialogue. Castaneda practised fruitlessly for years, until one day: "I had the shocking realisation that I had just walked for ten minutes without having said a single word to myself". After many years, Castaneda was able to enter 'the second attention' and became a 'man of power'.

Castaneda's books appeal to us because they make us aware of the latent power in all human beings. We remain passive, unfocused, never experiencing total control or clarity. We know that dogs hear sounds we cannot hear and that birds migrate thousands of miles, finding their way home year after year. The sorcerer, the *brujo,* through long years of discipline, has regained such powers. When the two halves of a man's brain are united, then the world is a different place. Everything is new, everything has never happened before. "For me, there is only the travelling", said Castaneda. "There I travel and the only worthwhile challenge is for me to traverse its full length, seeing, seeing".

Walking the Forked Path of Life

Ranjit Hoskote

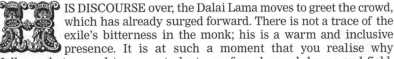IS DISCOURSE over, the Dalai Lama moves to greet the crowd, which has already surged forward. There is not a trace of the exile's bitterness in the monk; his is a warm and inclusive presence. It is at such a moment that you realise why Hollywood stars and teenage students, perfumed grand dames and field-hardened activists come under this spiritual leader's benevolent spell. Tenzin Gyatso, the fourteenth Dalai Lama, is at once a philosopher who weaves the intricacies of Vajrayana Buddhism and a shepherd who guides his flock through a hostile epoch. He is inspired by the metaphor of the two paths: the first, spiritual path leads the seeker to perfect knowledge; the second, temporal path is the one along which society evolves in the world of events. Some of us never see past the amiable 'laughing Bodhisattva'; others see only the head of the Tibetan government in exile negotiating his way among princes and envoys. But when he expounds the Kalachakra Tantra or Nagarjuna's *Ratnavali*, he is the Gyalwa Rinpoche, the stern custodian of his tradition.

The apparent duality of the Dalai Lama's personality epitomises the dilemma of the forked path in everyone's life. The Dalai Lama offers an example of how this shuttling between inner and outer lives can be managed with grace. He shows how we can maintain our serenity and nurture our joyfulness and creative powers, even when faced with the unnerving possibility that the world may be a great void. After all, the Dalai Lama's tradition regards the world as a mirage; the Buddha taught that the world had no permanent essence or abiding reality, that it was a phantasmagoria of images. As Nagarjuna glossed this theory: "The farther we are from the world/ The more real it appears to us/ The more we approach it, the less visible it becomes". The world nevertheless possesses apparent reality: a logic that demands action. The Buddha suggests that our lives would be fulfilled if we were guided by compassion, loving-kindness, joy in others' joy, equanimity and attentiveness to others' suffering. In so doing, the individual becomes wholly responsible for his or her own being. Therefore, the Buddha's proposition that there is no permanent essence in the self and the world is the first step not towards cynical nihilism but towards sensitive and constructive action.

Like every inheritor of the Buddha's insights, then, the Dalai Lama urges us to reflect on our unconscious motivations and on the acts to which we commit ourselves. He reminds us that our lives are conducted largely at the surface; we do not act independently, so much as we react to stimuli. Masters like the Dalai Lama have mapped the way to an inner sanctuary guarded with the discipline of prajna, wisdom, and *shila*, ethical practice. Manifesting as a continuous cycle of self-examination and positive action, the inner life gradually radiates through and transforms the outward life. This is the quality of ethical being that the Dalai Lama embodies, and which the Buddha had in mind when he said to his disciples: "Be a lamp to yourselves, seek refuge in yourselves".

Compassion & Concern
Show the Way to God

A D Pradeep Kumar

HE LIFE and work of Mata Amritanandamayi, a fisherwoman from Kerala who has blossomed into a saint of international fame, gives lie to the belief that spirituality breeds escapism. While ensuring the uplift of seekers who come to her, she stresses equally on social service. Her message is: Service to humankind is service to God. The life of Amma, as she is called by devotees, proves that self-realisation is possible even today, while her work shows the concern and compassion a real spiritual teacher must exhibit towards humanity.

In spite of opposition from her family members and village folk, she showed that self-realisation is possible if there is complete self-surrender, dedication and determination. "My goal is to inspire people with the desire for liberation through realisation of their Eternal Self. Miracles are illusory. That is not the essential principle behind spirituality", she told the sceptics who demanded a miracle to prove her divinity. Is it not a miracle that an unlettered woman is invited to address the 1993 Parliament of Religions in Chicago? She was also elected as a president of the Assembly of Global Religions and addressed the interfaith celebrations held in New York to commemorate the 50th anniversary of the United Nations in 1995. Her life and work gives a new hope for any true spiritual seeker. The most fascinating aspect of her is that she is living amidst us and not in the pages of history.

From childhood, devotion was an integral part of her nature. In spite of hardships she clung to her faith in Krishna. She accepted every obstacle as His blessings, and thus a way to bring her closer to Him. In her teens, through intense *sadhana*, she had a mystic union with Krishna. Her union was so complete that she could no longer distinguish between Krishna and her own self. In the second phase of her *sadhana*, she completely identified with the Divine Mother. She realised the Supreme Brahmn in its formless, attributeless aspect.

At 21, she outwardly manifested her state of God-realisation and at 22 began to initiate disciples. By 27, Amma had established the spiritual headquarters of her international mission in the house of her birth. Complete surrender to the Divine, constant contemplation and self-sacrifice are the three main things she advocates. She believes that "selfless service to God and ailing humanity is my life's goal. I am here not to earn anything but to renounce everything for the happiness of others". She asks her devotees to live like an incense stick which burns itself for spreading its fragrance.

Amma and her ashrams lay special emphasis on the uplift of society. Her charitable activities include a hospice for terminally ill cancer patients, a 500-bed superspeciality hospital for the poor, and the Amrita Medical Mission of Ayurveda that provides employment to tribal women. Indeed, Amma's life itself is a message to true seekers that spirituality is not something that is to be practised in the snow-clad mountains but amidst the trials and tribulations of everyday life.

Seer Who Spoke With the Help of Silence

Aruna Jethwani

HE ROAD going up the hillock is flanked by a cacti hedge. At the end, stolid in time and space is 'Retreat', the samadhi of Avatar Meher Baba. The tomb was conceived by Baba in 1927. He had instructed his devotees: "Wherever I drop my body, it should be brought here". The tomb had to wait for 30 years to embrace Baba's physical body. It was on January 31, 1969 that Meher Baba entered the realm of eternity.

Born on February 25, 1894, Meher Baba was a Zoroastrian. It was an era of 'perfect masters', notable being Shirdi Sai Baba, Upasani Maharaj and Hazrat Baba Jaan. Baba Jaan, a Muslim woman pir, was Meher Baba's first guru. Like Mira, Baba Jaan chose the path of spirituality. She had arrived in Pune, walked to the nearest tree and settled down under it. Meher used to pass her on his way to school. One day, when he was 12, Baba Jaan kissed him on the forehead, thus removing the first veil of maya and introducing him to the bliss of God-realisation.

The most striking quality of Baba was his silence, which he observed for 44 years. He went into *maun* (silence) on July 10, 1925 and remained silent till he left his body in 1969. In the beginning, he used to communicate through paper and pencil, then through gestures; finally he stopped communicating altogether. Mahatma Gandhi was so impressed by this that he began to observe *maun* every week. When asked why he observed silence, Baba said: "God does not speak, yet He communicates with all, all the time. Words are not necessary to communicate. It is the feeling that can vibrate and reach others without having to utter a word. For the unspoken has greater power than the spoken". The following words are inscribed on the wall outside the tomb: "Things that are real are given and taken in silence".

Baba's adherence to silence is remarkable. Even when he met with a serious car accident in 1952 in the US and another in India in 1956, fracturing his limbs, he did not utter a word despite the pain. He did not meet people. He rarely gave an audience. He worked for humanity through his 'love power'. Baba proclaimed: "I have come not to teach but to awaken. Because man has been deaf to the principles and precepts laid down by God in the past, I observe Silence. You have asked for and given enough words, it is now time to live them...When I break my Silence, the impact of my love will be universal and all life in creation will know, feel and receive it. The breaking of my Silence will help you to help yourself in knowing your real self".

When hearts are apart, words are needed to communicate, when hearts are together no words are needed. Words create differences and distances. Silence binds and brings harmony. Silence in its purest form is one's own self. It is the 'feeling' of God, within. Silence is meditation, silence is energy. Without words, without mind, it helps us to find answers to the questions, and paths to destination.

Festival of Lights and Prosperity

Pankaj Dixit

N THE Brihadaranyaka Upanishad, Janaka asks sage Yajnavalkya: "When the sun has set, the moon has set, and there is total darkness, what light does a person have?" The fire indeed is the light for human beings at that time, says Yajnavalkya. This philosophical discussion can be applied to Deepawali. There is total darkness on Deepawali night, not only due to Kartik *amavasya*, but also due to the weak position of the sun in the zodiac sign of Libra. Tradition has it that on this darkest night of the year there shines a mystic light like a single lamp's flame in the heart of moon. Lamps are lit to imitate that light. Janaka further asks: "If this fire also goes out, what light does a person have?" "Indeed", replies the sage, "one can make his existence felt in darkness only through sound". The bursting of crackers during Deepawali symbolises this. Janaka again asks: "If sound also stops, what light can a person have?" "The atman, the self, is his ultimate light", replies Yajnavalkya. So at midnight on Deepawali, yogis meditate in Lakshmi or Mahakali.

The earliest form of goddess related to wealth was known as Sri or Kamala. In Rig Veda Sri-Sukta, she is described as Hiranyavarna, ever radiating golden grace. Atharvaveda refers to Shatlakshmi, or a hundred forms of Lakshmi, which signify the fusion of Sri with Lakshmi. Traditionally, of these 100, only eight are worshipped on Deepawali. They are: Adi-Lakshmi who emerged from the ocean with the ambrosia pot; Dhanya Lakshmi who provides abundance of food; Dhairya Lakshmi who gives endurance; Gajalakshmi seated on an eight-petalled lotus who bestows fortune, wealth, power and beauty; Santana Lakshmi, who confers offspring; Vijaylakshmi who blesses with success; Vidyalakshmi who grants education; and Dhanalakshmi who gives wealth.

The most popular Deepawali legend of course is the return of Rama to Ayodhya after his victory over Ravana. According to Puranic beliefs, after the churning of the ocean, Mahalakshmi manifested herself on this day and accepted Lord Vishnu as her spouse, and this is the reason for worshipping Lakshmi on Deepawali. That's why the merchant class usually open their *bahi-khatas* or account books on this day. According to Jain traditions, when Lord Mahavira attained nirvana at Pava in Bihar, the occasion was celebrated with a lamp festival or Deepawali by the ruling Mallas and Lichavis.

On Deepawali, recitation of the Sri-Sukta of the Rig Veda or Adi Sankara's *Kanakadhara stotra* at midnight in front of Sri Yantra is said to confer prosperity, health, good fortune and wealth. One important point to remember is that there should always be an odd number of flames in front of the goddess, such as 1, 3, 5 or 7, as an even number of flames cancel each other's positive energy. The day after Deepawali is Govardhan Pooja, the foremost festival of the Vallabhacharya sect in Brij. Cows are worshipped on this occasion. The last day of this five-day festival is Bhai Dooj, when brothers visit their sisters. Taking bath on this day in the holy water of Yamuna is considered to be auspicious.

Knocking at the Door of Your Neighbour's Heart

Acharya Vidyananda

E WHO forgives sleeps untroubled; but he who does not spends restless nights, as though his bed were strewn with nails. The scriptures observe that "a spark will die of itself if it falls where there is not even a blade of grass. Similarly, he who has earned the mantle of peace cannot be harmed by evil". Forgiveness is the treasure of the conscience, the source of peace. The nectar of forgiveness nurtures many fruits: gratitude, humility, solidarity. As Mahavira said: "I forgive all living beings; may all living beings forgive me. To the entire world I show loving-kindness, I have not a single enemy". The beauty of our eyes is enhanced, not by kohl, but by the loving-kindness of our gaze. The Sanskrit word for forgiveness, *kshama*, may be traced back to the elements *ksha* and *ma*, which indicate a knot and a negation respectively. *Kshama* thus suggests that we must refrain from tying up our minds in knots of resentment. Forgiveness is a sign of courage and fortitude; it is not to be confused with the resignation of cowardice.

Forgiveness may be likened to the system of traffic signals and pedestrian crossings which regulate the flow of movement in great cities; it saves us from accidents, guides us along the appropriate path. Mutual forgiveness forms the foundation for the spiritual and social discipline of ahimsa, non-violence; it is the grove of serenity in which the self, purified of desires and ambitions, may meditate. The principle of forgiveness leads one to wish others good fortune, while desiring nothing for oneself. In the absence of forgiveness, it is the *matsya nyaya*, law of the fish that prevails: the big fish eats the small fish. Our only defence against the vicious terrors of this law is the simple aphorism that we must live and let live.

Do not merely broadcast the message of forgiveness over loudspeakers. Practise it so that it is as much a part of your natural being as your breath. You will find that those whom you could not cut down with a sword, you will win over through forgiveness; indeed, you will restore to wholeness what the sword has cut to pieces. Once this principle has been made a part of our lives, we will see the long queues outside our courts melt away, and the armed battalions standing vigilant at our borders make way for the happy reunion of friends.

Loving-kindness is of value only when it has truly taken root in the heart as a permanent condition of being; to limit it to certain days (while bristling with hostility the rest of the year) will only serve our complacent self-regard. It is through the practice of loving-kindness alone that we can share in our friends' joys and sorrows; such a sharing is crucial in a world that has been agitated by suspicion, jealousy and resentment. While we lust after commodities that guarantee us material comfort, we do not seem to value that rare thing, friendship. It is a tragedy that, today, while humanity stands poised to enter the very heavens; no one feels the need to knock at the door of his neighbour's heart.

A Prophet who Tilled the Field of The Soul

Marzban Hathiram

HOULD WE celebrate the birthday of someone who lived 9,000 years ago? Parsis do exactly that on Khordad Saal, birthday of their prophet Zarathushtra. Life and times of Zarathushtra have been obscured beneath the verbiage of philologists and historians. Tradition, however, recounts that he was born some 9,000 years ago to Pourushasp and Dugdau in the Iranian province of Rae. Zarathushtra's story is no different from those of many other prophets: the forces of evil made attempts on his life when he was a child; he went through a period of retreat and communion with God. His teachings gained acceptance after initial scepticism; and though false accusers tried to destroy him, he led to become a revered teacher. And he met a violent end.

Scriptures recount that all creation went into ecstasy at his birth, exclaiming: "Blessed are we, for our sake is born a priest who is Zarathushtra!" (Fravardin Yast, karta 23). Was he an ordinary man or was he a being of more than mortal flesh? He is in scriptures a yazata, a divine being worthy of worship and adoration. Zarathushtra is portrayed as the chosen one selected by Ahura Mazda to establish not only the specific Mazdayasni (or Zoroastrian) faith, but also to pave the way for future prophets and their religions. In the Tir Yast, karta 13, Ahura Mazda declares: "Just as I have appointed Tishtar as the Lord of the Stars, so also I have appointed Zarathushtra as the Lord of Men, whom neither the evil Angra Mainyu can smite, nor evil fairies nor sorcerers nor the entire multitude of evil beings". The prophet's name bears a special connotation. 'Zarathushtra' can be translated variously as 'golden camel' (Zarath-ushtra) or 'moulder of gold' (Zara-thushtra). Both suggest one who has achieved great wisdom, symbolised by the camel, or one who creates gold from dross. Zarathushtra is a transmuter, a converter in the sense of one who turns evil into good.

Coupled with this alchemical metaphor is the metaphor of cultivation. In a rather literal-minded interpretation of the Zoroastrian sacred texts notably the Vendidad, several scholars have suggested that Ahura Mazda recommends an agrarian way of life. It more likely points to an inward agriculture of the spirit. The texts recommend the wisdom of tilling the barren field of the soul, of weeding out lust and deceit and sowing the seeds of goodness, of nurturing them with the milk of kindness and fertilising them with religious observances until one can harvest the crop of everlasting happiness. To help man in this, Ahura Mazda has appointed Zarathushtra as humanity's friend and guide; in the Gathas, the Lord declares: "There is none other than Zarathushtra, whom I have appointed to teach man" (Gatha Ahunavaiti, Yasna 29.6). And so, amidst the revelry of Khordad Saal, each Parsi must find the time to retreat into his or her own private garden and reiterate his or her resolve to follow the directions of that great cultivator, Zarathushtra, certain in the belief that there is a rich harvest of blessings to be reaped.

Hajj: Pilgrimage to the House of God

Maulana Wahiduddin Khan

N 1982, I had the privilege of performing Hajj, the pilgrimage to Mecca. The message of Hajj, as I now comprehend it, is that man should make the Almighty the pivot of his existence, hastening to do His every bidding. When a man leaves home to go on such a pilgrimage, he brims over with emotions at the thought of embarking on a course to God. He sloughs off his own world and reaching out for the Almighty. He is on his way to the place where great deeds of God's messengers and his followers have been preserved for all eternity. The Haji, the one performing the Hajj, is filled with the realisation that he is bound for that very destination which God has specially chosen for His last revelation. The pilgrim is imbued with the awareness of God and His truths, as well as the feeling that it is imperative that he become God-oriented. The pilgrim also gives his mind to his death and the court of God. This trend of thought turns the ostensible physical journey of the pilgrim into an intense, spiritual venture.

For entrance into the Haram (sacred territory), pilgrims don an unstitched white garment, which heightens his consciousness of entering a new world. He finds himself uttering the *labbayk*, 'I have come'. *Labbayk* does not mean just that the pilgrim has come to Mecca. Rather, it means: "I am here, at your command, and with all my heart and soul, I am ready to obey you". The pilgrim must perform *tawaf* (circumambulation of Ka'bah). To do this, he enters the House of God (Baitullah), the great mosque in whose spacious central courtyard stands the Ka'bah, around which the pilgrim goes seven times to demonstrate his willingness to make God the pivot of his existence.

Next is *sa'i*, which entails walking from the hill of Safa to the hill of Marwa and back. This is repeated seven times in symbolic enactment of a covenant to expend all of one's energies in the path of God. The most important period of worship during Hajj is the day-long sojourn on the plain of Arafat. It is, indeed, an awesome spectacle, with people from all over the world, clad in identical, simple, white garments, chanting: "Lord, I am present". This serves to impress upon the pilgrim how great a gathering there will be in the presence of God on that Last Day of Reckoning. Once he becomes aware of its true significance, all his problems fall into their true perspective, and his life cannot but take a turn for the better.

Another Hajj practice is the casting of stones at Jamarat, the stoning pillars. This is a symbolic act through which the pilgrim renews his determination to drive evil away. The next step is to turn symbolism into reality, so that the pilgrim may be purged of all evils. After this, the pilgrim sacrifices an animal to God, an act symbolising the sacrifice of the self. His faith is such that even if it comes to giving his life, he will not hesitate to do so in the service of God.

A Healing Faith for Troubled Times

Amarjit Singh

URU NANAK lived in the turbulent period of the Delhi Sultanate through the reigns of four rulers: Bahlol Lodi, Sikander Lodi, Ibrahim Lodi and Babar. He was witness to political turmoil, social injustice, economic exploitation, and rampant superstition. It was also when Islamic and Hindu world views engaged in dialogue, giving rise to socio-religious movements like Sufism and Bhakti, which with their emphasis on worship and the equality of all before God, greatly influenced Nanak.

Nanak accepted the noblest principles of both Hinduism and Islam, while discarding their retrograde customs. He fused the two into a new synthesis, Sikhism, which was appropriate to the needs of the social milieu. A process of healing through cultural interaction was inaugurated, through which the two communities embarked upon mutual understanding. Nanak held discussions with pandits and kazis, urging them to question whether they had not, in attending to the letter of the tradition, killed the spirit of faith.

Nanak believed that there is only one God, whose name is Truth. He is immortal and self-existent; He was neither born nor will He die. God is *Karta Purukh, Sat Kartar,* the creator; He is *nirankar,* formless. Nanak emphasised that his God was a God of grace: the door to salvation is opened by His *nazar* or *kirpa* (grace). Nanak also preached the doctrine of *Hukam,* or divine will, which determines the position of man and directs his steps towards enlightenment. Nanak taught that *manmukh,* unregenerate man, is selfish and egoistic; his loyalty is towards himself alone. It was Nanak's mission to transform *manmukh* into *Gurumukh,* a human being who has heard the word of God through the Guru; a being who is compassionate and humane, the incarnation of love. *Manmukh* tends to get carried away by such evil impulses as *kama* (lust), *krodh* (anger), *lobha* (covetousness), *moha* (attachment to worldly things) and *ahankar* (pride): these impulses conspire to bring about violence, falsehood and man's fall. Nanak travelled extensively, spreading the message of love and humility. He adopted Punjabi and Hindi, the vernaculars, as the media of his ministry: in the Gurbani, therefore, the *loka-bhasa* replaced Sanskrit, the *deva-bhasa.*

Through his hymns, which express his devotional ecstasy, Nanak reached out to the Divine. To his disciples, he emphasised the importance of *simran:* the practice of thinking continually of God, which brings comfort, peace and solace. Nanak never turned his back on the world of events. His aim was to create a religion for householders, not for ascetics; he bent his optimism and energy to the goal of social emancipation, the ideal of an egalitarian society. He established the institution of Guruship, which provided cohesion and solidarity to the Sikh community. The Sikh *sangats,* or holy assemblies, and the institution of *langar*, or a common kitchen, brought people together across the distinctions of caste, gender and economic status. Guru Nanak infused a new hope and confidence into an age of crisis; one way of regenerating our afflicted society would be to attend, again, to his teachings.

In Praise of Jesus, the Prince of Peace

Tisy Jose

THE HUMAN history that Jesus Christ entered 2,000 years ago was no different from its unfortunate repetitions found today. Kingdoms were at war, religion had perverted into fanaticism, and the poor were crushed under an unjust social structure. Into such a chaotic world Jesus, the Prince of Peace, came with his liberating mission. Jesus is peace, announced the prophecies that preceded his birth. He was born in the serenity of a cold winter night when the twinkling stars mingled with the snow below. The white array of angels who sang under the jet black canopy of the starlit sky proclaimed him as the Prince of Peace: "Glory to God in the highest, and on earth Peace to People of Good Will" (Luke 2:14).

Jesus gave a tilt to the terms 'prince' and 'peace' and placed them on a new paradigm of sacrificial orientation. He replaced power with service, hate with love, revenge with forgiveness, judgment with mercy. He conquered hearts by serving others even to the extent of washing their feet, and finally laying down his life for the redemption of the world. He left no doubt in the mind of those who looked for a royal messiah in him when he said: "The Son of Man has come not to be served, but to serve, and to give himself as a ransom for the sins of many" (Mark 10:45).

Jesus's compassion embraced all as he worked for human liberation. No discussion on Jesus can be justified without skipping through the pages of his gospels which are replete with his message of peace. He said: "Peace I leave with you; my peace I give you...Do not let your hearts be troubled and do not be afraid" (John 14.27). Even his farewell discourse was filled with peace. "I have told you these things, so that in me you may have peace. In this world you will have trouble. But take heart! I have overcome the world" (John 16:33). Jesus's forgiveness never failed even the worst sinner: "Your faith...has saved you, go in peace" (Luke. 7:50). St Paul, once a persecutor of Christians, zealously spread the Good News of Jesus after his dramatic encounter with him on his way to Damascus.

Celebrating the Season of Hope and Joy

Nauzer Bharucha

AVROZ, (LITERALLY 'new day'), is an ancient Iranian spring festival celebrated each year when the sun enters the Zodiac Aries around March 21. India's Zoroastrian community and the Shia Muslims in Iran observe Navroz. In India, Parsis greet each other with 'Navroz Mubarak' and exchange presents. In Iran, families lay out a table containing seven items that begin with the letter 'S': *sib* (apple), *sabzi* (vegetables), *sir* (garlic), *serkeh* (vinegar), *sumac* (powder), *senjed* (olives) and *sikka* (coins). The legend of Navroz began about 2,000 years before the birth of Zarathustra, when Jamshed of the Peshadadian dynastywas anointed king: the day of his anointment was called Navroz. In ancient Zoroastrian scriptures, Ahura Mazda (the Supreme Creator) reveals to Zarathustra that Jamshed was the first to learn the principles of the Mazdayasani religion (the proper name for 'Zoroastrianism') from Him.

According to Firdausi's Persian epic, *Shahnama,* Jamshed discovered the art of extracting gold, silver and precious stones during his 700-year rule. For the first 300 years of his rule, peace and tranquillity prevailed. But Firdausi reveals that this state of bliss did not last long: pride entered Jamshed's soul, leading to his downfall. Phiroz Tavaria, in his *Manual of the Zoroastrian Occult Knowledge,* explains Jamshed's downfall as an allegory. "Animals and men were made undying. But this did not mean that the demons were rendered totally extinct, their devilry was only contracted to an embryonic state... the state of immortality and blissfulness created by Jamshed could last no longer and selfishness, lust, death reappeared, which is allegorically expressed as the downfall of Jamshed".

Greek historians have thrown light on Navroz celebrations conducted by Persian kings like Darius and Xerxes (550 BC-330 BC). Each year, on March 21, these kings visited Takht-e-Jamshed (Throne of Jamshed) or Persepolis, as it is known today, to take part in the festivities. Following a ritual and ceremony, representatives of about 23 satrapies under Persian domination (including north-western India), would pay tributes and offer gifts to the king. Remnants of rock carvings depicting the Navroz day parade at Persepolis, about 70 km from the garden city of Shiraz in Iran, bear mute testimony to the time when this festival was important not only for the Persians but for all humankind, as a day of spiritual rejuvenation. Jesus, the Prince of Peace, was born in Asia. India as a cradle of great religions has a historic mission to carry the peace of Jesus to the rest of the world. Apart from the Biblical tradition of peace, other sacred scriptures of India are not silent on peace. The last hymn of the Rig Veda has the following words to remind us of the need for unity and peace among us: "Walk together, speak in concord, and let your mind comprehend alike, let your efforts be united, let your hearts be in agreement, let your minds be united, that we all may be happy".

Hussein is an Eternal Source of Hope

Firoz Bakht Ahmed

UHARRAM COMMEMORATES the martyrdom of Hussein, grandson of Prophet Muhammad. Muharram is a day of mourning as Hussein and his 72 relatives and followers were brutally killed on the 10th day of Muharram for refusing to bow before Yazid, ruler of Damascus. Hussein was the son of Fatimah, the Prophet's daughter. It was said that the Prophet loved Hussein so much that he would say: "He who befriends Hussein befriends me; he who hurts Hussein hurts me".

The year 683 AD proved to be tragic for Islam, as the tyrant Yazid succeeded to the throne of the Caliphate and obliterated the democracy established by the Prophet. When he asked Imam Hussein to join hands with him, the Imam refused and urged him to mend his ways. Enraged, Yazid threatened Hussein with massacre. But Hussein remained firm. As he proceeded to the rebel city of Kufa, his caravan was intercepted by Yazid's soldiers. His tents were burnt and his source of water cut off. His sons, Ali Akbar and Ali Asghar, were killed before him. His daughter Sakina died of thirst. Yazid then asked Hussein if he would accept his authority, and once again, Hussein told him that his devotion was only for God. Hussein was then shot down and his body trampled upon.

Hussein's sacrifice is commemorated by Muslims everywhere, but nowhere except perhaps in Iran is it observed with such emotional intensity as it is in India. Benaras has a tradition of commemorating Muharram where Hindu families participate in the procession. This also happens in Allahabad, Kanpur and Hyderabad, observes Dr Khaliq Anjum, the famous Urdu writer. Many Hindus in these cities participate in the *majlis* (congregations), *salaams* (homages) and *marsiyas* (elegies); as also in the making of *taziyas* (replicas of the Imam's mausoleum in Karbala). Prof Gopichand Narang, renowned Urdu and Persian scholar, tells of the wonderful Imambaras Hindus built in Vijayanagara in the 16th and 17th centuries. They even wore garments of mourning during Muharram. Scindias of Gwalior and Holkars of Indore also observed Muharram to create harmony in their states.

In mourning processions, followers of Imam Hussein beat themselves with chains and daggers to recreate the torment that the Imam and his followers underwent. It is believed that the wounds incurred are cured without recourse to medicine. Among the Hindus of Lucknow, the *azadari* processions are no less revered than Ramlila. Many Hindus fast with Muslims on this day, while others distribute iced milk to those participating in the processions.

Hussein's message is not only for Muslims, but all humanity. As Narayan Das Talib says: *"Hum ne mana Musalmano tumharey hein Hussein/ Lekin humko yeh kehney do hamarey hein Hussein/ Roshni qayam hai jiski woh sitarey hein Hussein/ Aalam-e-insaniyat mein sab ke pyare hein Hussein".* That is: "We agree, O Muslims, that Hussein is yours but permit us to claim him as our own too. Hussein is that star whose light shines eternal; Hussein is best loved in the realm of humanity".

The Lesson of the Awakened One

Vivek Jain

HE BUDDHA was born in 563 BC, to Suddhodana and Mahamaya, king and queen of the Sakyas. The child was called Siddhartha, 'one whose aim is accomplished', after it was predicted that he would become a Buddha if he left home, or a universal monarch if he did not. It was as a boy that Siddhartha entered his first *dhyana* or absorption, as he sat beneath a jambu tree. The turning point in his life came at the age of 29, when (as the well-known story recounts) he saw an aged man, a sick man, a dead body and finally an ascetic. Greatly moved, he decided to leave home and go in quest of a solution to the problem of suffering.

In the *Tipitaka*, the 'three baskets' of the Buddhist canon, we find a detailed account of Gautama's enlightenment. He sat down one evening in what is today Bodh Gaya to meditate beneath an *assattha* tree (now universally renowned as the bodhi tree). As he entered a state of deep contemplation, Mara, the tempter, attempted to distract him with worldly seductions. In this ordeal, Gautama was protected by the *paramitas* ('great virtues') that he had perfected during his innumerable past lives as a Bodhisattva, a Buddha-to-be. Then, in the first watch, he gained the knowledge of his previous lives. In the middle watch, he attained the 'divine eye', the power to see the passing away and rebirth of beings. In the last watch, he directed his mind to the destruction of all defilements and attained enlightenment. At the age of 35, during the night of the full moon day of the month of Vaisakha, Gautama became the Buddha, the 'awakened one'.

The Buddha delivered his first sermon to the five ascetics who had been his companions in the early years of his life as a sanyasi. The substance of this sermon (known as the Dhammacakka Pavattana Sutta) is: Avoiding the extremes of self-indulgence and self-mortification, one must discover the 'middle path' (*majjhima patipada*). This is the Noble Eightfold Path of right view, right thought, right speech, right action, right livelihood, right endeavour, right mindfulness and right concentration. The Buddha departed from the main line of traditional Indian thought in not asserting an essential or ultimate reality. Contrary to Upanishadic thought, he maintained that atman (the self) does not exist: there is nothing within us that is metaphysically real. Along with impermanence, he affirmed the theory of *nairatmya*, the non-existence of an eternal 'I'.

Awareness of these fundamental realities led the Buddha to formulate the Four Noble Truths: the inevitability of misery; the origin of misery in the craving for pleasure; the elimination of craving; and finally, the achievement of such elimination through the practice of the eightfold path. This implies an understanding of the mechanism by which humankind's psychophysical being evolves, otherwise human beings would remain indefinitely in the continual flow of transitory existence. The ultimate goal to be achieved through the eightfold path is nirvana, a condition that is realised when karma and the consequential succession of lives and births have definitely been overcome.

Slaying the Demon that's Within Us

Shobha Viswanath

DUSSEHRA MARKS the day when goddess Durga killed the buffalo-demon Mahishasura, who had a boon from Brahma that he would not be slain by gods, men, spirits or any aspect of nature. Brahma, Vishnu and Shiva combined the energies of their consorts, Saraswati, Lakshmi and Shakti and created a beautiful woman, the 10-armed Durga, to kill the demon, as Mahishasura had not mentioned women in his boon. Durga fought Mahishasura for nine days, beheading him on the tenth day.

Durga and Mahishasura as aspects of our nature are relevant even today. Internally and externally, we face strife constantly. Durga, Saraswati, Lakshmi and Shakti represent aspects of energy which are manifest within us. But Mahishasura is also manifest within us. Yoga makes us aware of these energies and can help us harness the positive ones. It enables us to make ourselves any which way we want to be. Yoga deals with our inner nature, to create the right kind of interior to foster joyous and peaceful living. Sadhguru Jaggi Vasudev says, experience life beyond physical dimensions.

On the ninth day of Dussehra, Saraswati, the goddess of knowledge and learning, is worshipped. This day is also called Ayuda Puja, when all artisans lay down their tools before the goddess and seek her blessings so that their trade will do well. We should also remember that all this is symbolic of our self — that is, body, mind, emotion and energy — which is our biggest ayuda or tool. This festival is a time to transform our inner tools to their highest levels of functionality. Saraswati is propitiated for furthering knowledge and understanding to promote one's career and business. But the seeker of knowledge, instead of worshipping the crowbar, takes the opportunity to direct his attention inwards.

The science of yoga not only provides knowledge about the underlying basis of metaphysical principles and ethical values but it also provides the necessary tools to transform human nature. Its aim is to bring about perspectives beyond intellectual understanding and to foster experiences that bring life into a new dimension of perception.This knowledge or perception that yoga brings broadens and strengthens the visionary power of the mind. It opens the door of that realm of sensing beyond the five senses. Yoga is not something one does; it is the medium of becoming the crucible of self-transformation. It is not a practice or a certain way to be. Sadhguru Jaggi Vasudev offers a path to this self-transformation. His life is a continuous endeavour to help people manifest their divinity and experience something beyond the limited. He teaches a science through which, one can take the very process of life, death and rebirth into one's own hands. A tool, a transformative touch at your deepest core.

(Isha Foundation)

A Season of Reflection and Revelry

Rivka Sheinberg

CTOBER IN Mumbai. The city comes alive with Navaratri revelries. But in some corners of the city, a quieter celebration is taking place. For, this season is also the busiest time for another group of Mumbai's residents — the Jews. In the space of a few short weeks, Jews the world over celebrate four of their most important festivals: Rosh Hashanah, Yom Kippur, Sukkot, and Simhat Torah.

The season begins with Rosh Hashanah, the Jewish New Year, which marks the day that the world was created. Jews gather with family and friends for a festive meal to herald a year of blessing and prosperity. They attend prayers in the synagogue and hear the sounding of the shofar, the ram's horn. Its eerie, plaintive wail is a clarion call for taking stock of past actions and begin the process of *teshuvah* or repentance. Rosh Hashanah is followed immediately by the Yamim Nora'im, Ten Days of Awe, which culminate in the most solemn festival of the Jewish year: Yom Kippur, the Day of Atonement. Before Yom Kippur, Jews walk from home to home, asking forgiveness from friends and neighbours. They arrive at synagogue in the evening wearing white clothing. This is the White Fast, the day on which Jews neither eat nor drink nor wear leather or perfume. They emulate angels and focus on penitence, attaining 'at-one-ment' with God. By day's end, Jews believe, forgiveness has been granted, and they are written in the Book of Life for another year.

The mood now shifts to celebration. Four days later begins Sukkot, a harvest festival. In Israel during this season you will see in every backyard, on apartment balconies, in side alleys small enclosed huts called sukkot, or shelters, with palm branches for roofing. During Sukkot, Jews gather to study, sing, and eat in these shelters. The experience is intended to remind them of the time when their ancestors, escaped slaves, wandered homeless through the Egyptian desert. Hospitality is encouraged during this time: doors of the sukkot are always open to the hungry and poor. Every day during Sukkot, a bundle of branches known as a *lulav*, is shaken in all four directions while reciting special prayers. In the *lulav* is myrtle, willow, etrog and palm that represent the Jewish people, Israel, and the human body. Special prayers of joy, Hallel, are sung while waving the *lulav* in gratitude for a successful harvest. In Israel, Sukkot marks the end of summer, and the beginning of the rainy season. So, at the end of Sukkot, a special prayer for rain is recited.

The final day of Sukkot is a holiday called Simhat Torah, the joy of Torah. While Sukkot celebrates God's gift of a successful harvest which meets the needs of the body, Simhat Torah celebrates Torah, God's teaching, which meets the needs of the human spirit and mind. Jews take the Sefer Torah, a beautifully decorated handwritten parchment scroll containing the first five books of the Bible, out of the Ark where it is kept and parade it around the synagogue hall, singing and dancing. There can be as many as seven rounds of dancing and singing, and the celebration can last for hours. A fitting end to a season of joy!

Acquiring Immunity
to Temptation

Anselm Brito

SH WEDNESDAY marks the commencement of the period of Lent, the 40 days preceding Easter. Lent is a period of sobriety, reflection and customary fasting; its observance begins with special services, during which ashes are blessed and applied to the foreheads of the faithful. Lent carries a resonance of the 40 days of fasting that Jesus endured when as St Mathew tells us: "He was led by the spirit into the desert to be tempted by the Devil". This encounter prepared Jesus before the beginning of his public ministry.

We read of three temptations into which the Devil tried to draw Jesus, and which Jesus rejected. Seeing that Jesus was hungry, the Tempter said: "If thou be the Son of God, command that these stones be made bread". Jesus courteously retorted: "It is written, not in bread alone doth man live but in every word that proceedeth from the mouth of God". This is the spiritual logic of Lent. Then the Devil took Jesus to Jerusalem and set him on the pinnacle of the temple, saying: "If thou be the Son of God, cast thyself down, for it is written, That He hath given His angels charge over thee and in their hands shall they bear thee up". The Devil might quote scripture, but Jesus was equal to the occasion. "It is written again", he replied, "thou shalt not tempt the Lord thy God". This leads us to our own manner of dealing with God. By our sins, we tempt the Lord to punish us. On the other hand, in The Lord's Prayer, which Jesus taught His disciples, we pray: "Lead us not into temptation, but deliver us from evil".

Finally, Satan took Jesus up to a high mountain and showed him glorious kingdoms: "All these will I give thee if, falling down, thou wilt adore me". This gambit also failed. Jesus dismissed Satan sternly: "Begone Satan, for it is written: 'The Lord thy God shalt thou adore and Him only shalt thou serve'." This final response led Satan to realise that Jesus was a distinctive personality. Lent may be commemorated only once a year, but its lessons are meant to last us throughout the conduct of our lives. We often give way to pride; we are ready to bend and break others in the pursuit of our own goals; we permit ourselves to be blinded by the dazzle of wealth.

It is against these and other sins that Jesus cautions us; it should be our very literal and precise intention, during Lent, to search our souls. And if Lent begins with the blessing of ashes, this too reminds us that our corporal being will ultimately be consigned to the dust or the flames; it is spiritual rather than worldly riches that we must gather. Lent reminds us, essentially, of the ultimate purpose of our life: the attainment of unity with God. As we search our souls, we take stock of our actions, uncover our shortcomings, yet also discover ways of overcoming them. Above all, we learn to imitate Jesus, whose compassion for living beings caused him to quest for and share the wisdom of the true path.

Bringing the Manic
Mouse to Rest

Namita Devidayal

ANESH CHATURTHI signifies a flood of clay figurines of the elephant-headed God, only to be immersed in water a few days later. How many among the devout take the time to contemplate, during this fortnight of frenetic worship, on the reasons why Ganesha is God of wisdom? And why the appellation *vighna-harta*, remover of obstacles, resounds in boisterous prayer sung in his praise?

Most of us have heard stories about the beloved pot-bellied God. There's the one about Ganesha and Kartikeya in sibling competition over who could go faster around the world. While Kartikeya clambered on to his peacock and flew off, Ganesha walked briskly around his parents. His wisdom lies perhaps in recognising that, with the right values and a little ingenuity, you can effortlessly achieve what others strive endlessly to attain. Another story tells of his birth. Parvati created from her flesh a boy to guard her while she bathed. When Shiva showed up, he was not allowed in. In a fit of rage, he sliced off the boy's head. Parvati ordered her hapless husband to restore the child. He picked the first animal that came before him and brought Ganesha back to life.

It is no coincidence that an elephant ended up being the God of wisdom's better half. At the risk of making the unlikely connection between philosophy and anatomy, the elephant has enormous ears and a small mouth: the path to wisdom involves listening more, talking less. It has narrow, tiny eyes, like someone who carefully scrutinises things around him. A wise person, likewise, always examines a situation closely and attempts to understand its deeper resonances.

Ganesha has a big belly. He is able to digest all that is happening around him, good and bad, praise and criticism. Yet the rotund one is light enough to straddle a tiny mouse. For he does not hold grudges or ill will: feelings that make one heavy and unwieldy. Finally, why is Ganesha's *vahana* a mouse? Our anatomist-philosopher guru suggests that this scuttling creature represents the mind, which has a tendency to dart about, picking up fickle fantasies and devious desires along the way. Ganesha's true wisdom lies in the fact that he is able to control the mouse, to rein it in and bring it to rest at his feet. Control over one's mind is thus the ultimate sign of wisdom. The Bhagavad Gita speaks of a stable mind — one which does not jump around chasing ephemeral and base desires, but remains in a state of placidity, and eventually, attains to bliss.

Yet Ganesh Chaturthi in its current avatar is the antithesis of contemplation. It has become a festival of one-upmanship (my Ganapati is bigger and more shiny than yours); of insensitivity (let's make some noise and wake up the neighbourhood); and even greed, if one is to believe complaints about local thugs in Mumbai turning this festival into yet another means of extorting money from a long-suffering citizenry. Let us, rather, pray to Ganesha to enable us to rein in our thoughts, channelise our energies and bring the manic mouse to rest.

Fasting as Spiritual Discipline

Saniyasnain Khan

AMADAN (OR Ramzan as it is known in India), ninth month of the Muslim year, spent in ritual fasting, encourages the devout to do good and desist from evil. Following the lunar calendar, Ramzan may occur in extremes of cold and heat, or in seasons when the days may be very long or very short. However adverse the physical conditions, its rites are dutifully observed since to the true believer, fasting applies not just to the body but also to the soul. Prophet Muhammad called fasting "a shield", saying: "Let not him who fasts behave immodestly, or engage in vulgar speech; and if someone abuses him or quarrels with him, let him say: 'I am fasting, I am fasting'" as he is abstaining, as a matter of strict self-discipline, not just from food and drink but from all pernicious thoughts, intentions and acts. Indeed, during the entire month of Ramzan, the believer is expected to give himself up entirely to prayer, contemplation, piety and charity. Those who merely observe outward forms are warned that Allah is in no need of their fasting.

Fasting begins with *suhur*, a light meal before dawn. The Prophet described this meal as 'blessed'. He also reminded believers to delay in eating this meal, but to hasten with the *iftar*, food taken at sunset, for the entire day is spent without taking the smallest morsel of food or a drop of water. With the sharp pangs of hunger and thirst brought on by day-long fasting, and the consequent fatigue, the believer develops the strength of patience and endurance. Protracted abstinence from basic necessities not only heightens awareness of bodily needs, and of the sufferings of fellow human beings, but also intensifies feelings of gratitude for the Creator's benevolence.

On breaking the fast in the evening, prayers of thanksgiving to the Lord arise spontaneously. The Prophet cherished these moments. As the food and water touched his tongue, he would say: "The thirst has gone, the veins are moistened and the reward has been established, insha Allah". During the last 10 days of Ramzan, the Prophet would keep a vigil each night, asking his family to increase reading of prayers because one of the last nights falling on odd dates could be the 'Lailatul Qadr', or Night of Power on which the Qur'an began to be revealed to him. Surah 97, devoted to this significant event, says that worshipping on this night is better than worshipping for a thousand months. The sincere devotee, who has spent Lailatul Qadr in worship, would have his past sins forgiven. When the Prophet's wife Aishah asked what request one should make on this night, the Prophet taught her a short prayer: *Rabbana inaka affuwun tuhibbul affwa, fa affwanni* or, 'O Allah, you are the One who forgives. You love forgiveness, so forgive me'.

Ramzan begins with the first sighting of the waxing moon and concludes when the moon is first seen for the next month, Shawwal. If the moon cannot be seen, it ends with the completion of 30 fasts. Perhaps one of the most positive features of Ramzan is that it is a time for Muslims not only to refrain from bodily satisfactions, but also to come to grips with the whole range of their religious duties.

Colours of the Mind

Ayesha Irani

COLOUR IS integral to all spring festivals: whether it be the *abir-gulal* of Holi or the fruits and flowers that deck the Navroz table. As a lot of us cower indoors to keep away from street hooliganism, it is comforting to think of the inner beauty of Holi. As the Upanishads inform us, all things have a rhythmic existence, vibrations of sound and colour. Even though our sense organs catch only a fraction of the range of light and sound waves, the moment we think of something, we can see its colour and perhaps even hear its sound. Every object has innate colour or *varna*, which is a matter of individual psychology, not caste identity. Dominant thought patterns emanate colour vibrations. For instance, a person with a martial mentality is said to emanate a red aura, one whose focus is money is said to emit yellow; one who lives the life of the mind has a white colour, whilst one who is preoccupied with the struggle for survival has a dark aura. These are held to be subtle colours, not readily visible to the human eye.

Whilst all created things have *varna*, the creator of it all lies beyond vibrational existence, as *avarna*, untouched by the play of colour: "With its power, the colourless one/ Makes numerous colours/ Imbuing them with secret meaning". This subtle science of colour, like the science of sound was discovered in the laboratory of Tantra, the ancient system of spiritual practice that expands the mind by liberating it from bondage. It was Mahaprabhu Chaitanya, nearly 500 years ago, who cast Tantra in a Vaishnav mould. Chaitanya, like other Bengalis of his time, knew nothing of Holi until he arrived in Vrindavan. There, he saw how the fires were lit the night before Holi, and demoness Holika and her kind, the demons of our past, the dead weight of the old year, consigned to flames. So enchanted was Chaitanya that, on his return home, he introduced the festival to his people, charging it with new meaning. Holi festivities would begin in the Krishna temple, by smearing the beloved deity with red. After this, they revelled in the colour themselves. Participation was voluntary, and all who joined in were fed *malpua*, Chaitanya's favourite sweet.

In Vaishnava bhakti, *raga sadhana* is significant. Though raga can be used as a synonym for *varna*, it has a different nuance of meaning. Raga is 'a colour that can dye other things with its colour'. In addition to its innate *varna*, the individual mind is liable to be dyed with *ragas* of the objects of its desire. *Raga-sadhana,* then, is the psycho-spiritual offering of those things we most desire, in the form of colour, to the Lord; so that we set the mind awash instead with the colour of the Lord.

Devotion is a fragile treasure of the human heart. To guard it from the perpetual onslaughts of materialism, which all too easily make cynics of us, we need to turn our gaze inwards from time to time and understand the colours of our mind and ultimately move beyond them.

Easter Hallelujahs For a new Beginning

Erasto Fernandez

HE GREAT Easter proclamation: "Christ is risen, he is not here" shattered the shroud-like silence that engulfed Jerusalem's inhabitants about 2,000 years ago. It still echoes in our midst each year on the joyous feast of Easter. The essence of the Easter message is of life, love and generous self-giving. The dreams of the apostles lay lifeless with the gruesome death on the cross. Some of these devoted followers had even taken his death to be the end of the road and had returned to their former way of life. But with the Easter proclamation they found themselves hurrying to new and inspired beginnings.

In whatever form they come, such beginnings are unmistakably a gift that surprises, enthralls, excites, even delights us. It has been happening from time immemorial because life is stronger than death and love is greater than hate. The man who comes out of hospital with a different approach to life; the mother of four who, after some serious soul-searching, decides to go back and finish her studies; the college student, an awkward adjustment behind him, who begins to feel at home and finds his or her major field of study interesting and gripping; the youthful rebel who discovers a cause worth dedicating his life to; the lonely individual who finds someone challenging enough with whom to share his or her life with; the adolescent who now begins to see himself as a responsible adult; the agnostic who begins to believe in precisely what he ridiculed before; the alcoholic who starts constructing a new life; the middle-aged man who embarks on a second engaging career; the bored retiree who works out a new way to employ his God-given yet buried talents: all these people experience the Easter call to newness.

Unfortunately, not all follow this gift of a call through. Some smother it in endless dreaming and talk, others pull back with the first inevitable roadblock. A good many wait for a 'break', for some good samaritan to lend a helping hand. Inspiring and impelling as the gift of inspired beginnings may be, we cannot afford to feel and act as if the creative inspiration by itself is all that matters. Rather, life is meant to be a never-ending journey, and once we are convinced of this, we are no longer survivors, but adventurers.

To the one who seriously commits himself or herself to being true to the Easter newness of life, finds the power of the Risen One creatively at work in his/her seemingly insignificant lives. It is awesome to be caught up in the divine work of a new creation, and to experience the freedom that comes from the 'not having' and 'not doing' of the little 'painful endings' we gladly accept; to experience the new life coming from the 'nothingness' of our 'letting be', to experience the artwork of our life unfolding day-by-day in ways we could never even have dreamt of. When we see all this begin to happen, it is the springtime of our lives. Easter Hallelujahs are the repeated refrain of our joyous days. It is a time of new life, a new season of graceful growth. Our energies well upward and outward, to make a creative difference in the world.